Praise for *Fame and Fortune:*

"A strong reputation is an enduring source of competitive advantage. In *Fame and Fortune*, Fombrun and van Riel show how successful companies mobilize the support of employees, consumers, and investors to strengthen their reputational capital. An excellent read!"

—FREDERICK W. SMITH
Chairman, President, and CEO, FedEx Corp

"At Philips, we care a lot about our reputation. In their latest book, Fombrun and van Riel provide an excellent roadmap for companies who care as much about their reputations as we do and want to improve how they are regarded by others."

—GERARD J. KLEISTERLEE
President and CEO, Royal Philips Electronics

"*Fame and Fortune* is a searching examination of a company's elusive yet valuable asset: its reputation. At Johnson & Johnson, we agree with the authors' thesis: A powerful reputation begins with organizational values that are clearly stated and rigorously upheld. Employees, consumers, and customers of businesses today, while still expecting quality and price, increasingly value integrity. So do we."

—WILLIAM C. WELDON,
Chairman and CEO, Johnson & Johnson

"A consistent and authentic brand is the foundation for a strong reputation in a world where trust is more important than ever. The authors tell a compelling story about the roots of reputation and show how companies should never underestimate the need to nurture their reputation in relation to all stakeholders."

—KJELD KIRK KRISTIANSEN
CEO and Owner, LEGO Company

"The ING corporate brand is a powerful symbol that distinguishes us from other aggressive competitors in financial services. *Fame and Fortune* provides invaluable ideas for senior managers interested in building a more sophisticated approach to reputation management in their own companies."

—EWALD KIST
CEO, ING Group

How
Successful Companies
Build Winning
Reputations

CHARLES J. FOMBRUN CEES B.M. VAN RIEL

FAME & FORTUNE

How Successful Companies Build Winning Reputations

FT Prentice Hall
FINANCIAL TIMES

An Imprint of PEARSON EDUCATION
Upper Saddle River, NJ • New York • London • San Francisco • Toronto • Sydney
Tokyo • Singapore • Hong Kong • Cape Town • Madrid
Paris • Milan • Munich • Amsterdam

www.ft-ph.com

Library of Congress Cataloging-in-Publication Data

Fombrun, Charles J.
  Fame and fortune: how successful companies build winning reputations / by
Charles J. Fombrun and Cees B.M. van Riel.
    p. cm.—(Financial Times Prentice Hall books)
  Includes bibliographical references and index.
  ISBN 0-13-093737-1
    1. Corporate image. 2. Corporations—Public relations. 3. Brand name
products—Management. I. Riel, C. B. M. van Riel. II. Title. III. Series

HD59.2.F657 2003
659.1—dc21   2003049853

Editorial/production supervision: *Kerry Reardon*
Cover design director: *Jerry Votta*
Cover design: *Anthony Gemmellaro*
Art director: *Gail Cocker-Bogusz*
Interior design: *Meg Van Arsdale*
Manufacturing manager: *Alexis Heydt-Long*
Manufacturing buyer: *Maura Zaldivar*
VP, executive editor: *Tim Moore*
Editorial assistant: *Allyson Kloss*
Marketing manager: *John Pierce*
Full-service production manager: *Anne R. Garcia*

FINANCIAL TIMES
Prentice Hall

© 2004 Pearson Education, Inc.
Publishing as Financial Times Prentice Hall
Upper Saddle River, NJ 07458

Financial Times Prentice offers excellent discounts on this book when ordered in
quantity for bulk purchases or special sales. For more information, please contact: U.S.
Corporate and Government Sales, 1-800-382-3419, corpsales@pearsontechgroup.com.
For sales outside of the U.S., please contact: International Sales, 1-317-581-3793,
international@pearsontechgroup.com

Printed in the United States of America
10 9   8   7   6   5   4   3   2

ISBN 0-13-093737-1

Pearson Education LTD.
Pearson Education Australia PTY, Limited
Pearson Education Singapore, Pte. Ltd.
Pearson Education North Asia Ltd.
Pearson Education Canada, Ltd.
Pearson Educación de Mexico, S.A. de C.V.
Pearson Education–Japan
Pearson Education Malaysia, Pte. Ltd.

FINANCIAL TIMES PRENTICE HALL BOOKS

For more information, please go to www.ft-ph.com

Business and Technology

Sarv Devaraj and Rajiv Kohli

    The IT Payoff: Measuring the Business Value of Information Technology Investments

Nicholas D. Evans

    Business Innovation and Disruptive Technology: Harnessing the Power of Breakthrough Technology…for Competitive Advantage

Nicholas D. Evans

    Consumer Gadgets: 50 Ways to Have Fun and Simplify Your Life with Today's Technology…and Tomorrow's

Faisal Hoque

    The Alignment Effect: How to Get Real Business Value Out of Technology

Economics

David Dranove

    What's Your Life Worth? Health Care Rationing…Who Lives? Who Dies? Who Decides?

John C. Edmunds

    Brave New Wealthy World: Winning the Struggle for World Prosperity

Jonathan Wight

    Saving Adam Smith: A Tale of Wealth, Transformation, and Virtue

Entrepreneurship

Oren Fuerst and Uri Geiger

    From Concept to Wall Street: A Complete Guide to Entrepreneurship and Venture Capital

David Gladstone and Laura Gladstone

    Venture Capital Handbook: An Entrepreneur's Guide to Raising Venture Capital, Revised and Updated

Erica Orloff and Kathy Levinson, Ph.D.

    The 60-Second Commute: A Guide to Your 24/7 Home Office Life

Jeff Saperstein and Daniel Rouach

    Creating Regional Wealth in the Innovation Economy: Models, Perspectives, and Best Practices

Finance

Aswath Damodaran
  The Dark Side of Valuation: Valuing Old Tech, New Tech, and New Economy Companies

Kenneth R. Ferris and Barbara S. Pécherot Petitt
  Valuation: Avoiding the Winner's Curse

International Business

Peter Marber
  Money Changes Everything: How Global Prosperity Is Reshaping Our Needs, Values, and Lifestyles

Fernando Robles, Françoise Simon, and Jerry Haar
  Winning Strategies for the New Latin Markets

Investments

Zvi Bodie and Michael J. Clowes
  Worry-Free Investing: A Safe Approach to Achieving Your Lifetime Goals

Harry Domash
  Fire Your Stock Analyst! Analyzing Stocks on Your Own

David Gladstone and Laura Gladstone
  Venture Capital Investing: The Complete Handbook for Investing in New Businesses, New and Revised Edition

D. Quinn Mills
  Buy, Lie, and Sell High: How Investors Lost Out on Enron and the Internet Bubble

D. Quinn Mills
  Wheel, Deal, and Steal: Deceptive Accounting, Deceitful CEOs, and Ineffective Reforms

John Nofsinger and Kenneth Kim
  Infectious Greed: Restoring Confidence in America's Companies

John R. Nofsinger
  Investment Blunders (of the Rich and Famous)…And What You Can Learn from Them

John R. Nofsinger
  Investment Madness: How Psychology Affects Your Investing…And What to Do About It

H. David Sherman, S. David Young, and Harris Collingwood
  Profits You Can Trust: Spotting & Surviving Accounting Landmines

Leadership

Jim Despain and Jane Bodman Converse
  And Dignity for All: Unlocking Greatness through Values-Based Leadership

CONTENTS

Chapter 6   BE VISIBLE   103

Chapter 7   BE DISTINCTIVE   133

Chapter 8   BE AUTHENTIC   161

Chapter 9   BE TRANSPARENT   185

Chapter 10   BE CONSISTENT   217

Chapter 11   BECOMING A TOP COMPANY: THE CASE OF FEDEX   243

ACKNOWLEDGMENTS

Few worthwhile projects are possible without the unflinching support of a lot people —partners, colleagues, analysts, assistants, and friends. This one is no exception.

Over many years of conferencing and joint projects, people in and around the Reputation Institute contributed heavily to the development of these ideas. We are particularly indebted to Majken Schultz (Copenhagen Business School), Davide Ravasi (Bocconi University), Klaus-Peter Wiedmann (University of Hannover), Keith MacMillan (Henley Management College), Gary Davies (Manchester Business School), and Frank Thevissen (Vrie University of Brussels) for their efforts in bringing the RQ Project to life. Bill Margaritis of FedEx has been a constant and encouraging champion of our work—how not to be grateful to him. Other early believers who supported us at various times along the way include Carol Ballock and Leslie Gaines Ross (our reputation "groupies" at Burson Marsteller), Scott Meyer at Weber-Shandwick, and our earliest supporter of all, Harold Kahn, then at PricewaterhouseCoopers. The road hasn't always been smooth in getting reputation research off the ground, but what a ride it's been!

Dennis Larsen labored mightily to support us with online research and financial analysis, and did so with his usual diligence and charm. In the last two years, Kasper Ulf Nielsen and

Nicolas Georges Trad have become indispensable members of the Reputation Institute, helping us breathe life into reputation projects in Denmark, Norway, and Sweden. Majken Schultz was visionary to get them involved with us. From his perch in London, Daryn Moody has been a real collaborator in helping us to build the Reputation Institute's quarterly publication—the *Corporate Reputation Review*— into a noteworthy multi-disciplinary publication that releases a growing amount of thoughtful academic research and practitioner case studies. Many of our ideas get tested out in that early forum for knowledge exchange.

At the center of our work, however, sits Joy Sever—the "beating heart" of RQ research, and our thoughtful partner, ally, and friend at Harris Interactive®, the market research firm responsible for safeguarding methodological rigor in the development of representative consumer samples around the world and our partner in carrying out empirical research using the RQ instrument. Don't let anyone fool you—it's not easy carrying out complex multi-country, multi-party, multi-lingual research and we've been happy to see her succeed in building the "Reputation Practice" at Harris. We're grateful to her and her team for the painstaking work they deliver in annual and custom RQ projects around the world. They've stimulated us to probe more deeply the interface between data and knowledge, to negotiate the many issues involved in carrying out research, and to untangle the complex alliance that RQ projects require among companies, academics, and consultants. Bravo to the core team that has had the round-the-world and round-the-clock support of Oliver Freedman in Australia, and Rama Botlagadur and Deirdre Wanat in New York! The sun never sets on the RQ.

Former students Violina Rindova and Naomi Gardberg contributed to our work, both methodologically and creatively, often unknowingly, as did the many master's level students and executives who participated in our classes and seminars, and often posed interesting research questions and conducted partial analyses that helped us question, confirm, or modify our thinking.

Obviously we benefited heavily from time itself—something made possible only when others pick up the slack at the office and at home. Joke's administrative support kept Cees organized. For a good while, our part time office staff in Brussels (led by Robin Lokerman, Catherine Hartmann, Michael Podt, Arnaud Ponsard, and Natalie Reynaud) helped keep things aligned for us externally. While on the home front, Hannaeke Aerts and Michael Bevins did what no others can do: provided peace of mind —and the occasional food and wine—that sustained the long hours spent solo sitting at the computer.

All told, a book is both labor and love. Constant pressure from our editors, Tim Moore and Russ Hall, kept us securely focused on the labor of it all, thereby preventing us from falling too deeply in love with our own project and unable to finish it. We are grateful that they firmly prodded us into completing this book and thinking about the next.

Thank you, all.

INTRODUCTION

KNEE DEEP IN THE REPUTATION BOG

As we go to press, corporate reputations are very much in the news around the world. Sadly, much of the reporting is negative and involves allegations of fraudulent behavior by senior executives accused of misleading investors and consumers. Witness the following news items from spring 2003:

■ Ten of Wall Street's biggest financial firms agreed to pay about $1.4 billion and adopt reforms to resolve allegations that they issued biased ratings on stocks to lure investment-banking business. The unprecedented industrywide settlement called for one of the largest penalties ever levied by securities regulators. The settlement will change the way major investment firms do business, and focused particularly on Citigroup, Merrill Lynch. J.P. Morgan Chase, and Credit Suisse First Boston. Most significantly, the brokerage firms agreed to sever the troublesome links between financial analysts' research and investment banking, to pay a total $432.5 million over five years for independent stock research for their customers, and to fund an $80 million investor education program. A fund of $387.5 million is intended to compensate customers of the ten firms; $487.5 million in fines will go to states according to their population.

- The U.S. Securities and Exchange Commission announced that it planned to file civil-fraud charges against accounting giant KPMG LLP for its role in auditing Xerox Corporation, which last year settled SEC accusations of accounting fraud amounting to some $6.4 billion, one of the largest restatements in corporate history. At the heart of the SEC's investigation of KPMG's role as auditor of Xerox was an examination of whether the auditor had become so closely aligned with Xerox that its role as public watchdog had became largely secondary. KPMG is already a target of shareholder lawsuits involving drugstore chain Rite Aid Corporation, which admitted overstating income by more than $1 billion over a two-year period, as well as Lernout & Hauspie Speech Products NV, which collapsed after admitting to massive fraud, including fabricating 70 percent of the sales in its largest unit.
- The SEC charged US healthcare provider HealthSouth Corporation and its Chairman and CEO Richard M Scrushy with substantial accounting fraud. The Commission's complaint alleges that since 1999 HealthSouth systematically overstated its earnings by at least $1.4 billion in order to meet or exceed Wall Street earnings expectations. The false increases in earnings were matched by false increases in HealthSouth's assets. By the third quarter of 2002, HealthSouth's assets were overstated by at least $800 million. Weston L Smith, HealthSouth's chief financial officer pleaded guilty on March 20 to criminal charges of securities fraud, and conspiracy to commit securities and wire fraud. He also pleaded guilty to criminal charges of certifying false financial records designed to inflate the company's revenues and earnings by hundreds of millions of dollars. Eight senior HealthSouthexecutives to date have admitted guilt in the fraud.
- The world's number two communications giant Interpublic demoted its chairman and CEO John Dooner following Interpublic's disclosure that the company would have to restate its earnings downward by $181.3 million

because of accounting irregularities in its ad agency Mc-Cann-Erickson, spurring a federal investigation. In previous weeks, ratings services had downgraded its corporate debt numerous times, reducing it to one level above junk status.

■ Email records appeared to demonstrate that Credit Suisse First Boston's star banker Frank Quattrone knew that the firm was under various regulatory inquiries and a criminal probe for its IPO practices when he urged colleagues to purge files and dispose of notes, valuation analyses, and other internal memos to protect the firm against lawsuits. Such destruction is strictly forbidden once a lawsuit or investigation has begun. Mr. Quattrone had gained fame as one of the most powerful investment bankers during the tech-stock boom when he and a cadre of investment bankers in Silicon Valley brought some of the era's biggest and most profitable IPOs to market, including those of Netscape, Amazon, and Linux.

■ Ahold's chief executive officer Cees van der Hoeven and chief financial officer Michael Meurs resigned over assumed accounting irregularities at the Dutch grocery giant's U.S. operations. Ahold said the accounting problems caused it to overstate operating earnings by $500 million for 2001 and 2002. Its shares plunged 67 percent and are now worth only a tenth of their value at the peak of the company's fortunes in mid-2001. Ahold is now under investigation by the U.S. attorney's office in New York, the Securities and Exchange Commission, and the Euronext stock exchange in Amsterdam. On May 8, 2003 the company reported that earnings at its U.S. Foodservice unit had actually been overstated by $880 million through the actions of two of its executives. That figure was $380 million more than the Dutch retailer had initially estimated.

■ The German giant of chemicals and drugs Bayer A.G. announced continued efforts to settle over 7,200 lawsuits filed against the company because of its anticholesterol drug Baycol. Baycol was withdrawn in August 2001 after hundreds of deaths worldwide. Company documents, including email messages, memorandums, and sworn depositions, suggest that some Bayer executives were aware of the possible dangers of Baycol long before the company withdrew it from the market. If negligence is proven, the lawsuits are expected to expose the company to claims of over $5.4 billion. As a result, the company's shares have been on a downward spiral as investors flee the uncertain liabilities.

■ German prosecutors confirmed charges against Deutsche Bank's chief executive, Josef Ackermann, charging breach of trust stemming from his approval of more than $100 million in payments to executives of Mannesmann in the final days of its takeover battle with the Vodafone Group of Britain. Mr. Ackermann is one of six former board members of Mannesmann accused of improperly using the conglomerate's funds to pay severance and bonuses to top managers. If the defendants are found guilty, they could face up to 10 years in prison.

The list goes on, each one more damaging than the next. Reports of these alleged corporate crimes come on the heels of an avalanche of revelations throughout 2002 about executive excess and fraud that led to the demise of major corporate names such as Enron, Andersen, and Adelphia, jeopardized the continued existence of others such as WorldCom and Martha Stewart's Omnimedia, and produced a serious crisis of confidence in the corporate sector.

Yet not all the news has been bad. In February 2003 the latest ratings of companies by a representative sample of American consumers were developed by Harris Interactive and the Reputation Institute. The results revealed some interesting findings. For one, despite awesome turmoil, a downbeat economy, corporate financial scandals, and growing prospects of war in Iraq, the American public continued to show confidence in many of its largest companies. Major corporate names such as Johnson & Johnson—the perennial leader on these surveys—as well as Coca-Cola, Maytag, Dell, Sony, P&G, FedEx, Disney, Wal-Mart, Anheuser-Busch, and Southwest Airlines maintained their strong reputations. Not surprisingly, as this book shows, these are also the companies that know the value of their reputations and manage them accordingly. Reputation is proving to be a resilient asset to some companies in a difficult marketplace.

A second finding involved recognition of exemplary customer service. At a time when corporate focus and product reliability are being questioned by many corporate customers across sectors, who better to join the list of the highest rated companies in the United States than Harley-Davidson, a company whose single-minded devotion to customers brought it back from the brink of bankruptcy to reclaim an exemplary and dominant position in the motorcycle business. UPS's climb into the top 10 as well as Home Depot's upward surge to number eight also pointed to the company's success at pleasing the customer, whether in the reliable delivery of packages or in providing quality goods at an affordable price. General Mills also joined the list for its consistent and persistent emphasis on delivering quality products to happy consumers.

Finally, despite a turbulent economic climate, some companies still managed to make gains in reputation in 2002. They were Bridgestone/Firestone, DaimlerChrysler, Home Depot, Sears, UPS, and Xerox. Bridgestone/Firestone edged out of the tire debacle in slightly better form than its one-time partner Ford. Though still weak, the tire-maker gained ground since last year, whereas Ford did not. Retailers Home Depot and Sears both inched ahead, buoyed by cost-conscious consumers. Luxury automaker Daimler Chrysler got a boost from smoothing out its internal rifts between the United States and Germany. UPS successfully navigated past the threat of an employee strike, and Xerox settled its huge accounting irregularities with the government. Both got favorable and significant upward bumps in reputation.

Figure I-1 shows an analysis that combines the consumer poll with the results of a separate analysis of media coverage conducted by Delahaye-Medialink and the Reputation Institute. The electronic content analysis of media coverage of top U.S. companies in 2002 shows how the media (both print and broadcast) portrayed the corporate reputations of the top-

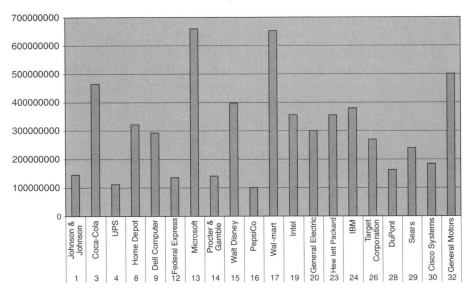

Media Reputation Index

Figure I-1 Linking media coverage to consumer perceptions.

rated companies in the consumer survey. The companies that topped the media ratings were Microsoft and Wal-Mart, with General Motors and Coca-Cola not far behind.

Figure I-2 compares the two sets of rankings obtained from consumers and from the media. The results indicate that:

- Microsoft, Wal-Mart, and General Motors get better media coverage than consumers think they deserve. Assuming media have a better grasp of a company's real situation, it suggests that these three companies could improve their public standing by more carefully and effectively framing their communications with consumers.
- Coca-Cola, Home Depot, Dell Computer, Procter & Gamble, FedEx and PepsiCo earn more balanced reputations from consumers and the media. It suggests that their communications strategies are being consistently implemented across channels.

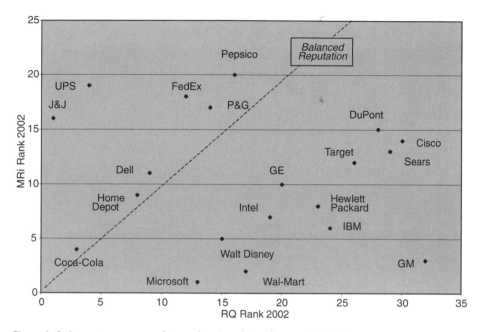

Figure I–2 Comparing consumer rankings and media rankings of companies in 2002.

■ Johnson & Johnson and UPS get relatively weaker media ratings than consumers think they deserve. It suggests the potential gains for these companies of focusing on improved media relations to reinforce the stronger perceptions in which they are held by consumers. They face significant reputational risk of losing ground with the public over time from not generating better media coverage.

The combined analysis provides useful insights. It suggests the point of view we uphold in this book: That reputations reflect how companies are perceived across a broad spectrum of stakeholders,. And that's a function of how companies communicate both with the media and with the public. When authenticity, consistency, and transparency come through from a company, it earns kudos from both the public and the media. If Johnson & Johnson gets top marks from the public, it's because of powerful messaging that bring out emotions of customer care and emotional attachment –features that appear less relevant to the media. If Coca-Cola earns high marks from both the media and the public, it's for persuasive messaging that conveys its ubiquity and refreshment and appeals to both the public and the media. If FedEx earns balanced grades from both the public and the media, it's because of consistent and credible messaging that conveys the company's consistency, reliability, and service.

That's the thesis we demonstrate in *Fame and Fortune: How the World's Top Companies Develop Winning Reputations.* We hope you enjoy it.

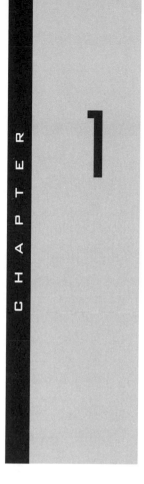

WHY REPUTATIONS MATTER

Anyone who follows the news knows that reputations matter. A banker gets caught with his hand in the till; a manager is accused of passing insider information to friends and family, enabling them to make money by trading his company's stock; an oil company is accused of burying poisonous chemicals that have filtered into a region's water supply and caused outbursts of cancer. Journalists and publicists bombard us daily with such bits of information.

What gets our attention? Often, our eye is caught by bold headlines that announce cataclysmic events and issues: scandals, accidents, deaths, and crises—negative events that cast a dark shadow on the reputations of companies and individuals. A disproportionate share of that attention goes to people whose names we recognize, often they're captains of industry or political leaders. We are a celebrity culture, after all, and celebrity also attaches to companies that have become familiar to us because of the products they make. We recognize these people and companies because of the reputational halos that surround them—halos of past actions that have created more or less "reputational capital" around their names.

But do these reputations really matter? That's always the first question we are asked by critics and enthusiasts alike. Should we bother thinking about reputations at all, or should we focus only on the key things that earn you reputation—things like revenues and costs? If we say yes, if we say of course reputations matter, we inevitably get the more deeply probing question: Can you prove it—scientifically? Here's what we have to say about it.

WHY DO REPUTATIONS MATTER?

To the question, Do reputations matter? the short answer is yes. That's good news, or else we wouldn't be writing this book. To the question, *Why* do reputations matter? the answer is more complex. The truth be told, to trained academics the question itself always seems surprising, given the existence of a voluminous research literature on the topic. It explains how people make decisions and shows that people make decisions not only on the basis of reality itself, but on the basis of their *perceptions* of reality, whether accurate or not. That it is a fragmented, multidisciplinary literature doubtless has something to do with why it's not better known. Surely everyone knows this, you say. It's common sense. Well, apparently not, given prevailing business logic that insists on the exclusively rational and economic aspects of decision making, a logic that shortchanges the influence of perceptual, and social factors on the decisions we make.

Behavioral psychologists like to remind us that we are all heavily influenced by such nonrational elements in our purchasing decisions: We act on rumors and hearsay in choosing which television set or CD-player to buy; we are swayed to a product based on a self-serving magazine ad we saw; we watch a movie based on a critic's endorsement. In none of these decisions are we making careful calculations about the objective features of the products themselves. Rather, we are acting on *perceptions* of these products—perceptions which themselves are heavily influenced by our own highly personal, emotional, nonrational reactions to the way the product is presented to us by companies, journalists, or friends.

The reputations of people and companies influence our investment decisions in much the same way. We often turn to well-known analysts for professional opinions about a promising stock; we ask friends for advice; we pick companies to invest in whose products are familiar to us; and we speculate about their future prospects based on reports by insiders, experts, and others whose knowledge we assume to be better than our own and whose advice serves as a substitute for careful, rational analysis on our part. Clearly, their own reputations affect the judgments we make.

So it is too in the jobs we take. When students select jobs, the most attractive jobs are invariably the ones offered by the best-regarded companies of the moment. Generally, they are offered by companies whose names are well known, whose reputations are strong and positive. For comparable jobs, these highly regarded companies regularly get a larger share of the best applicants. Although top companies could easily take advantage of the situation and offer lower pay than their rivals, they are often the ones who offer substantially *higher,* more generous pay packages to graduates in order to further distinguish themselves and generate positive word of mouth—and reputation—with others who won't get the job. Consulting firms and investment banks are particularly attuned to this "mystique factor" and have become well versed in managing it. They profile themselves carefully at on-campus gatherings and manage off-campus visits that candidates make to the company's offices. Recruiting events at leading business schools are carefully choreographed reputational events that companies take very seriously because they understand the ripple effects on the firm's reputation that their campus visits produce.

A good reputation acts like a magnet: It attracts us to those who have it. That's why so many of us are prepared to spend large sums of money to eat in Michelin-starred restaurants, to sleep in Ritz-Carlton hotels, to drive BMWs, to wear designer clothes, to carry an American Express Platinum Card, and to live in Paris or New York. A good reputation is an excellent calling card: It opens doors, attracts followers, brings in customers and investors—it commands our respect.

It's often true, therefore, that a good reputation sits on the bedrock of a strong product or corporate brand. However, brand and reputation are *not* synonymous—and they differ in important ways. On one hand, a brand describes the set of associations that customers have with the company's products. A weak brand has low awareness and functional appeal to customers, whereas a strong brand has high awareness and functional appeal. Reputation, on the other hand, involves the assessments that multiple stakeholders make about the company's ability to fulfill their expectations. A company may have strong product brands or even a strong corporate brand—its brands have high awareness and appeal—but can still have a weak or poor reputation. A strong brand like Nike, for instance, consistently rates poorly on public reputation surveys because of perceptions by many consumers that the company chooses low-labor countries in which to produce but does too little to prevent child labor in its subcontractors' factories. A weak brand, in contrast, can still have a strong reputation: Its products and services may be relatively unfamiliar to most people but are held in high regard by its own stakeholders. Succinctly put, branding affects the likelihood of a favorable purchase decision by customers. Reputation, however, affects the likelihood of supportive behaviors from all of the brand's stakeholders. Branding is therefore a subset of reputation management.

Figure 1–1 specifies how reputations influence the decisions that people make. It suggests that a good reputation affects the decisions of *customers* about which company's products to buy; it influences the decisions of *employees* about which company to work for; and it affects the decisions of *investors* about which company's shares to accumulate.

Figure 1–1 also indicates that reputations affect the judgments of *media journalists* and *financial analysts*. Evidence shows that reporters write more frequently about highly regarded companies and tend to cover them more favorably. Evidence

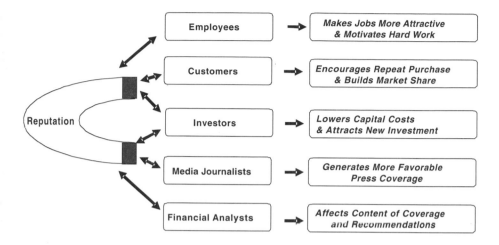

Figure 1-1 Reputations are magnets: They help a company attract resources.

shows that financial analysts have a "herd mentality" in following lead analysts who themselves are affected by the established visibility, notoriety, and reputations of established companies. The plight of Enron in 2002 certainly demonstrated the fragility of opinion making by financial analysts: It exposed the frail, inherently human, social biases and filters that reporters and analysts use to judge companies. How could a company whose financial position was as questionable as Enron's otherwise have been so widely and universally praised just before its stock crashed—especially by all those mainstream Wall Street insiders whose street savvy and numbers focus are legendary? Clearly, analysts are affected by a company's established reputation, whether that reputation is justified or not.

REPUTATIONS CREATE DIFFERENTIATION AND COMPETITIVE ADVANTAGE

Ultimately, a good reputation matters because it is a key source of *distinctiveness* that produces support for the company and differentiates it from rivals. Differentiation based on reputation has become more important to companies because of various environmental trends:

■ *Globalization*. Rivalry is on the rise due to the blurring of national boundaries and to the multimarket operations that companies develop to capitalize on regional differences in labor and logistical costs. When companies enter new markets, they carry with them the strengths and weaknesses of their foreign reputations: When McDonald's, Shell, or Coca-Cola enter a market, their reputational halos are a major force in negotiating attractive deals with local taxing authorities and suppliers. Foreign companies with weaker reputational halos have far less strength in building their distinctiveness against local rivals.

■ *Information Availability.* The proliferation of information sources and instantaneous transmission of information via print media, broadcast media, and the Internet have created an environment in which people find it difficult to distinguish the quality of a company's products and services. In these circumstances, customers, investors, and potential employees turn disproportionately to the more highly regarded companies.

■ *Product Commoditization.* Globalization has fostered increasing homogeneity in the products and services offered across markets. You can't escape the proliferation of franchises around the world, whether in purchasing fast foods, beverages, or other consumer products. In most countries local businesses imitate the practices of the more reputable foreign companies—you can eat McDonald's-like hamburgers in local Quick outlets throughout France; drink Heineken-like beers throughout Asia. When product and service differences between offerings are slight, reputations become a powerful and salient source of differentiation.

■ *Media Mania*. In recent years the media have widened their sphere of influence to encompass the business world. Companies and their top executives now perform in the media spotlight, making corporate reputations a major source of distinction—or concern. Images of indicted executives led away in handcuffs to face charges of securities fraud clogged the airwaves throughout 2002 and into 2003, helping to foster an atmosphere of crisis in corporate governance that has raised the visibility and importance of reputation as an economic asset.

■ *Ad Saturation*. From banners to billboards to radio and television commercials, we are mentally assaulted with corporate messaging. As overloaded publics pay less attention to these messages, purchased advertising space has lost some of its historical effectiveness. Broader reputation-building strategies rooted in public relations, event management, sponsorships, and corporate citizenship have grown in importance in the media mix for influencing consumer perceptions and cutting through the crowded media marketplace.

■ *Stakeholder Activism*. It's not often that executives get to see a rabbi chauffeured by a nun in a car emblazoned with the slogan "What Would Jesus Drive?" But such was the scene in November 2002 when a coalition of Christian and Jewish religious leaders went to Detroit to press automakers for more fuel-efficient vehicles and were ferried from General Motors to Ford by nuns driving small Toyota Prius vehicles that rely on a combination of gas and electric power. The slogan was the work of the Evangelical Environmental Network, a small grassroots group. It epitomizes the growing activism by nongovernmental groups (such as Greenpeace, Alliance for Better Foods, and numerous others) who are using increasingly sophisticated marketing and public relations tactics to make their messages heard. They do so principally by attacking the reputational foundations of some of the world's most visible companies.

These trends reinforce the fact that reputations matter a great deal and must be nurtured and protected. For large firms, they are the basis of continued competitiveness. For smaller, younger firms, they are the foundation on which to build business. For all firms, reputations matter because they are both valuable and vulnerable.

CAN YOU PROVE THAT REPUTATIONS MATTER?

A lot of research has been done by academics and consultants seeking to demonstrate that reputations actually influence key decisions of stakeholders—and vice-versa.[1] The circularity of the causal relationships is important to our understanding of reputational dynamics, and we examine some of that work here.

CUSTOMERS: REPUTATION AFFECTS PURCHASE DECISIONS

Students of marketing generally focus on consumers' purchase decisions. They try to show that through careful branding, a company can get consumers to buy more of its products than those of its rivals. Branding is a marketing concept that focuses on how companies can increase their visibility and reach by creating memorable associations between a product and a group of customers it targets. Customers purchase and repurchase the product because they associate strong, favorable, unique characteristics with the product brand. The branding effect is particularly strong when consumers cannot adequately gauge product attributes before the purchase decision. So they draw inferences from the company that stands behind the product.[2]

Corporate branding applies the standard branding process developed for products to the whole company. It proposes that building strong emotional associations between a company and its customers increases customers' identification with the company and therefore the likelihood of product purchases. Entertainment giant Walt Disney and toy-maker Lego rely heavily on a single corporate brand name to market their products. Insofar as consumers make positive associations with the corporate name, they transfer positive or negative attributes to the company's products. Among the more persuasive studies to document this "halo effect" are comparative studies of *identical* products bearing different brand names. Car companies, for instance, often market identical vehicles produced in the same plants with only a nameplate to differentiate the products. A study by McKinsey & Company showed that these cars often meet dramatically different fortunes. General Motors and Toyota produced identical cars through their NUMMI joint venture in California. The Toyota Corolla and Chevrolet Prizm, though built side by side from identical components and with only minor trim differences, had quite different fates: Only one-quarter as many Prizms were sold, their trade-in value depreciated more quickly, and the Prizm required up to $750 more in buyer incentives to support its sales. Having Toyota's name on the Corolla attracted customers, while the Prizm was lost among the Chevy dealer's other offerings. [3]

In other words, from a branding point of view, there's evidence that a company's reputation affects the attractiveness of its products to potential customers and so influences the company's ability to generate revenues. High-reputation companies are more likely to be credible to consumers when they make extreme claims about their products in their promotional campaigns.[4] The reputation effect on sales is stronger when the company's reputation is based on core competencies (e.g., product quality or innovation) rather than on perceptions of its social responsibility.[5] A good reputation improves a company's credibility and transfers positive effect from the company to the product, whereas a poor reputation detracts from product sales.

EMPLOYEES: REPUTATION AFFECTS DECISIONS TO ENGAGE, COMMIT, AND STAY

Employer branding is the label given to the reputation-building tactics being used by a rising number of companies to make themselves more attractive to prospective and current employees.[6] In a February 2001 Conference Board report sponsored by financial services giant Charles Schwab, managers in 138 leading companies replied to a survey about their branding experiences and practices. They indicated that the challenges to employers were not only to make potential employees aware of the company as a good place to work and bring the best applicants successfully through the recruitment and hiring process, but to *retain* them and ensure their understanding of the company's goals and commitment.

Virtually all the surveyed companies with distinct employer-branding efforts had launched those efforts in the previous five years. Respondents overwhelmingly said that funding for employer-branding efforts had increased in the past two years and further growth was expected for the next two years. For the employer brand, the communications and marketing executives identified the following top goals:

- Helping employees internalize the company's values
- Achieving a reputation as an employer of choice
- Recruiting and retaining employees
- Instilling brand values into key processes

The human resources executives picked a similar set:

- Helping employees to internalize the company's values
- Recruiting employees
- Retaining employees
- Achieving a reputation as an employer of choice

Although becoming an "employer of choice" involves improving recruitment and retention, true employer branding goes farther and involves motivating employees and generating improved alignment between personal goals and the vision and values of the company. Ultimately, employer branding gets involved with all the people-related processes that create organizational excellence, including the human resource systems for appraising, rewarding, and developing individual performance.

The war for talent has moved onto the web. In a July 2000 report, the Association of Graduate Recruiters in the United Kingdom reported that 88 percent of students had used the internet to seek employment, with 44 percent completing online applications. Many companies now consider online recruitment vital in maintaining their corporate reputation and competing in the graduate market.

The Web provides candidates with a clearer idea of both companies and jobs. If Web-surfers don't like what they see, they can deselect themselves. If a Web site is uninformative, confusing out-of-date, or simply duplicates a brochure, it can turn off the best qualified candidates. Moreover, a company's Web site makes a very public statement about its values, aspirations and corporate culture—something the company has to live up to. As the report points out, a striking finding of the study was that those companies who were most successful in using the Internet to recruit graduates had built a strong internal team of managers from corporate communications, marketing, information technology, and human resources to coordinate the activity.

Few studies actually document the effect of a company's reputation on its success in recruiting and retaining employees. A study of 200 business undergraduate students found them more attracted to jobs in companies whose workplaces were featured among the "100 Best Companies to Work For."[7] The reputational effect appears to hold true for MBA students as well. Universum is a Swedish company that conducts annual surveys of MBA students to assess their perceptions of top employers. In April 2001, the top 10 companies and their 2000 and 2001 ranks are shown in Table 1.1.

Except for the brief detour into e-commerce startups in the late 1990s, MBA graduates are consistent in their nominees for most desirable employer: Their top choices are typically the high-reputation firms in consulting, investment banking, and high technology.[8]

Table 1—1 Top 10 Companies and Their 2000 and 2001 Rankings

COMPANY	RANK 2000	RANK 2001
McKinsey & Co.	1	1
Boston Consulting Group	4	2
Cisco Systems	7	3
Goldman Sachs	3	4
Bain & Co.	5	5
Accenture	13	6
Booz-Allen & Hamilton	8	7
Intel	12	8
Hewlett-Packard	22	9
Morgan Stanley Dean Witter	9	10

In fall 2001, a similar poll of 6,000 final-year students at 42 universities around the United Kingdom asked them to name five organizations for which they would most like to work. The BBC topped the list. The Foreign and Commonwealth Office, British Airways, Accenture, and Andersen were the other big, blue-chip organizations that made up the top five.[9]

But, in the company of so many big graduate recruiters, why did the BBC come out on top? After all, the BBC doesn't actually have a formal graduate recruitment process and re-cruits only some 300 people a year. It can perhaps be explained by the BBC's efforts to revamp its brand as an employer. In 2001 the BBC cosponsored Media Days, a program held at var-ious campuses around the country designed to dispel the notion that the corporation is elitist and encourages nepotism. Simi-larly, the company ran BBC Talent, a recruitment program tar-geted to young presenters, producers, and technicians that portrayed the BBC as risk-taking and innovative rather than elitist and established.

Clearly, a good reputation attracts interest from potential employees, even if you don't hire much. It also reinforces the commitment of in-house employees to the company's values, beliefs, mission, and objectives. By building identification with the company, reputation as a good employer fuels employee loy-alty, motivation, engagement, and commitment.

INVESTORS: REPUTATION AFFECTS INVESTMENT DECISIONS

There are two basic types of investors: Individual investors and institutional investors. Individual investors are people like us who occasionally and recklessly decide to gamble with their sav-ings and trade corporate shares for their own account. Some in-dividual investors are savvy, do extensive research, and study carefully the records of the companies in which they are con-sidering investing. Others, less sophisticated perhaps, choose the companies and shares they buy on the basis of casual research, hype, and hearsay. To identify good prospects in which to invest, some individual investors actually examine the shareholdings of institutional investors—and mimic them. In general, institutional ownership is a sign of the legitimacy and liquidity of a company's shares. It implies that the company has gained access to large pools of capital, which might not be available otherwise.

For their part, institutional investors are firms or individuals that hold more than $100 million in assets for investment. They include managers of pension funds, banks, trusts, unions, endowments, and mutual funds. Institutional investors do not buy on the hype and purchase signals that many brokerage houses release to the public. Instead, they do their own inhouse analyses, carry out extensive research, and rely on specialists to study the numbers.

Institutional investors actually control some 40 percent of all investment funds. The remainder are fragmented in the hands of millions of individual investors. Institutional investors account for an estimated 80 percent of all U.S. trading activity in stocks, bonds, mutual funds, and commodities. Their influence also extends abroad. In 1996 the financial assets of U.S. institutional investors were six times those of the United Kingdom, ten times those of France and Germany, and nearly four times those of Japan. As a result, the financial assets of U.S. institutions make up the majority (61.9 %) of the five-country total. This concentrated pattern of institutional shareholdings is important because their actions can fuel large capital movements in and out of a company's shares.

Major companies are well aware of the importance of maintaining their corporate reputations with institutional shareholders. When institutional investors lose confidence in a company, when they develop negative perceptions of the company's prospects, they increasingly press for a change in leadership. In recent years a number of major institutional investors have flexed their muscles on various corporate governance issues, questioning the reasoning behind executive pay packages and in some instances taking active steps to split executive roles. Doing so invariably provokes a media fest, with a feedback effect on the company's reputation. Vision and leadership often are at the heart of the crisis of confidence—and the company's reputation ultimately depends on it. The call is invariably made for increased transparency from corporate leaders.

THE MEDIA: REPUTATION AFFECTS COVERAGE

The media have a powerful effect on the issues we pay attention to. In a well-known study conducted in 1972, professors Max McCombs and Don Shaw interviewed 100 undecided voters in North Carolina and asked them to identify five issues they were most concerned about in the coming presidential election. The researchers then examined the content of the main media serving Chapel Hill (both print and broadcast), and found an almost perfect correlation between media coverage and the concerns that voters expressed.[10] Their study was the first in a stream of research that confirms the "agenda-setting" role of the media— that the media has a strong effect in shaping the public's view of events and their importance; that the *number of times* a story is repeated in the news affects peoples' perception of an event's importance, regardless of what is said about the topic.

At the same time, the media are run of the mill people who are themselves affected by the world around them: Journalists have to select the topics they cover; editors have to anticipate what will be of interest to their readership. Publishers and producers rely heavily on advertising dollars and so are willy-nilly affected by the companies whose advertising they carry—even when no overt efforts are made either by publishers seeking to court favor with advertisers or by advertisers seeking to influence media content. To prevent undue influence, most well-regarded publishers build a wall of sorts between news and advertising.

Pressured by competition and the need to attract revenues, however, the barrier between editorial and marketing occasionally comes down. Consider the much criticized relationship between the *Los Angeles Times* and the office supply retailer Staples. In 2000 the newspaper released a 168-page Sunday magazine full of soft stories and advertising about the opening of Staples Centre, a downtown arena financed by the retailer. Investigative reports indicated that the *Times* shared handsome profits on magazine sales with Staples itself, raising widespread concern about a possible lapse in journalistic values at the *Times*.[11]

Anecdotal accounts like these abound, documenting how corporate tactics are used systematically to directly influence media content. After all, the media relations industry as a whole exists to do just that. However, hard empirical evidence is more difficult to locate. In reality, the influence of reputation on the media is likely to be much more covert, much less traceable than mere examples can account for. And that's far harder to trace.

Common sense suggests that the reputations of companies and of the executives who run them are likely to play a powerful role in attracting reporters to cover specific companies, in predisposing reporters to cover better-regarded companies more favorably, and in positioning a story more or less visibly in print and on the air.

FINANCIAL ANALYSTS: REPUTATION AFFECTS LANGUAGE

Sir Richard Branson is no fan of financial analysts. In 1986, he sold shares in his $5 billion Virgin Group empire to the public, making it one of Britain's most hotly subscribed initial public offerings. Two years later, frustrated by their shortsightedness, he took Virgin Group private once again. As he put it, "The delightful thing about not being a public company is that we don't have to worry about foolish analysts who say stupid things."[12] Surely his comments were prescient, given the virtual maelstrom analysts have found themselves in since the fall of Enron and its domino-like effect throughout 2002 on Arthur Andersen, WorldCom, Xerox, and the public's loss of confidence in Wall Street in general.

Following a presentation about how corporate reputations are built, we once received a call from a mid-sized advertising agency in New York who asked how we might show that the ads it produced for some major companies had a *measurable* effect on financial analysts who covered those companies. Naturally, they wanted us to demonstrate that the campaigns they created had generated more and better analyst recommendations for the company's shares.

Although showing such an effect would be wonderful indeed, it's actually very difficult to do. Analysts are influenced by many factors, including each other, and by ongoing financial and operating results as well as strategic changes that affect the company's prospects and trust in the company's leadership. It's hard to control for such effects in any meaningful quantitative fashion—not to mention that financial analysts pride themselves on their entirely rational ["it's a numbers issue"] assessment of a company and would hardly welcome evidence to the contrary.

Instead, along with colleague Violina Rindova, we proposed to examine whether analysts were influenced by ad campaigns on a subliminal level. Since ad campaigns are generally trying to change qualitatively the perspective of the person exposed to the ad or to generate some emotional reaction, we decided to examine whether the actual words they used in their quarterly and annual reports changed after an ad campaign. To do so, we used software that chunked the electronic text used in these analyst reports into strings of words, recognized synonyms, classified the entire text into these words, and catalogued the counts of words used by the multiple analysts who covered the company. Specifically, for *each* ad campaign, we followed these steps:

Step 1: Create a list of all words used in an ad campaign.

Step 2: Select as keywords those that were repeated more than three times in the ads.

Step 3: Create a dictionary of words used in analysts' reports before and after the ad campaign.

Step 4: Compare how often analysts used the keywords from ads before and after the ad campaign.

Step 5: Calculate the multiplier effects of the campaign on word usage in analysts' reports before and after the ad campaign.

We did so for a number of ad campaigns that the agency had created for four different companies. Analyst reports were compiled for a year *before* the campaign and a year *after* the campaign. We also brought together the agency's campaign creators and managers to identify key hypotheses reflecting their strategic objectives for the campaign—what they were trying to change. Figure 1–2 uses the example of a company whose ads were intended to change the company's image from that of an old-fashioned financial printer relying on mechanical technologies to that of a high-tech advisor whose activities involved as much information manipulation across multiple media. The company was also growing heavily through acquisitions of related businesses. As Figure 1–2 indicates, the ad agency hypothesized that if the campaign was successful, it would *decrease* the word count associated with the old image and *increase* the word count of descriptors of the new, high-tech aggressive image.

The campaign was carried out in the late 1990s. We identified, retrieved, and analyzed the electronic texts of all analyst reports about the company over a two-year period. The core of the analysis involved creating reliable dictionaries to capture the keywords and ideas expressed by the management team (listed in Figure 1–2). The results of the study are summarized

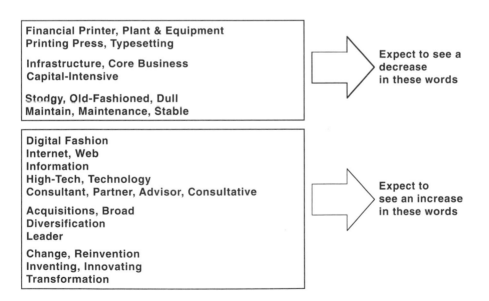

Figure 1–2 Hypothesized effect of an advertising campaign on word counts in analyst reports.

in Figure 1–3 and indicate that analysts continued to use words associated with the old image of the company, such as "stodgy" and "printing-based," at about the same rate as before the campaign. However, it also documents that in writing about the company, financial analysts began using significantly more words associated with the new image *after* the ad campaign had run than they had before, suggesting that the transformation of the company was picked up by financial analysts and confirming that even analysts are influenced by the context within which they interpret a company's operating results. In short, we demonstrated that analysts are human after all.

A small but neglected literature in finance actually documents some of these human foibles of the financial community. By examining the recommendations that analysts make, these researchers demonstrate that analysts constitute something of a social group in which some act as leaders, others as followers. In this social group, leading analysts often set the tone by recommending or downgrading a stock, only to be quickly followed by lesser analysts who behave all too much like lemmings

	Before Campaign	After Campaign	Multiplier Effect
EXPECTED DECREASES			
Financial	3	23	
Printer	4	45	
Plant & Equipment	0	2	
Infrastructure+Core Business+Capital Intensive	0	1	
Stody+Old Fashioned+Dull	0	0	
Maintain+Stable	0	4	
OVERALL MULTIPLIER OF DECREASES	7	75	0.97
EXPECTED INCREASES			
Digital/Internet/Web	0	17	
Information	0	22	
High-Tech+Technology	0	4	
Consultant+Consultative+Partnership+Advisor	0	1	
Acquisitions+Diversification+Broad	1	70	
Leader	0	7	
Change+Reinvention+Inventing+Innovating	0	6	
Transformation	0	1	
OVERALL MULTIPLIER OF INCREASES	1	128	11.57
TOTAL WORDS IN ANALYST REPORTS	527	5828	

Positive Effect of Campaign

Figure 1–3 The effects of an advertising campaign.

and demonstrate the herd mentality that is known to prevail in most social groups.

That analysts are influenced by social and political factors has hardly gone unnoticed in recent years. Arthur Levitt, former chairman of the U.S. Securities and Exchange Commission, commented pointedly that there had to be a reason why in 1999 there were eight times as many analyst "buy" as "sell" recommendations. In the early 1980s, that ratio had been roughly one-to-one. As Levitt put it, "Part of the explanation could be what more and more studies are showing: A direct correlation between the content of an analyst's recommendation and the amount of business his firm does with the issuer."[13]

A study by four economists at Stanford University documents just how wrong analysts were at the end of the Internet technology bubble in 2000. As the study's authors conclude, "During that year, the stocks least recommended by analysts earned an annualized market-adjusted return of 49 percent, while the stocks most highly recommended *fell* 31 percent, a return difference of 80 percentage points."[14]

Another empirical study shows that analysts are clearly biased when they work for an investment bank that underwrites a new issue of shares, a so-called IPO (individual placement offering). The conflict of interest gets manifested in the fact that the recommendations of analysts in such firms are demonstrably less reliable than those of other firms in predicting the future performance of the IPO.[15] It suggests that there's internal pressure on these analysts to justify their bank's investment in the IPO shares—all of which justifies our understanding of financial analysts as people whose recommendations are constructed from their efforts to interpret what companies are doing operationally and strategically, and whose opinions are also shaped by the strategic communications of various institutional colleagues seeking to influence how analysts interpret a company's activities and prospects.

Throughout 2002, as companies like Enron, WorldCom, Global Crossings, Tyco International, and Andersen toppled into bankruptcy, we were bombarded daily with scandalous revelations that financial markets are peopled by very human analysts and executives whose guile, self-interest, and opportunistic outlook had never before been quite so apparent—very human indeed. Hence the call for reform of the banking system, found most visibly in the push for removing research and analysis out of the investment bank's portfolio of legitimate activities. In May 2003 the United States' largest brokerage firms agreed to pay $1.4 billion in fines to end investigations into whether they issued misleading stock recommendations and handed out hot new shares to curry favor with corporate clients. The firms also agreed to sweeping changes in the way research is done on Wall Street and the way new stocks are distributed, moving away from the practices they used during the stock boom of the 1990s. As part of the settlement, the firms also agreed to pay an additional $500 million over five years to buy stock research from independent analysts and distribute it to investors.

CONCLUSION: REPUTATIONS MATTER BECAUSE THEY AFFECT STRATEGIC POSITIONING

If reputations matter, it's because they are intrinsically connected to the strategic positioning of the company as a whole. A corporate reputation is a mirror that reflects a company's relative success at convincing upstream, downstream, and diagonal stakeholders about the current and future validity of its strategic direction. But the mirror is also a magnet: If stakeholders like what they hear and see, they support the company—and an upward spiral results that attracts more resources to the company. If stakeholders withdraw their support, a downward spiral results that can lead to bankruptcy, as demonstrated by the speedy demise of the giant auditor Arthur Andersen following its reputation-damaging criminal indictment in the United States in 2001.

In an analysis that seems almost quaint now because it focused on two high-tech darlings of the Internet boom, our colleagues Violina Rindova and Suresh Kotha [both were then at the University of Washington] examined the crucial role that reputation played in the frenzied battle between Yahoo! and Excite, the two most popular search engines of the mid-1990s. As they point out,

In building its brand, Yahoo! magnified its existing organizational attributes, especially the cool image based on its playful culture and somewhat iconoclastic stance toward the technical community that had dominated the Web in its early years.... For example, the firm's name, supposedly an acronym for "Yet Another Hierarchical Officious Oracle," parodied the language of computer programming." [16]

To support its reputation-building efforts, Yahoo! invested in a $5 million television ad campaign that was designed to reinforce the company's playful identity with the tagline *Do You Yahoo!?* and that established the company as a consumer brand rather than a technology company.

Those efforts were quickly matched by rival Excite's own brand-building efforts, which ultimately proved less successful than Yahoo!'s. One reason it was less successful is that it lacked the cool consumer image and employee advocacy that Yahoo! had created. Excite's own $8 million television campaign was built around Jimi Hendrix's 1967 rock classic "Are You Experienced?" but its effectiveness was widely questioned. A poll conducted by *BusinessWeek* in 1998 indicated that Yahoo!'s name was recognized by 44 percent of Internet users and about 2 percent of non-Internet users, whereas Excite was recognized by only 11 and 0 percent respectively.

Yahoo!'s established reputation had clearly factored into its success. But as history teaches us, the competitive terrain continuously shifts. No sooner had both Yahoo! and Excite built strong reputations as search engines than they were faced with the need to change how they were perceived, and both companies had to morph from mere search engines into full-fledged media companies. And morph they did—only to find themselves challenged by new developments in the Internet space that almost drove Excite out of the market entirely, leaving Yahoo! in a battle with newer rivals like Go and Google.

If reputations matter, then what are they worth? In the next chapter, we examine some of the evidence that relates corporate reputation to real financial value and show why and how this occurs.

ENDNOTES

1. Stakeholders are "groups or individuals who can affect, or are affected by, the achievements of an organization's mission." R. E. Freeman, *Strategic Management: A Stakeholder Approach*. Boston: Pitman, 1984, p. 52.

2. T. J. Brown, "Corporate Associations in Marketing: Antecedents and Consequences." *Corporate Reputation Review, 1*(3), 1998: 215–233.

3. A. Chatterjee, M. E. Jauchius, H.-W. Kaas, & A. Satpathy, "Reviving Up Auto Branding." *The McKinsey Quarterly, 1,* 2002: 134–144.

4. M. E. Goldberg & J. Hartwick, "The Effects of Advertiser Reputation and Extremity of Advertising Effectiveness." *Journal of Consumer Research, 17,* 1990: 172–179.

5. T. J. Brown & P. A. Dacin, "The Company and the Product: Corporate Associations and Consumer Product Responses." *Journal of Marketing, 61,* 1997: 68–84. See also K. L. Keller & D. A. Aaker, "The Impact of Corporate Marketing on a Company's Brand Extensions." *Corporate Reputation Review, 1*(4), 1998: 356–378.

6. The Conference Board, "Engaging Your Employees Through Your Brand." Report 1288, February 2001.

7. C. J. Fombrun & C. B. M. Van Riel, "The Reputational Landscape." *Corporate Reputation Review, 1*(1), 1997: 5–13.

8. M. Boyle, "So Where Do MBAs Want to Work?" *Fortune,* April 16, 2001: 408.

9. I. Wiley, "BBC Tops News List as Ideal Employer: Big Brands Dominate Survey of Graduates." *The Guardian,* March 16, 2002: 3

10. M. E. McCombs & D. L. Shaw, "The Agenda-Setting Function of Mass Media." *Public Opinion Quarterly,* 1972: 176–187.

11. Jim Naughton, "No Newsroom Is an Island." February 2000. Online:http://www.poynter.org/Research/lm/lm_jbvisland.htm.

12. *New York Times,* May 26, 2002, p. C-1.

13. Quoted by P. Martin, "Who Pays the Piper?" *Financial Times,* May 20, 2002: 11.

14. Barber, Lehavy, McNichols, & Trueman, "Prophets and Losses: Reassessing the Returns to Analysts' Stock Recommendations." Research Paper 1692, Stanford Graduate School of Business, 2001.

15. Michaely & Womack, "Conflict of Interest and the Credibility of Underwriter Analyst Recommendations." Online: http://mba.tuck.dartmouth.edu/pages/faculty/kent.womack/workingpapers/bost.pdf.

16. V. Rindova & S. Kotha, "Continuous 'Morphing': Competing through Dynamic Capabilities, Form and Function." *Academy of Management Journal, 44*(6), 2001: 1261–1281.

2

WHAT ARE REPUTATIONS WORTH?

No matter how receptive executives are to the idea that reputations matter, there's no denying them the inevitably punchy question, so, what's a reputation *really* worth? Everyone wants an answer, from the communications chieftains to the heads of marketing and finance, from the senior C-level staff to the company's board of directors. Indeed, this remains by far the most frequent question we're asked and the most problematic issue facing business researchers. It involves demonstrating a quantitative relationship between a public company's reputation and the financial value of its shares. Unfortunately, as this chapter shows, proving such a relationship is no simple matter, and quantifying the financial value of a company's reputation remains the holy grail of all reputation research. We offer evidence that the holy grail is in sight.

In fact, reputation and financial value are related in three ways. First, reputation affects the *operating performance* of a company and therefore its profitability. Second, profitability affects market perceptions of the company's future prospects—and so influences the level of demand for a public company's shares, that is, its market capitalization. Third, the company's operating activities themselves contribute to building "reputation capital"— a *shadow asset* whose value encompasses the intangible equity hidden in both a company's product brands and corporate brand, and that describes the positive regard in which it is held by all of the company's stakeholders. Positive regard, in turn, attracts people to work for and invest in the company—and so increases profitability. We address these three financial impacts in turn.

REPUTATION AFFECTS A COMPANY'S OPERATING PERFORMANCE

Consider a highly respected company. Respect and admiration create considerable goodwill for the company on a day-to-day basis. For one, being admired is likely to mean it can recruit the highest potential employees, people willing to go the extra mile for the company—and often at a better wage than lesser regarded rivals. In turn, working there boosts the productivity of both new and existing employees. This reinforcing loop enhances operating performance immeasurably: Employees are motivated to work, to solve problems, to generate creative solutions, to service customers. As pride in work grows, efficiency and innovation result, fueling corporate growth.

A study of the New York Port Authority conducted in the late 1980s demonstrated this effect. Employees of the quasi-private agency that runs New York's buses and airports were alienated by the rise in the population of homeless inhabiting the agency's urban terminals. Employees' self-concept as caring, helpful, and effective contradicted the external image displayed in the media that portrayed the agency as inhumane in its efforts to jettison the homeless and as ineffectual in managing the issue. The result was growing alienation, a demotivated staff, and productivity decline.[1]

In general terms, a good reputation can improve a company's efficiency and effectiveness by stimulating employee productivity. It also creates a reservoir of goodwill toward the company that derives from partners, suppliers, dealers, creditors, and regulators whose support often manifests itself in the form of lower input prices, including a lower cost of capital, and translates into higher margins. The company's lower input costs are supported by its ability to charge better prices for its offerings, a factor that enhances the company's margins, encourages financial analysts to give favorable ratings to the company and fuels demand for its shares. Figure 2–1 diagrams the straightforward logic of reputation's effect on a company's operating performance and its subsequent effect on the company's market value.

A study of 125 U.S. manufacturing businesses compared the relative effects of industry structure, competitive strategy, and company-specific differences.[2] The results confirmed the powerful effects of reputation on operating results. Factors associated with the industry's overall structure accounted for only a small percentage of observed variation in business performance.

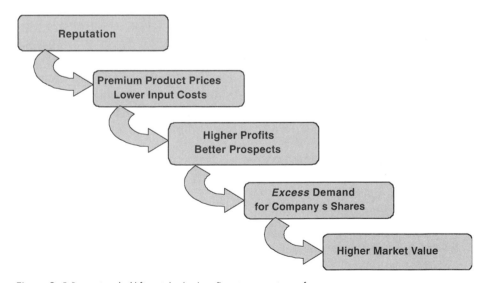

Figure 2–1 Reputations build financial value by influencing operating performance.

Competitive strategy variables such as product quality and sales force expenditures were not statistically significant in explaining variance in business performance, but company market share was. Finally, of all the company-specific variables, reputation and brand equity of the business unit were found to be the best predictors of variation in business unit performance.

Most researchers who have examined the relationship between reputation and operating performance have relied on *Fortune's* annual survey of "most admired companies" as a measure of reputation and correlated that measure with various financial measures of risk and return. Since the survey instrument is filled out by analysts and executives, it naturally demonstrates that corporate reputation is highly correlated with measures of both prior operating performance and subsequent operating performance, although they are generally more closely related to prior financial performance than to subsequent financial performance.[3]

In this view, reputation acts like a resource to the company—one that is difficult to gain and difficult to imitate, and that enables the company to achieve superior levels of performance. Two professors at the University of New South Wales in Australia examined the effects of reputation on a company's profitability by looking at the group of 435 companies rated in *Fortune's* most admired companies between 1984 and 1995. They concluded that there was a significant effect that operated in two ways: First, companies with better corporate reputations are better able to sustain superior operating performance over time, and second, companies with better reputations are better able to improve their operating performance over time.

REPUTATION CREATES FINANCIAL VALUE THAT BUILDS REPUTATION

The higher levels of operating performance that result from having a good reputation virtually guarantee that a company will receive favorable endorsements from stakeholders and the media. Charles Fombrun and Mark Shanley showed that reputations measured by *Fortune's* most admired company ratings were heavily influenced by a company's size, advertising, operating performance, market value, and media visibility—thereby confirming the idea that a company's operating performance, market value, and strategic behavior are heavily intertwined.[4]

We describe the relationship in Figure 2–2 in terms of the reputation value cycle. It illustrates how financial value and stakeholder support are dynamically intertwined: Endorsements build value and enable a company to expense funds on corporate activities such as advertising, philanthropy, and citizenship that generate media endorsements, attract investors, and add financial value. The net effect is a *reinforcing loop* through which recognition, endorsement, and support from stakeholders produce equity and financial value.

Of course, the downside of such a reinforcing loop is that a *decline* in operating performance is generally followed by cutbacks in communications and initiatives that alienate stakeholders, reduce operating performance, and fuel a downward spiral in both fame and fortune. Clearly, reputation and performance are linked through the reputation value cycle, and the cycle has to be managed carefully to capitalize on the upside gains it can generate while minimizing the downside risks of value loss that can result.[5]

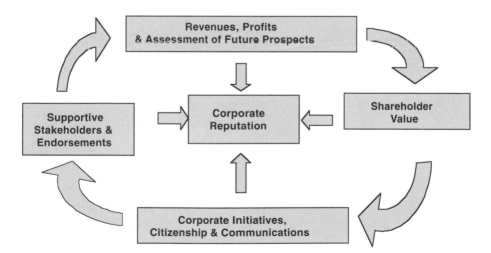

Figure 2–2 The reputation value cycle.

The link between fame and fortune has been partially documented in various other academic studies.

- Brad Brown's research at the University of Virginia found a strong relationship between *Fortune's* measure of corporate reputation and the market values of those companies in the years 1984 through 1996.[6]
- A Connecticut-based consulting company founded by Jim Gregory tracks "brand power" for 700 publicly traded companies using mailed surveys sent to business decision makers. Taking advantage of a three-day period of unusually high U.S. stock price volatility (October 24–28, 1997), they hypothesized that corporate reputation would act as a relative buffer for companies facing market volatility: Companies with stronger reputations should experience less volatility and less market decline than those with weaker reputations. The study showed that all stocks fell significantly on Monday October 27, but by the close of the market on Tuesday October 28, the strongest brands had regained nearly all of their losses from the previous day. The weaker brands had not come close to recovering from Monday's precipitous drop. In addition, from Friday to Tuesday, the strongest brands had actually *gained* a total of $7.09bn in market capitalization, while the passive brands lost a total of $19.79bn.[7]
- A team of researchers compared 10 groups of companies that had similar levels of risk and return, but different average reputation scores from *Fortune's* most admired company survey. They found that a 60 percent difference in reputation score was associated with a 7 percent difference in market value. Since an average company in the study was valued at $3 billion, that meant a 1-point difference in reputation score from 6 to 7 on a 10-point scale would be worth an additional $51.5 million in market value.[8]
- Another team of researchers examined the relationship between market value, book value, profitability, and reputation for all the firms rated in *Fortune's* most admired company survey between 1983 and 1997. They report that a 1-point difference in reputation is worth about $500

million in market value. They concluded that "...our findings add support to existing research that internally generated intangibles not currently recognized as assets contribute to firm value and thus are viewed as assets by investors."[9]

Looking across these studies, clearly, there is evidence of a consistent link between fame and fortune. Although the coefficients vary from study to study, we can identify an approximate equation between ratings and market values. It suggests that a 10% improvement in reputation is worth between 1% and 5% of a company's market value. The equation sets a benchmark of sorts: It provides a rough guideline for the kinds of expenditures a company should be willing to engage in to improve its reputation. In the next section, we explore the shadow value a company can associate with its total pool of reputational assets—what Charles Fombrun described as its reputational capital.[10]

REPUTATION HAS FINANCIAL VALUE AS A CORPORATE ASSET

Conservative accounting rules require that companies expense most of the operational activities that build reputation. By doing so, accountants implicitly tell us that advertising, public relations, sponsorships, and corporate philanthropy are so uncertain in their effects as to have no long-term value to the company. They are therefore best treated not as investments in building an asset but as direct costs of doing business. This is clearly prudent. But in a post-Enron world, it's certainly ironic that accountants have been so conservative in their treatment of all reputation-building activities yet so willing to facilitate the capitalization of unearned income that enabled Enron, WorldCom, and Xerox to claim inflated returns for so long. There would seem to be greater certainty and more measurable effects from brand-building and reputation-building activities than some of these other forms of capitalization that accountants allow.

Although no one claims *complete* certainty about branding and reputation-building, some portions of these activities clearly help to build a company's visibility, familiarity, and fame. It's therefore not inappropriate to conceive of them as *investments in creating reputational assets*. After all, a company's advertising and communications campaigns are intended not only to influence current sales and support but to build customer loyalty and repeat business. One can only wonder, therefore, at extreme policies that completely deny a role for intangibles as value-creating assets in their own right. At the very least, we should be accounting for them as valuable shadow investments, a set of off–balance sheet items worthy of tracking systematically.

To make direct estimates of the shadow financial value of corporate reputations, it's useful to decompose the market value (MV) of a publicly traded company into four components:

- Physical capital (PC): The replacement value of the company's non-financial tangible assets
- Financial capital (FC): The liquid financial assets of a company
- Intellectual capital (IC): The value of the company's know-how
- Reputational capital (RC): The value of the company's brands and stakeholder relationships

Figure 2–3 describes these four forms of capital. *Physical capital* consists of net plant and equipment—the company's hard assets net of costs incurred in acquiring them. *Financial capital* represents the net liquid assets of the company. *Intellectual capital* describes the wealth of the company that resides in its accumulated wisdom and know-how, in the company's routines, and in its employees' skills. *Reputational capital* embodies the company's stock of perceptual assets and social assets—the quality of the relationships it has established with stakeholders and the regard in which the company and its brands is held—positive regard increases the probability of supportive behavior from those stakeholders, be they investors, customers, or employees. Together, they add up to the company's market capitalization.

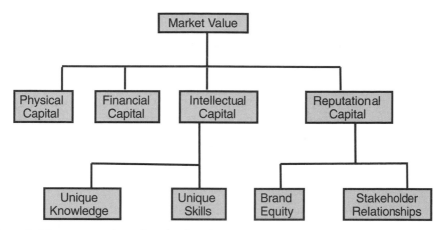

Figure 2–3 Reputation capital is a subset of market value.

Physical capital, financial capital, and market value are easily estimated. However, estimates of reputational capital require deep knowledge of the company's stock of intellectual capital—something that's as difficult to estimate as reputation itself. Failing that, it's possible to assess the company's pool of intangible assets as the joint value of its reputational and intellectual capital.

The accumulated value of a company's intangible assets has grown dramatically over the last 50 years, not least cause of which is accounting rules that force either expensing or rapid depreciation of goodwill-related items. In large public companies, these intangibles amount to an average of some 55 to 60 percent of market value—justifying the heightened interest in the management of knowledge, brands, and reputation.

Another estimate of reputational capital results from asking, How much would you be willing to pay to *lease* a corporate name? Licensing arrangements are actually royalty rates for corporate names. The greater the drawing power of the company's reputation, the more a licensee should be prepared to pay to rent a corporate name. Royalty percentages on corporate licenses generally range between 8 and 14 percent of projected sales. One way to estimate the value of a company's reputation is to calculate the present value of expected royalty payments over an arbitrary life of, say, 20 years.

Consider consumer goods giant Gillette. In 1993 the consulting firm Interbrand suggested that an 8 percent royalty rate might be expected from licensing the Gillette name. Applied to Gillette's $4.7 billion in sales, it meant potential royalty revenue of $375 million in the first year. Assuming sales growth of 5 percent a year over 20 years (an arbitrary term ascribed to use of the Gillette name) and discounting the royalty revenues back to the present at Gillette's own cost of capital of 10.12 percent produces a financial estimate for Gillette's corporate name of about $4.5 billion in 1993, a significant proportion of Gillette's total market value.[11]

Consider a similar analysis for Coca-Cola in 2002. With sales of $20 billion in 2002 and assuming a higher royalty rate of 14 percent for the respected Coke brand means potential royalty income on the brand of $2.4 billion a year. Cumulating these royalties over an arbitrary 20 years, assuming an 8 percent growth rate and discounting them back at a 5 percent rate, produces a financial estimate for the Coca-Cola brand of $69.9 billion. This compares rather well with the $69.6 billion value ascribed to Coca-Cola by valuators at Interbrand and *Business Week*.[12]

CRISIS COSTS INCLUDE LOSS OF REPUTATION CAPITAL

Crisis costs provide another way of estimating reputation capital. An Exxon oil tanker hits a reef in Prudhoe Bay on a moonless night. A terrorist bomb rips open the belly of a Pan Am jet over Lockerbie, Scotland. A lethal gas cloud seeps from a Union Carbide plant in Bhopal, India. The flames from a Phillips Petroleum refinery fire engulf block after block in Pasadena, California.

The value of a corporate reputation is magnified at such times because of the tragic loss of physical assets and human lives that occur and the expected clean-up and legal costs associated with the crisis. Comparable market losses occur, however, even when no physical assets are actually lost and the crisis can be attributed solely to changed perceptions of the company by key resource-holders.

Consider what happened to the actual market values of the following companies listed in a one-week window after they were plunged into unnatural crises that made headlines around the world:

- Johnson & Johnson dropped $1 billion in market value, or 14 percent, after some of its Tylenol bottles were laced with cyanide in 1982. J&J took another $1 billion hit when malicious tamperers struck again in 1985.
- The discovery that Intel Corporation's new Pentium chip couldn't handle some simple math calculations knocked $3 billion, or 12 percent, off Intel's market value in 1985.
- Exxon Corporation's stock was devalued by $3 billion, or 5 percent, in the first week after the oil gushing from the *Exxon Valdez* fouled Alaska's Prince William Sound in 1989.
- Salomon Brothers watched the bears take $1.3 billion, or 30 percent, of its value after one of its own traders was caught trying to corner the bond market in 1991.
- Motorola saw its capitalization fall by $6 billion, or 16 percent, after scientists hinted at a link between cell phones and brain cancer in 1995.

These market losses can be traced to the changed expectations of resource-holders about the company's future profitability. They are equally staggering, whether they involve material losses of physical capital or consist purely of changes in how the company is perceived in the marketplace. Exxon's subsequent clean-up and legal costs were approximately $2.5 billion. But in 1995, Motorola's $6 billion losses from the brain tumor scare were purely intangible, as were most of Intel's from the Pentium chip.

Over time, some companies recover dissipated value quickly and the crisis fizzles. Others experience more extended damage. Research suggests that the enduring difference may well lie in how the crisis is handled and what the reputation of the company was beforehand.

Academics at Oxford University conducted event studies to chart the impact of manmade catastrophes on the market values of 15 companies. They ranged from the first Tylenol tampering in 1982, to Source Perrier's recall of its gassy, green-bottled water because of benzene contamination in 1990, to a Heineken recall due to rumors of broken glass in its beer bottles in 1993. As the authors put it, catastrophes "provide a unique opportunity to evaluate how financial markets respond when major risks become reality." On average, all 15 stocks they studied took an initial hit of 8 percent of their market value. However, the companies quickly sorted themselves into two distinct groups that the Oxford professors called the "recoverers" and "non-recoverers."[13]

The recoverers' stock sagged only 5 percent in the first weeks, while the non-recoverers' stock lost 11 percent. After 10 weeks, the recoverers' stock actually rose 5 percent and stayed comfortably in positive territory for the balance of the year. In contrast, the non-recoverers' stock stayed down and finished the year off by a sobering 15 percent. The conclusion: All catastrophes have an initial negative impact on price, but paradoxically, "they offer an opportunity for management to demonstrate their talent in dealing with difficult circumstances."

Event studies like these support the thesis that reputations have considerable hidden value as a form of insurance—they act like a reservoir of goodwill. The insurance value derives from an ability to buffer better-regarded companies from taking as large a fall as companies with lesser reputations. J. R. Gregory examined the stock prices of companies on the New York Stock Exchange following the market crash of 1997.[14]Consistent with the reservoir hypothesis, he argued that better-regarded companies would be cushioned from the crisis. Their results confirmed that the market values of high-reputation companies were less affected by the market crash than those of a comparable sample of companies with weaker reputations.

Bridgestone/Firestone and Ford are a case in point. A media fest occurred in 2000 as information was uncovered suggesting that Firestone tires were to blame for numerous deadly accidents around the world involving Ford Explorer sports utility vehicles. Ford announced that it would take a $2.1 billion charge to replace Firestone tires on its vehicles with Goodyear tires. However, the financial *impact* of the crisis on both companies was considerably greater than its financial cost: Each company saw its market value drop by over 50 percent from its value in early 2000—Bridgestone to $11 billion from $22 billion and Ford to $16 billion from $29 billion. Ford may have benefited initially from a somewhat better handling of the crisis, as Jack Nasser, Ford's CEO at the time, launched an aggressive media campaign that focused on blaming Firestone's tires. In contrast,

Japanese-based Bridgestone conveyed secrecy and guile by failing to communicate information in a timely fashion, which may have penalized it in financial markets. But both have suffered heavily, with market values now at their lowest level in years.

More recently, an interesting study examined the effects of Andersen's reputation loss from its link to Enron and revealed that it indirectly affected the market value of Andersen's *other* clients. As the authors show, on the three days following Andersen's admission that a significant number of internal Enron documents had been shredded, Andersen's other clients experienced significant and negative market losses, suggesting that investors downgraded the quality of all audits performed by Andersen. Consistent with that notion, the effect was even more pronounced for companies that had been audited by Andersen's Houston office, where Enron was based.[15]

Finally a crisis for one can therefore become a crisis for many. Some years ago, Charles Fombrun examined the prices of oil company shares surrounding the Exxon Valdez spill in of 1989. Figure 2–4 diagrams the results. Controlling for market conditions and

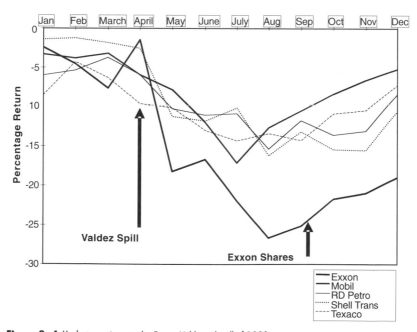

Figure 2–4 Market reactions to the Exxon Valdez oil spill of 1989.

the oil price index, it shows that Exxon's shares were most affected by the spill. However, the oil shares of Shell, Mobil, and Texaco were also swept downward by association and recovered only slowly to their pre-crisis levels. Overall, reputational losses associated with crises are substantial and, on average, amount to 8-15% of the market values of affected companies.

COURT AWARDS RECOGNIZE
CORPORATE LIBEL AND DEFAMATION

Crises often propel companies into the courts, where students of the judicial system generally concede that financial value attaches to a company's good name. In a court case that the lead author was called on to testify, a garment manufacturer sued one of its contractors for producing lower quality garments than it had ordered. The manufacturer argued to the courts that its premium-pricing strategy was based on customer perceptions that its garments were high quality. Having experienced high returns from customers attributed to low-quality products, the company argued that it had experienced an adverse reputational effect that could undermine future business. The courts found in favor of the company and awarded substantial financial damages to the manufacturer.

In another case on which the lead author was asked to testify, a major television network was sued for defamation when it erroneously linked a company to a terrorist group following the September 11, 2001, bombing of the World Trade Center in New York. A member of the company's board was misidentified as having a relationship with a leading terrorist leader and the mistake was broadcast without adequate verification. In an unprecedented move, the network read an on-air apology note the next day. Nonetheless, damage was done: the company found itself besieged with hate mail, lost contracts, and innuendo, and so claimed reputational injury in the courts. As often happens in these cases, the matter was settled out of court, so the size of the financial settlement itself cannot be known—but given the costs incurred, we know it was not trivial.

In general, the courts have proven to be sympathetic to demonstrations of reputational loss due to libel and defamation. In such cases, plaintiffs demonstrate reputational damage in two ways:

1. by calculating direct financial losses incurred because of the defamatory act—for instance, by showing a timeline with an abrupt change in revenues and costs timed with the occurrence of the act;
2. by calculating the necessary investment in advertising or communications required to remedy the negative perceptions created by the defamatory act.

When projected over a finite horizon of months and years, the costs that companies incur from reputational damage are clearly substantial and often comparable to the losses associated with crisis events—some 5 to 15% of the market values of the injured company.

Linking Fame and Fortune

The analyses we described in this chapter demonstrate a link between measures of reputation and measures of financial value. They constitute a mosaic of evidence for the link between fame and fortune. To examine the question more systematically and cross-nationally, the next two chapters describe a research project that we have been involved in that was designed with three purposes in mind:

1. to create a robust measure of a company's reputation,
2. to measure the reputations of visible companies around the world, and
3. to examine the link between reputation, financial value, and corporate practices.

In Chapter 3, we report the results of international projects through which we identified some of the best-regarded companies in the world. The process relied on rigorously conducted representative surveys of the general public in various countries.

In Chapter 4, we return to the question of financial value and examine whether being tops in these surveys is linked to measures of financial value. The remaining chapters of the book are then devoted to examining how those companies have come to be so well regarded.

ENDNOTES

1. J. E. Dutton, & J. M. Dukerich, "Keeping an Eye on the Mirror: Image and Identity in Organizational Adaptation." *Academy of Management Journal, 34*(3), 1991: 517–554.

2. S. G. Bharadwaj, "Industry Structure, Competitive Strategy, and Firm-Specific Intangibles as Determinants of Business Unit Performance: Towards an Integrative Model." Texas A&M University, Ph.D. Dissertation, DAI-A 55/07, 1995.

3. J. B. McQuire, T. Schneeweis, & B. Branch, "Perceptions of Firm Quality: A Cause or Result of Firm Performance," *Journal of Management, 16*(1), March 1990: 167–181.

4. C. J. Fombrun & M. Shanley, "What's in a Name? Reputation Building and Corporate Strategy." *Academy of Management Journal, 33*(2), 1990: 233–250.

5. C. J. Fombrun, N. A. Gardberg, & M. L. Barnett, "Opportunity Platforms and Safety Nets: Corporate Citizenship and Reputational Risk." *Business and Society Review, 105*(1), 2000.

6. B. Brown, "Do Stock Market Investors Reward Companies with Reputations for Social Performance?" *Corporate Reputation Review, 1*(3), 1998: 271–280.

7. J. R. Gregory, "Does Corporate Reputation Provide a Cushion to Companies Facing Market Volatility? Some Supportive Evidence." *Corporate Reputation Review, 1*(3), 1998: 288–290.

8. R. K. Srivastava, T. H. McInish, R. A. Wood, & A. J. Capraro, "The Value of Corporate Reputation: Evidence from the Equity Markets." *Corporate Reputation Review, 1,* 1997: 62–68.

9. E. L. Black, T. A. Carnes, & V. J. Richardson, "The Market Valuation of Corporate Reputation." *Corporate Reputation Review, 3*(1), 2000: 31–41.

10. C. J. Fombrun, *Reputation: Realizing Value from the Corporate Image*. Cambridge, MA: Harvard Business School Press, 1996.

11. C. J. Fombrun, *Reputation: Realizing Value from the Corporate Image*. Cambridge, MA: Harvard Business School Press, 1996.

12. G. Khermouch, "The Best Global Brands; BusinessWeek and Interbrand Tell You What They're Worth." *Business Week*, August 5, 2002: 92.

13. R. F. Knight & D. J. Pretty, "Corporate Catastrophes, Stock Returns, and Trading Volume." *Corporate Reputation Review, 2,*(4), 1999: 363–381.

14. J. R. Gregory, "Does Corporate Reputation Provide a Cushion to Companies facing Market Volatility? Some Supportive Evidence." *Corporate Reputation Review, 1*(3), 1998: 288–290.

15. P. K. Chaney & K. L. Philipich, "Shredded Reputation: The Cost of Audit Failure." Working Paper, Vanderbilt University, 2003.

3 WHO'S TOPS— AND WHO'S NOT?

You can't build your reputation
on what you're going to do.

—HENRY FORD

If you were asked to name two or three companies that you most respect, trust, and admire, which companies would you put on your short list? Would you name a huge company like General Electric? Or a small company like Bang & Olufsen? A computer company like IBM, or the Internet auctioneer eBay? Would the companies be American or Japanese, German or Dutch, French, Danish, or Italian? The maker of your television set (Sony), the coffee retailer who sells you your café latte (Starbucks?), or the company whose name probably first pops up when you turn on your laptop (probably Microsoft)?

Questions like these are interesting to think about because they speak to the visibility that some companies achieve over others and to the trust and respect we have for the many things they do. They therefore speak to a company's *reputation* with consumers. Companies rightly care about being recognized (as well as what they are recognized for) because a good reputation attracts support from customers, investors, and potential employees.

THE WORLD'S MOST VISIBLE COMPANIES

In the fall of 2000, with the help of various market research companies, we gathered nominations from consumers in 12 countries: Australia, Belgium, Denmark, France, Germany, Greece, Italy, the Netherlands, Spain, Sweden, the United States, and the United Kingdom. They represent three major regions of the world: the United States, Europe, and Australia.[1]

In each country, we asked participants to name two companies that stood out as having the best and worst reputations. We then compiled the open-ended nominations from representative consumers to identify the most visible companies in each country.

WHO'S MOST VISIBLE IN THE UNITED STATES?

Figure 3–1 identifies the 30 companies at the upper end of the distribution of nominations. Also shown on the chart are the 10 companies U.S. consumers were most aware of, for both good and bad reputation, in summer 2001.

The results are instructive. For one, companies become visible for different reasons. Among the most visible companies were some that attracted enormous *negative* public attention throughout 2000 and 2001. This was the case for Bridgestone/Firestone and Ford, because of the accidental deaths caused when Firestone tires exploded on Ford Explorers. It was also true of Philip Morris due to its protracted court battle over the company's past efforts to disguise from the public the negative health effects of tobacco. ExxonMobil continued to display a negative halo—reflecting the persistent association consumers make between the company and the decade-old Valdez spill of

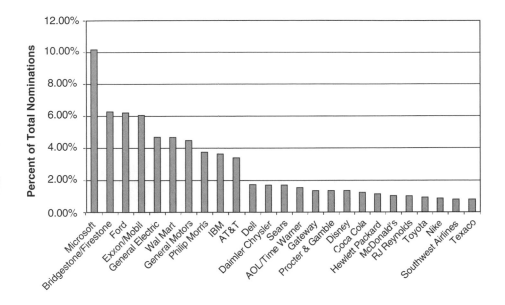

**U.S. Companies Nominated
for Best Reputation (2001)**

1. Microsoft
2. General Electric
3. Wal-Mart
4. IBM
5. General Motors
6. Ford
7. AT&T
8. Dell
9. Sears
10. Gateway

**U.S. Companies Nominated
for Worst Reputation (2001)**

1. Bridgestone/Firestone
2. Exxon Mobil
3. Ford
4. Microsoft
5. Philip Morris
6. AT&T
7. General Motors
8. RJ Reynolds
9. AOL/Time Warner
10. DaimlerChrysler

Figure 3–1 The most visible companies in the United States (summer 2001).

1989. Clearly, ExxonMobil has not benefited from any positive carryover from Exxon's merger with Mobil, a company that has long enjoyed more positive regard from the public. None of these companies attracted positive nominations.

Two companies earned nothing kudos: Wal-Mart and General Electric (GE). The fact that Wal-Mart took the number three spot on positive counts is remarkable, given recurrent media and activist criticism about the company's damaging effects on small local stores that are driven out of business when a Wal-Mart store opens in a community. Clearly the public thinks very favorably of what Wal-Mart has achieved from providing high-quality products at affordable prices, efficiently and effectively. GE also makes the grade for mostly positive nominations, often as not for its continuing ability to generate high returns and for the acclaimed style of GE's former CEO, the legendary Jack Welch.[2]

Finally, two companies received mixed nominations: Microsoft and General Motors (GM). Microsoft's nominations mirror the polarized public debate over its actions. On one hand, some respondents react negatively to the company because of its highly publicized tussle with the U.S. Department of Justice over allegations of monopolistic practices. On the other hand, many respondents clearly think highly of Microsoft, its products, and leaders. The ambivalent pattern combined to elevate Microsoft to the status of 2nd most visible company in the United States after Bridgestone/Firestone. In contrast, GM earned its mixed pattern of nominations from very different perceptions of its divisions: Most of GM's positive nominations reflect public enthusiasm about its Saturn division. Consumers generally perceived other parts of GM in negative terms.

WHO'S MOST VISIBLE IN EUROPE?

We asked the same two questions of nearly 10,000 people in 10 European countries in the fall of 2000. Initially, we expected that some of the same global multinationals would probably receive the bulk of the nominations. In fact, we were wrong. Across countries, quite different companies were nominated—and patriotic fervor had much to do with the replies. For Germans, auto-maker DaimlerChrysler (the makers of Mercedes) reigned supreme. The French frequently thought of Renault, Italians applauded Fiat, Spaniards named telecom giant Telefonica, and Greeks praised their mobile phone company Panafon. Clearly, then, no demonstration of European integration emerged from these data: Instead, the results demonstrated that consumers in most European countries tend to praise their homegrown brands over those of other countries. Of the non-European companies nominated, Coca-Cola, McDonald's, and Sony were the most frequently mentioned corporate brands.

In each European country, however, consumers were also quick to recognize their own companies' faults: The French haven't forgiven Total-Fina-Elf for the oil spill that devastated part of its Atlantic coastline in spring 2000 following the sinking of the tanker *The Erika*; the Danes chastise the former government telephone monopoly TeleDanmark (now known as TDC) for its ongoing difficulties in servicing consumers, as well as Cheminova for its involvement in producing insecticides and pesticides that harmed consumers and forced people to relocate from affected areas in the 1980s and 1990s. Finally, the Dutch have yet to forget the fireball collapse of World Online, the Dutch Yahoo! wannabe that imploded dramatically in 1999 from its inflated promises to investors and from brash overexposure.

To identify a pan-European set of the most visible companies, we compiled the results *across* all 10 European countries in which we carried out the study. Figure 3–2 summarizes the results. The most visible company based on total nominations received across all 10 countries was the French food retailer Carrefour. The company owns leading supermarket chains in Europe and earns most of its nominations for its visible retail outlets in France and Spain. Philips runs a close second and owes its nominations to the Netherlands, Belgium, and France. Both Carrefour and Philips, as well Ford (whose nominations come mostly from nominations to its Volvo-branded cars) and DaimlerChrysler, owe their top spots to the high number of positive nominations they received. In contrast, the most highly named U.S. companies in Europe were McDonald's and Coca-Cola, both of which also received a large number of negative votes. The pattern is different than the one we observed in the United States, where negative publicity often fuels the highest levels of corporate visibility.

Across Europe, people think most highly of companies that have powerful consumer brands: Car companies are heavily represented, as are food producers, retailers, and electronics—the companies that consumers are most likely to interface with in their daily lives. Named for best reputation status are each country's top

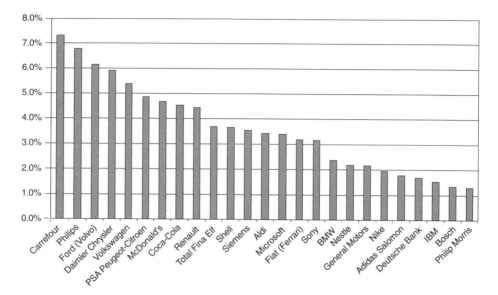

European Companies Nominated for Best Reputation (2000)

1. Carrefour
2. Philips
3. DaimlerChrysler
4. Ford (Volvo)
5. Volkswagen
6. PSA Peugeot-Citroen
7. Renault
8. Coca-Cola
9. Siemens
10. Sony

European Companies Nominated for Worst Reputation (2000)

1. McDonald's
2. Total Fina Elf
3. Shell
4. Deutsche Bank
5. Microsoft
6. Aldi
7. Fiat
8. PSA Peugeot-Citroen
9. Nike
10. Deutsche Telekom

Figure 3–2 The most visible companies across ten countries in Europe (fall 2000).

suppliers of retail goods, including companies like Siemens, Sony, BMW, and GM (for its Opel brand), whose reputations are wholly national. Named for worst reputation were companies that cross geographies, reaching well beyond Europe, with negative auras surrounding American icons McDonald's, Microsoft, Nike, and (to a lesser extent) Wal-Mart. Also negatively viewed were France's Total-Fina and Germany's Deutsche-Telekom. On both sides of the Atlantic, consumers clearly have a profound distaste for companies whose actions they perceive to pose enduring threats to health, safety, and the environment.

Finally, the most visible companies in Europe have quite different national origins, and most of them earn their standing on a nationalistic basis—nominations from more than three countries are very rare indeed. It suggests that few companies are truly well-positioned in the hearts and minds of consumers across Europe. In other words, the reputational marketplace in Europe is still wide open, and there's no company yet that can claim legitimate reputational standing as pan-European.

As in the United States, some European companies received mixed nominations as both good and bad companies. In the United States tobacco was the chief villain and Philip Morris its poster child. In Europe, by comparison, Philip Morris earned no negatives and even received above average nominations for 'best reputation'. In the United States, Wal-Mart was unanimously praised, whereas in Europe it earned a significant number of nominations for worst reputation. The duality of the reputations of these companies is a recurring pattern that holds true in Europe for Microsoft, Shell, PSA-Peugeot-Citroen, and GM as well. These splintered images, we suspect, probably do affect the operating performance of these companies: Polarized consumers are unlikely to deliver the kind of unfailing support that managers need in order to generate sales. It suggests a latent tension that executive teams in these companies should address if they are to improve their market results with consumers.

WHO'S MOST VISIBLE IN AUSTRALIA?

In fall 2000, 1,019 Australian consumers were asked to nominate best and worst companies in Australia. Figure 3–3 shows the results. The most visible company in Australia was Telstra, the country's semi-private telecommunications monopoly. Commonwealth Bank (the country's oldest commercial bank) and the well-known retailer Coles-Myer took second and third place respectively. Like Philip Morris and Microsoft in the U.S., Telstra's reputation was heavily splintered—being nominated as tops on both positive and negative counts. In contrast, Commonwealth Bank owed its visibility

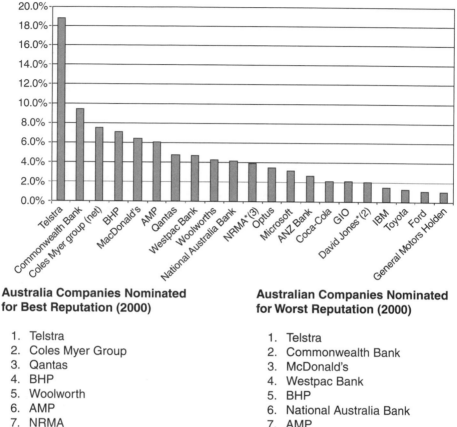

Australia Companies Nominated for Best Reputation (2000)

1. Telstra
2. Coles Myer Group
3. Qantas
4. BHP
5. Woolworth
6. AMP
7. NRMA
8. Commonwealth Bank
9. Microsoft
10. David Jones

Australian Companies Nominated for Worst Reputation (2000)

1. Telstra
2. Commonwealth Bank
3. McDonald's
4. Westpac Bank
5. BHP
6. National Australia Bank
7. AMP
8. Optus
9. ANZ Bank
10. Coles Myer Group

Figure 3–3 The most visible companies in Australia (fall 2000).

mostly to negative nominations, whereas Coles-Myer enjoyed the strongest positive halo of all.

Cross-country comparisons of the most visible companies suggest some generalizations:

■ Companies are often nominated more positively when they market very popular consumer products and services, when they own key products that carry the corporate brand name

(Coca-Cola), or when they rely on a very recognizable logo (Mercedes), all of which are heavily advertised.

■ Most companies that top the negative nomination charts often do so because their names have become indelibly tied to products that cause harm—they damage health (Philip Morris, RJ Reynolds), kill people (Ford and Bridgestone/Firestone), have damaged the environment (Total-Fina, ExxonMobil, Shell), or are thought to take advantage of consumers (Microsoft, Telstra).

■ Public impressions are driven partly by the visibility of the industries in which these companies operate. They're also influenced by the visibility of the companies themselves—many have huge advertising and communications budgets, and so develop high public profiles. Some are catapulted into visibility because of scandal or crisis.

Most clearly, however, visibility is only a *precursor* to reputation. The question before us is therefore this: If we focus on any single company, *what specific criteria* do people think about when they evaluate the company? And how do companies really compare when we go beyond the "beauty pageants" that characterize the nominations-process, and actually ask people to rate companies on a standardized list of criteria?

Various instruments have been proposed to address this issue.[3] *Fortune* magazine publishes one of the best-known measures of corporate reputation, one that is derived from answers to eight questions about the company's products, leadership, and results. Over the years, many have criticized *Fortune*'s instrument and data collection methodology.[4] To overcome some of these problems, we created the Reputation Institute in 1999 to undertake careful research and develop a standard indicator that could be used worldwide with different types of stakeholders. The Reputation Quotient[sm] (RQ) instrument is what emerged from joint work with our research partner Harris Interactive. In the next section, we describe the RQ and how we have used it since 1999 to develop detailed ratings and analyses of some of the most visible companies in the world.

THE REPUTATION QUOTIENT

Pick a well-known company—one you hold in high regard. Fix it in your mind. Now try to explain *why* you named that company. If you're like most people we've asked this question of individually and in focus groups in 6 countries, your explanations will fall into one of the following six categories:

- *Emotional Appeal:* You simply like, admire, or trust the company.
- *Products and Services:* You think the company sells products or services that are high quality, innovative, reliable, or a good value for the money.
- *Financial Performance:* You've been happy with the company's profitability, believe it has strong future prospects, and isn't too risky to invest in.
- *Vision and Leadership:* You feel the company has a clear vision for the future and strong leadership.
- *Workplace Environment:* You believe the company is well-managed, has topnotch employees, and would be great to work for.
- *Social Responsibility:* You think the company is a good citizen—it supports good causes, doesn't damage the environment, and does right by local communities.

Through our collaboration with Harris Interactive, we systematically tested these dimensions and attributes on thousands of people, online, by phone, and in personal interviews. Based on these tests, we created a standardized instrument from which we calculate an overall reputation score—the Reputation Quotient, or RQ.[5] Simply put, the RQ is the sum of the answers people give when they are asked to rate a company on 20 questions. Figure 3–4 diagrams the structure of the RQ. The questionnaire survey based on these items is designed to be filled out by all kinds of respondents, be they managers, investors, employees, or consumers—people who have a minimal level of familiarity with the companies they are asked to rate.

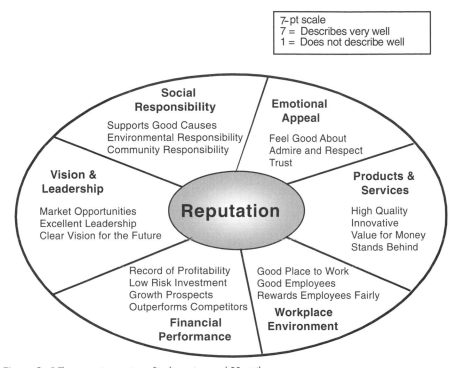

7-pt scale
7 = Describes very well
1 = Does not describe well

Social Responsibility
Supports Good Causes
Environmental Responsibility
Community Responsibility

Emotional Appeal
Feel Good About
Admire and Respect
Trust

Vision & Leadership
Market Opportunities
Excellent Leadership
Clear Vision for the Future

Reputation

Products & Services
High Quality
Innovative
Value for Money
Stands Behind

Financial Performance
Record of Profitability
Low Risk Investment
Growth Prospects
Outperforms Competitors

Workplace Environment
Good Place to Work
Good Employees
Rewards Employees Fairly

Figure 3–4 The reputation quotient: Six dimensions and 20 attributes.

THE REPUTATIONS OF THE MOST VISIBLE COMPANIES IN THE U.S.

Knowing the companies that were most visible in each country, we set out to measure in detail the reputations of those companies. In 2001, over 20,000 American consumers were asked to answer the 20 standard RQ questions in order to obtain detailed ratings of the 60 most visible U.S. companies.

Figure 3–5 shows the 2001 results. As it had in each of two prior years' ratings, Johnson & Johnson again topped the U.S. ratings of 2001. And Microsoft, Coca-Cola, Intel, 3M, and Sony were also among the public's top 10 companies—they had the highest RQ scores among the most visible companies.

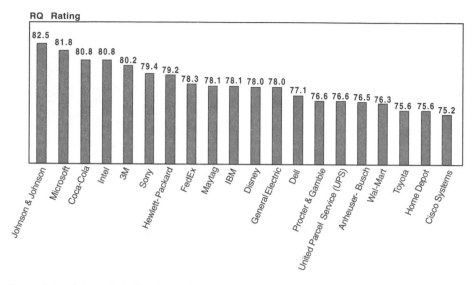

Figure 3–5 Who's tops in the United States (2001)?

THE REPUTATIONS OF THE MOST VISIBLE COMPANIES IN EUROPE

In fall 2001, we also invited representative samples of consumers in the Netherlands, Italy, and Denmark to rate the reputations of the most visible companies in each country.

The Netherlands's Top-Rated Companies   The 30 most visible companies in the Netherlands were rated by a representative sample of over 5,000 consumers. The giant food retailer Ahold topped the Dutch ratings, with Sony, Unilever, Heineken, and Microsoft running close behind. In consumer electronics, it came as something of a surprise that Sony outdid Philips in the Netherlands. It suggested the need for closer examination of the reputation strategy Sony has pursued in international markets, and possible areas of improvement for Philips in its own home market. Figure 3–6 summarizes the Dutch results.

Italy's Top-Rated Companies   Around the same time, we asked close to 3,000 Italian consumers to rate the 20 most visible companies in Italy using the RQ. Figure 3–7 shows that Italy's most

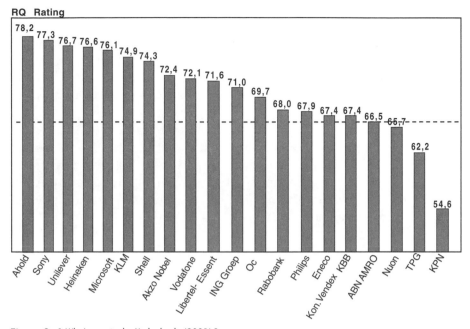

Figure 3–6 Who's tops in the Netherlands (2001)?

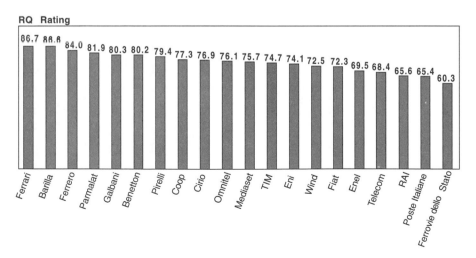

Figure 3–7 Who's tops in Italy (2001)?

visible companies are grouped in three tiers. The top tier is led by prestige car maker Ferrari, food producer Barilla, the chocolate confectioner Ferrero, and includes food giants Parmalat and Galbani, retailer Benetton, and tire-maker Pirelli. Clearly, Italian consumers applaud the flagship performance of Italy's top-branded Ferrari cars, most visible for its successes in Formula One racing.

The second tier is led by Coop Italia and includes the regulated telecommunications, media, and publishing groups, as well as Eni, the Italian utility company—the highest performing state-operated company. The third tier is anchored by Italy's problem-ridden automaker Fiat and includes the state-owned and operated postal services and railways.

Denmark's Top-Rated Companies Some 2,700 Danish consumers were asked to rate the reputations of Denmark's 15 most visible companies using the RQ. The results shown in Figure 3–8 indicate that in 2001 toy and entertainment provider Lego was the top-rated company in Denmark, followed by high-end consumer

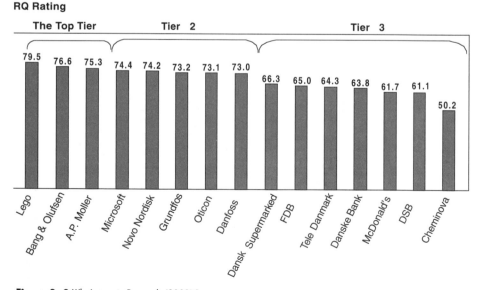

Figure 3–8 Who's tops in Denmark (2001)?

electronics developer Bang & Olufsen—world famous for its sleek designs of stereo and video equipment—and the transport-based conglomerate A. P. Moller, the parent company of the Maersk family of businesses involved in commercial shipping and air transport. The second tier was led by Microsoft and Novo Nordisk, the well-known maker of insulin products. The third tier consisted of a mix of consumer product companies, anchored at the low end by Cheminova, the chemical company involved in the production of insecticides and pesticides.

THE REPUTATIONS OF THE MOST VISIBLE COMPANIES IN AUSTRALIA

Finally, in fall 2001, our colleagues at AMR Interactive invited over 4,000 consumers to rate the 20 most visible companies in Australia. In contrast to Europe, where national companies earn the top ratings, Figure 3–9 shows strong mindshare by American companies: Microsoft topped the rankings, along with three other U.S.-based multinationals: McDonald's, Coca-Cola, and IBM. The

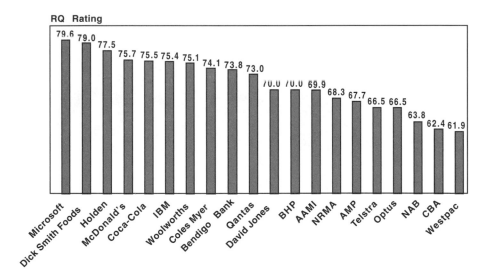

Figure 3–9 Who's tops in Australia (2001)?

only Australian companies that were rated in the top tier were retailers Dick Smith Foods, Holden, Woolworth, and Cole-Myers. In contrast, Australia's three major banks fared relatively poorly (NAB, CBA, and Westpac), performing less well than BHP, Australia's major mining company. The only standout among banks was tiny Bendigo Bank, notable for its widely-publicized community-based banking strategy. Disappointing results were also obtained by Australia's telecom operators Optus and Telstra.

LEARNING FROM THE WORLD'S TOP-RATED COMPANIES

Rankings are always titillating, creating as they do an Oscar-like atmosphere of red-carpet winners and side-show losers. The research question that inspired us to launch the RQ project, however, is not who wins and loses—but why. What drives reputation among the world's top-rated companies? From our observations, it's probably safe to say that they do things differently. But what?

The RQ project demonstrates that consumers are quite good at sensing what companies are up to. In both the United States and Australia, Microsoft earned praise from consumers for carrying out a smooth leadership transition from Gates to Balmer and for emerging relatively unscathed from the government's antitrust efforts. Similarly, in all countries Coca-Cola was given credit for conveying invigorated leadership under CEO Douglas Daft and for unveiling an effective global advertising campaign. On the other hand, the public was not fooled by either DaimlerChrysler's rocky intercontinental marriage or by Lucent's flawed business model. Nor did American consumers fail to blame both Ford and Bridgestone/Firestone for the tire debacle that led to the loss of so many human lives.

To examine the underlying drivers of reputation, we conducted detailed statistical analysis of the RQ measures taken in 2001. In cross-national comparisons, very comparable results were actually obtained. Figure 3–10 summarizes the statistical pattern that was uncovered from analysis of the U.S. data.

The model in Figure 3–10 can be read to say that:

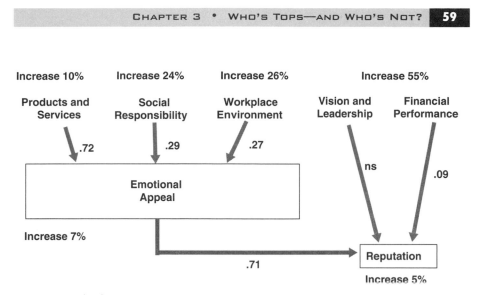

Figure 3–10 What drives corporate reputation?

- Most consumers ascribe high reputations to companies they like, trust, and admire—the components of a company's 'emotional appeal'.
- Perceptions of a company's products and services are the key factor driving emotional appeal and hence overall reputation. The communications initiatives of companies seeking to improve their reputations should therefore heavily emphasize product quality, innovation, and value.
- Perceptions of a company's workplace environment and social responsibility are significant predictors of how well consumers rate a company. Knowingly or not, consumers psychologically support companies that they perceive as behaving fairly and responsibly towards employees and communities.
- Interestingly, differences in perceived financial performance and leadership had little effect on consumer ratings of corporate reputation. In forming impressions of companies, these core business factors are clearly discounted by the public.

At the risk of over-quantification, the model also suggests that to increase its reputation by 5 percent, a company would have to improve its emotional appeal to consumers by 7 percent, which in turn would require improved perceptions either of the company's products and services by 10 percent, workplace environment by 24 percent, or social responsibility by 26 percent. Favorable perceptions of the company's financial performance would have to be improved by 55 percent to generate a comparable change in reputation. Take General Electric, with an RQ of 78 in 2001. To improve its RQ by 5% or 3.9 would catapult General Electric to the highest tier of U.S. companies at 81.0 (close to Johnson & Johnson and Microsoft). Such a change would require significant improvement in how consumers rate the company's emotional appeal. To get consumers to improve their ratings, GE would have to invest in costly initiatives, and would get the highest leverage from generating improved perceptions of its products and services. However, that may also be the most difficult set of attributes to change—most people already have high opinions of the value they get from buying GE products. In contrast, the results suggest that it's possible the company could get the greatest return from investments that position GE as a more socially-responsible company—something consumers don't yet associate with the company, and that therefore present a greater opportunity for improvement.

You'll recall that at the end of Chapter 2 we concluded from various studies that a 10 percent change in reputation was worth at least a 1 percent change in market value. Given GE's $300 billion market capitalization, the 5% improvement needed to carry GE to the top of the consumer ratings would be worth approximately $500 million in value creation. *In a real sense —the number represents the maximum budget a company like GE should be willing to allocate specifically to improve consumer perceptions of the company by 5 percent, whether through advertising, public relations, or philanthropic initiatives.*

CONCLUSION

Overall, we've shown that consumers are as sophisticated as investors, but interpret the corporate world in terms of multiple signals that companies broadcast about their *non-financial initiatives*. Reputation-building with consumers is therefore about making sure a company communicates clearly, not just about its quarterly financial results—the purview of analysts and investors—but about how it treats its employees and about how it contributes to society. It signals that reputations act as mirrors to the public about a company's managerial excellence.

In the next chapter, we examine the relative contribution that corporate reputation has made to the financial performance of the most visible companies. To explore excellence more deeply and provide reputational benchmarks to others, the rest of the book then focuses on the top-rated companies. In successive chapters, we show that top companies actually manage their reputations systematically by building strong reputation platforms—a strategic positioning they achieve in the marketplace through a combination of sustained leadership, internal and external communication, citizenship, and workplace initiatives—the drivers of the RQ.

METHODOLOGICAL APPENDIX TO CHAPTER 3

We created the Reputation Institute in 1999 to study corporate reputations. The annual consumer polls that we've sponsored since then have been conducted with our market research partner Harris Interactive and other affiliated companies. Harris relies on a 7 million person panel of voluntary participants to identify and poll representative samples of consumers in the United States. The opinions of those sampled are weighted to be representative of what the general public thinks in each country. In Europe, we relied on telephone sampling to carry out the studies.

Projects unfolded in two stages in each country: a nominations phase and a rating phase. In the nominations phase, we began by asking two basic questions:

- Of all the companies that you're familiar with or that you might have heard about, which TWO—in your opinion— stand out as having the BEST reputation overall?

■ Of all the companies that you're familiar with or that you might have heard about, which TWO—in your opinion—stand out as having the WORST reputation overall?

Polls of the general public were conducted in 12 countries and three regions of the world between fall 2000 and spring 2001. Over 20,000 people participated in these initial polls. From their nominations, we extracted a list of the companies that were "most visible" to the public in each country—for better or worse. These companies are the ones whose reputations were measured in detail in the second phase of research—the rating phase.

Detailed studies sponsored by Harris Interactive and the Reputation Institute using the RQ have been featured annually in the *Wall Street Journal* since 1999. Here we discuss the results of parallel studies completed in 2001 in the United States, Australia, Denmark, Italy, and the Netherlands. The projects involved close collaboration with the market research firms of Harris Interactive, Blauw Research, and AMR Interactive, as well as close working relationships with the Corporate Communications Center at Erasmus University, with SDA-Bocconi in Italy, and with Copenhagen Business School and Interplay in Denmark.

As interesting as they are, nominations are not accurate depictions of the reputations of companies. To fully examine corporate reputations requires more detailed measurement—hence the launch in 2000 of a worldwide project to measure corporate reputations accurately—we call it the rating phase. To carry out the rating phase, we needed a reliable instrument to *measure* the reputations of the nominated companies. The instrument we used to rate those companies was the Reputation Quotient (the RQ), a measure developed by Charles Fombrun and Harris Interactive that was designed to overcome weaknesses in existing instruments and that we have proposed as a useful benchmark for reputation measurement.

More than 30,000 people participated in the rating phase across the five countries. We relied on these RQ interviews to obtain accurate ratings of the most visible companies in each country. The ratings enabled us to calculate reputation scores for these companies and set the stage for us to explore the underlying reasons why they are thought to be tops by the public.

Sampling Process in the United States: A total of 10,038 U.S. respondents were polled in seven separate polls conducted between April and August 2001: Of these, 5,975 were done online and 4,063 by telephone. An identical nomination phase was conducted during summer 2000 with 5,661 respondents, of which 4,651 were interviewed online and 1,010 by telephone. The online respondents were randomly selected from a large online panel that Harris Interactive created to carry out online research. At the time, the Harris online panel included over 7 million voluntary participants. To ensure that the study was not biased to online respondents, a separate set of telephone interviews was conducted with a representative sample of the general public. The nominations for best and worst corporate reputation were tallied and summed, and the 60 most visible corporate reputations in the United States were identified.

A total of 21,630 consumers then rated the reputations of the 60 most visible companies using the RQ instrument. All interviewing was conducted online in October 2001, and all companies were rated by respondents who indicated that they were at least somewhat familiar with that company. Respondents were asked to rate up to two randomly chosen companies with which they were familiar. Respondents who were familiar with more than two companies were randomly assigned to rate two companies. After the first rating was completed, they were given the option to rate their second company, and interviews lasted an average of 22 minutes.

Sampling Process in Europe: Sampling was done on a country-by-country basis. Various research firms were used to obtain phone nominations from representative samples of 750 to 1,000 people in each country in fall 2000. Commercial brands, purely financial holdings, and subsidiaries were excluded. The nominations enabled creating lists of the 20 to 30 companies with the most visible corporate reputations in each country. RQ interviews in each country were conducted by telephone, between February and April 2002, and companies were rated by respondents who had indicated that they were "very familiar" with, "somewhat familiar" with, or "had heard the name of" that company.

Sampling Process in Australia: A similar process was used to sample the general public in Australia for both the nominations phase and the rating phase. The Australian sample was national in scope, and stratified to represent the population of the States and Territories, and then split between urban and rural populations. Data collection was conducted by AMR Interactive, based in Sydney, Australia.

The comparable sampling and rating methodologies used in the United States, Europe, and Australia enable us to compare the relative RQ scores given to companies across the regions.

ENDNOTES

1. For interested readers, we have appended a note at the end of this chapter that describes in greater detail the methodology that guided our research.

2. Even Mr. Welch fell victim to public outrage in 2002 following revelations of retirement perks awarded by General Electric judged as unseemly by many critics and uncovered during his high profile divorce proceedings.

3. A number of major media publish corporate ratings on a regular basis. *Fortune*'s annual survey of America's Most Admired Companies (AMAC) is probably the best known of these and has spawned a small industry of followers in publications such as the *Financial Times*, *Asian Business,* and the *Far Eastern Economic Review*. Social ratings agencies like the former Council on Economic Priorities and investment funds like Kinder, Lydenberg, & Domini (KLD) also rate companies on their social performance.

4. Academics conducting research on corporate reputations have relied heavily on practitioner ratings in their modeling efforts, particularly the *Fortune* AMAC and KLD ratings. Although everyone routinely acknowledges many limitations to the data, most

also acknowledge that it has been difficult to develop a valid, standardized database of corporate reputational ratings (see *Corporate Reputation Review,* Vol.1, 1997). Unfortunately, the result has been a patchwork quilt of analyses whose inconsistent findings are invariably blamed on methodological shortcomings attributable to measurement issues. Hence our effort with Harris Interactive to systematize the measurement process.

5. C. J. Fombrun, N. A, Gardberg, & J. M. Sever, "The Reputation Quotient: A Multi-Stakeholder Measure of Corporate Reputation." *Journal of Brand Management,* 2000: 241–255.

4

FROM FAME
TO FORTUNE

*"Not everything that can be counted counts,
and not everything that counts
can be counted."*

—ALBERT EINSTEIN

Is there a financial return to companies that develop strong reputations? As we showed in Chapter 2, "What are Reputations Worth?" the general answer to that question is yes—reputation is closely tied to bottom-line returns, so research tells us. Financial performance results because, in line with the reputation value cycle, a good reputation induces supportive behaviors from customers, employees, investors, and the public that improve operating performance and grow market value.

Despite having presented these results in many management forums, however, doubt persists. Senior executives are reluctant to believe that the "business case" for reputation management is fully documented, and it has become a sort of holy grail for communications-minded executives—there's doubt, and they want more robust proof with which to sell the idea internally. In our view, if doubt persists about the relationship between reputation and financial performance, it is largely because empirical measures of reputation used in past studies have been inconsistent and because of thorny methodological problems: A company with the same level of financial performance is evaluated in different ways by different groups of respondents. Naturally, then, it proves difficult to establish a single, strong correlation between financial results and reputational ratings across studies.

In this chapter we focus on the specific companies measured as part of the RQ Project described in Chapter 3, "Who's Tops—and Who's Not?" and examine their financial results compared to peer companies. We do so because, for the first time, the *same* RQ instrument was used to measure reputation consistently across multiple countries, and the study was conducted with comparable consumer samples in each of those countries. The RQ Project therefore provides credible data with which to assess the link between reputation and performance, between fame and fortune.

The top-line answer from our analysis? Yes, corporate reputations, as measured by consumer RQ ratings of companies, is indeed related to indicators of a company's financial well-being. Figure 4–1 reminds us why: The chart indicates the

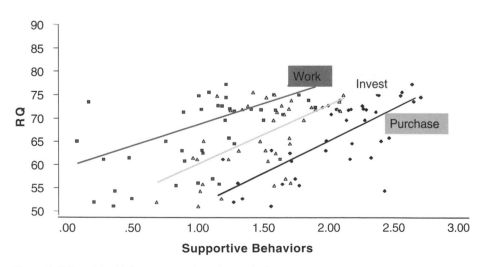

Figure 4–1 The relationship between reputation and supportive intent.

observed correlation between RQ scores of rated companies and the public's intent to recommend the companies' for its products, as a place to work, and as an investment. The scatter plot of correlations indicates a strong propensity for people to support better-regarded companies.

As Chapter 2 suggested, public support is likely to put strong upward pressure on a company's operating performance and on all financial measures. To demonstrate this, we examined the observed relationship between RQ scores and various key indicators of these companies' financial well-being in the same year during which their RQ scores were obtained between 2000 and 2001 in the U.S., Australia, Denmark, Italy, Netherlands: earnings, liquidity, cash flow, growth rate, and market value. The analysis is based on data about the 60 companies listed in Table 4–1, all of which were taken from the companies measured in

TABLE 4–1 Contrasting Higher and Lower RQ Companies

LOWER RQ COMPANIES	HIGHER RQ COMPANIES
ABN AMRO	3M
Akzo Nobel	Ahold
AMP	Anheuser-Busch
Coles Myer	Bang & Olufsen
Commonwealth Bank	Cirio
Danske Bank	Coca-Cola–Australia
David Jones	Coca-Cola–USA
DSM	Dell
DuPont	FedEx
Eni	General Electric
Fiat	Heineken
General Motors	Honda
ING	IBM-Australia
KPN	IBM-US
Laurus	Johnson & Johnson
Libertel Vodafone	McDonald's-Australia
McDonald's-DK	Microsoft-Australia
Merck	Microsoft-Denmark
Novo Nordisk	Microsoft-Netherlands
Shell	Target
Southwest Airlines	Telecom Italia
Tele Danmark	Toyota
Telecom Italia	Unilever
Telstra	UPS
Vendex KBB	Wal-Mart
Westpac Banking	Woolworth

the RQ Project in 2001. The RQ scores used were those of the countries in which they were measured, and the financial data used were the publicly released results for the company as a whole.

Fame Breeds Fortune

Table 4–2 compares the two groups of companies on various measures of financial health. The results suggest a clear difference in the financial strength of the two groups: On average, companies with stronger reputations have higher intangible wealth, significantly higher return on assets, lower debt-to-equity ratios, and higher 5-year growth rates, in each case dominating lower rated companies by a factor of nearly two to one. These findings are a strong endorsement of the idea that reputation is related to financial outcomes. We examine them in greater detail below.

Reputation and Earnings

Of the 60 companies in the study, pharmaceutical giant Pfizer had the highest return on assets (ROA) at 24.29 percent. Coca-Cola ranked second with an ROA of 20.21 percent, and Merck came in next with 19.01 percent. Below them, with strong returns of 12 to 16 percent, is a cluster comprised of Denmark's top insulin maker Novo Nordisk, Australia's telecom giant Telstra,

TABLE 4–2 Performance of Companies with Higher and Lower RQs (2001)

	Lower RQ Companies	Higher RQ Companies
RQ Rating	68.8	77.3
Market Value to Book Value	4–01	5.73
Long-Term Debt to Equity	144–7	74.9
Return on Assets	5.30%	9.52%
5-Year Growth Rate in Earnings per Share	8.46%	12.07%
1-Year Growth in Employment	2.82%	6.96%

Italy's Eni, and the United States' Home Depot and Anheuser-Busch. The companies with the weakest earnings results in the 2001 sample were Laurus, the food retailer, and KPN, the troubled Dutch telecom.

The positive relationship between reputation and earnings is documented in the scatter plots of Figure 4–2 and the associated

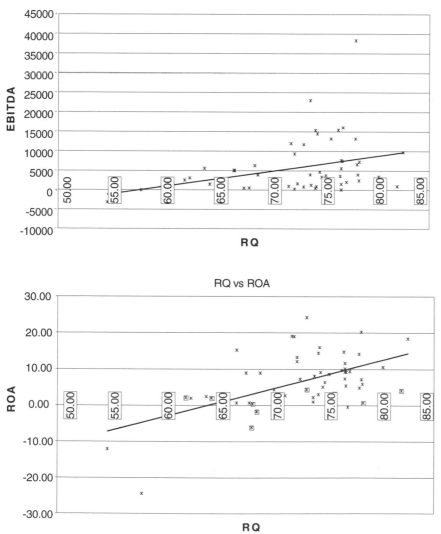

Figure 4–2 The relationship between corporate reputation and earnings.

trend lines that relate reputation to both the company's EBITDA (earnings before interest, taxes, depreciation, and amortization) and to its ROA. The charts confirm what we expected: On one hand, financial returns build reputation; on the other hand, reputation contributes to financial returns.

REPUTATION AND CASH FLOW

A key indicator of financial well-being is the amount of free cash flow a company generates. Of the companies measured in the RQ Project, those with the highest ratio of cash flow to sales in 2000 were Microsoft and Italy's Mediaset. They were followed by a cluster of companies that consisted of Intel, Coca-Cola, Johnson & Johnson, Cisco Systems, Westpac Bank, Pfizer, and Telecom Italia. Lowest in cash flow were Rabobank, AMP, and Fiat. Figure 4–3 shows the scatter plot of cash flow against RQ scores. The results confirm the positive relationship between corporate cash flow and reputation: Companies with higher cash flows tend to earn higher praise from the general public—and vice versa.

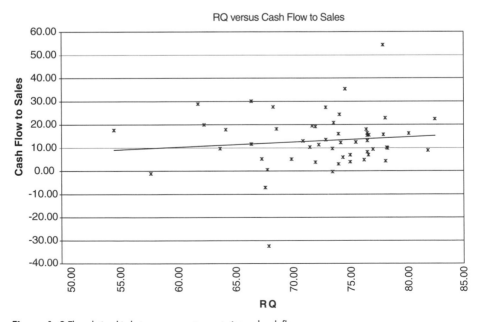

Figure 4–3 The relationship between corporate reputation and cash flow.

REPUTATION AND GROWTH

Financial markets generally reward sustained growth. To investors and analysts, growth indicates competitiveness, a continuing ability to attract customers. Growth therefore signals strong future prospects. The scatter plot in Figure 4–4 documents the positive relationship between RQ scores and one of a slew of measures of growth (in this case, the one year change in the company's total assets). In the 2001 data BHP Billiton and Vodafone lead the way in asset growth, followed by Southwest Airlines, Ahold, and Telstra.

REPUTATION AND MARKET VALUE

The ratio of a company's market value to its book value is an indicator of a company's accumulated pool of reputational and intellectual capital—its intangible assets.[1] Large numbers indicate investor appreciation for their invisible capital—a willingness

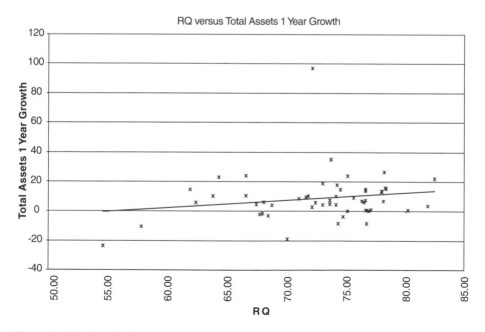

Figure 4–4 The relationship between corporate reputation and growth.

to bid up the share prices of companies with valuable intangibles. In 2001 Maytag, Coca-Cola, Unilever, Dell, and Pfizer had top ratios of market value to book value, an indicator of the significant holdings of intangible capital in their portfolios. By contrast, Fiat had the lowest ratio among automakers, a factor that clearly helps understand its lower reputational rating in Italy. Figure 4–5 shows the scatter plot and confirms the positive link between reputation and market value.

WHAT DRIVES MARKET VALUE?

Numerous factors influence market value. To isolate specific factors and their relative effects on market value is therefore a significant challenge. In this section we examine whether reputation has a marginal impact on market value after controlling for other key financial drivers. We begin by looking at the direct effect of a change in reputation on market value, controlling for

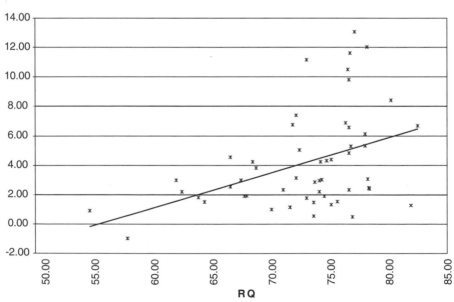

Figure 4–5 The relationship between reputation and market value.

size and age (the simple fact that older, larger companies have higher market value). We then examine whether reputation has any additional impact on value.

THE EFFECTS OF AGE, SIZE, AND REPUTATION ON MARKET VALUE

Statistical analysis indicates that reputation and market value have a significant correlation of 0.43. Figure 4–6 describes an analysis that we conducted on the U.S. companies in the study that examined the relationship between a change in reputation (measured in 2000 to 2001) and market value (in 2001) after

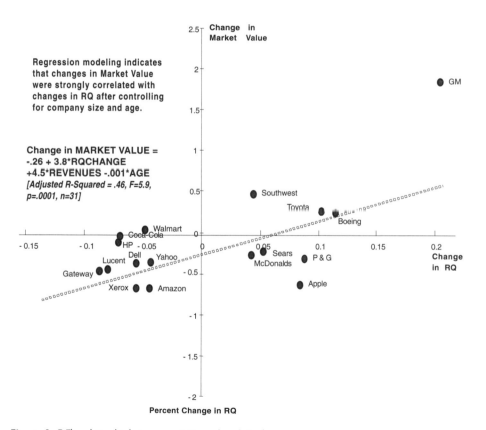

Figure 4–5 The relationship between reputation and market value.

controlling for company size and age since founding. The results clearly demonstrate that investors reward companies with improved reputations: After controlling for age and size, we observed that the shares of companies with improved RQ scores are bid up by the financial markets. A positive change in RQ is a reasonable surrogate measure of other latent factors that investors probably attend to—most likely underlying improvements in corporate results.

COMPARING EXTREMES IN REPUTATION: HIGHEST RQ VERSUS LOWEST RQ

If we focus strictly on the extremes of the RQ distribution, we should expect to confirm the general findings described in the previous section relating reputation and financial performance. Table 4–3 shows the specific companies whose high and low RQ scores justified closer inspection. The two sets of companies obviously differ: Across all three years 1999, 2000, and 2001, the low RQ companies are dominated by companies faced with stakeholder challenges—whether from consumer lawsuits (tobacco), continuing environmental crises (energy), bankruptcies (K-Mart), or a specific product crisis (the exploding Firestone tires on Ford Explorer vehicles).

In contrast, the high RQ companies consist of perennial press darlings—the powerful corporate brands of consumer giants Coca-Cola, Intel, Hewlett-Packard, Johnson & Johnson, and Sony.

Table 4–4 compares these two groups of companies drawn from the extremes of the RQ distribution on various measures of financial health. The results confirm our previous finding of a clear difference in the financial profiles of the groups. Despite similarities in market risk (beta and price volatility are comparable), companies with stronger reputations have, on average:

- higher intangible wealth (market to book, and price-earnings ratios),
- significantly higher returns on all measures of profitability (return on assets, equity, and net margin),

TABLE 4–3 Comparing the Extremes: Low RQ Companies Versus High RQ Companies (1999—2001)

YEAR	LOW RQ	HIGH RQ
1999	Amway (Malaysia) Holdings	Coca-Cola
	Apple Computers	Hewlett-Packard
	Bank Of America	Intel
	Exxon Mobil Certificate	Johnson & Johnson
	General Motors	Wal-Mart Stores
	K-Mart	
	Philip Morris	
	WorldCom MCI Group	
2000	BP	Anheuser-Busch
	Bridgestone	BMW
	ChevronTexaco	Eastman Kodak
	Exxon Mobil Certificate	Home Depot
	K-Mart	Intel
	Philip Morris	Johnson & Johnson
	Royal Dutch Petroleum ADR	Maytag
	Shell T&T ADR	Sony
	Unilever NV ADR	
2001	Bank Of America	3M
	Bridgestone	Coca-Cola
	DaimlerChrysler AG	FedEx
	Philip Morris	General Electric
	Reynolds Tobacco Holdings	Hewlett-Packard
	UAL	Intel
	Worldcom MCI Group	IBM
		Johnson & Johnson
		Maytag
		Microsoft
		Sony
		Walt Disney

TABLE 4–4 Relating RQ to Financial Performance

	Low RQ	High RQ
RQ Rating	60.1	80.2
1 Year Measures		
Cost of Goods Sold	60.8	49.0
Growth in Employment	2.82%	6.96%
Market Value to Book Value	0.81	1.1
Net Margin	4.3	8.0
Return on Assets	4.3%	8.4%
Beta	1.07	1.11
Share Price Volatility	26.3	25.5
5 Year Averages		
Cash Flow to Sales	12.8	18.1
Price-Earnings Ratio	21.7	32.5
Return on Equity	16.8	38.4
Equity as % of Total Assets	35.3	44.9
Long-Term Debt to Capital	29.9	24.8
Quick Ratio	0.82	1.01
EPS Growth	7.3	16.5
Sales per Employee	$2.46 million	$4.55 million

- lower debt-to-equity ratios (lower capital risk),
- higher growth rates in employment, earnings, and sales, as well as
- higher productivity

In each case, better rated companies dominate lower rated companies by 50 percent or more. These findings are a strong endorsement for the idea that reputation is related to financial outcomes. We examine them in greater detail below.

ARE HIGH RQ PORTFOLIOS
A SOUND INVESTMENT?

What if an investor had put $1,000 in a portfolio of stocks rated using the RQ score as a guideline? How well would that investment have fared compared to the market basket of companies included in the S&P 500?

To examine the issue, we created three portfolios of companies defined by the extremes of the RQ distribution and whose shares were traded on the New York stock exchange in each of the three years in which RQ measurements were taken in the United States:

- *The High-RQ Portfolio*: A group of companies whose RQ scores were higher than the mean of the companies rated in that year by at least one standard deviation.
- *The Low-RQ Portfolio*: A group of companies whose RQ scores were lower than the mean of the companies rated in that year by at least one standard deviation.
- *The S&P 500 Portfolio*: The well-known index that consists of the largest 500 publicly traded companies.

We then examined the performance of each portfolio during the subsequent 12-month period. The results for 1999–2000 are shown in Figure 4–7 and demonstrate that an investment in a High RQ Portfolio in fall 1999 performed better than an equivalent investment in the S&P 500. Indeed, an investment in the Low RQ Portfolio consistently under-performed both of the others.

Anyone who had made an investment of $1,000 in the High RQ Portfolio on October 1, 1999, and left it there would have seen that investment rise in value to a high of $1,334 on August 14, 2000. A similar investment in the Low RQ Portfolio would have been worth $1,066 at that time. By comparison, a $1,000 investment in the S&P 500 would have been worth $1,163. The date of August 14, 2000, was not magically selected—it is the date on which the trend line of the S&P 500 turned downward and marks the beginning of the bear market. Clearly, this is the point at which the portfolio should have been liquidated in favor of a portfolio that consisted of low RQ companies.

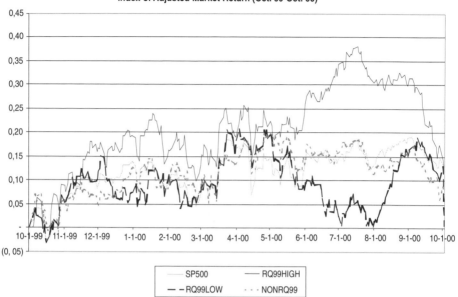

Figure 4–7 The financial performance of RQ portfolios against the S&P 500 (1999–2000).

Would the same hold true for comparable $1,000 portfolio investments made following release of the RQ 2000 and RQ 2001 results? Figures 4–8 and 4–9 show the financial performance of those portfolios in both years. The results offer a dramatic contrast to those of 1999 and suggest that the relationship between RQ and financial performance is even more complex than anticipated—and must take into account the movement of the market as a whole. In 2000, for instance, the High RQ Portfolio largely followed the steadily declining S&P 500. More dramatically, however, it significantly underperformed the Low RQ Portfolio throughout the year. This indicates that high RQ companies are likely to outperform the average *in a rising market*. However, a company with a lofty RQ is also *more vulnerable* than a low RQ company *in a declining market*. In a sense, the high RQ company benefits from the rising tide—and investors gain more from investing in them in a bull market. In a bear market, however, the high RQ company has more to lose—and investors are wiser to buy the shares of low RQ companies.

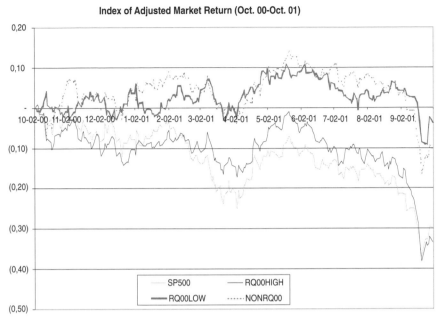

Figure 4–8 The financial performance of RQ Portfokios against the S&P 500 (2000–2001).

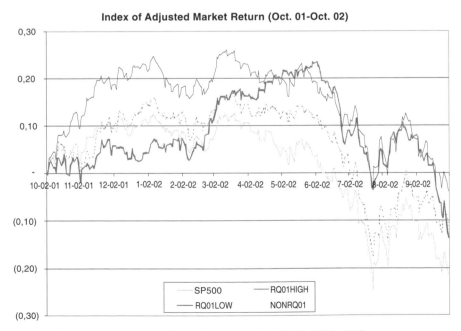

Figure 4–9 The financial performance of RQ portfolios against the S&P 500 (2001–2002).

The findings are confirmed when we examine the 2001 port-folios in Figure 4–9. Here, in the relatively steady or slightly rising first six months of the year (October 2001 to February 2002), the High RQ Portfolio outdistanced both the S&P 500 and the Low RQ Portfolios. Investors who stayed with the High RQ Portfolio steadily outperformed the two alternatives. As the overall market turned sour from March 2002 to October 2002, the Low RQ Portfolio caught up, and occasionally even outperformed the High RQ Portfolio.

The results of these analyses are fascinating in that they provide unprecedented evidence that public perceptions are indeed systematically related to a company's stock market performance. But they also demonstrate the complexity of that relationship: Higher reputation companies attract investors in bull markets but are also more vulnerable to market downturns, during which they can underperform lower reputation companies. An investment strategy predicated on reputation monitoring must therefore take into account the *market context* in which trading is taking place. The relationship that links reputation to market value is neither simple nor static.

THE BOTTOM LINE?

As we demonstrated throughout this chapter, being well regarded is closely associated with a company's earnings, liquidity, cash flows, and growth—its operating results. Consumer ratings of reputation are therefore tied to familiar indicators that a company is well-managed. However, when we examine the tie-in between reputation and a company's stock market results, being well regarded appears to pay off heavily in bull markets where a company's valuation improves more quickly than the valuation of lower rated rivals. In bear markets, being well regarded does not hurt valuations, but savvy investors do better by investing in lower-reputation companies—to capture greater upside potential. In all cases, however, the results show that investors who bet on the most visible U.S. companies (the companies rated in the RQ Project) *always outperformed the S&P 500 by a significant margin,* suggesting that consumer visibility and therefore 'fame' —in and of itself— pays off handsomely for investors. We elaborate further on this theme in Chapter 5, "The Roots of Fame," after we describe our StellarRep model—an integrative framework that describes the core practices for reputation-building that we have observed in many of the companies that have topped RQ surveys around the world.

ENDNOTE

1. C. Fombrun, *Reputation: Realizing Value from the Corporate Image.* Cambridge, MA: Harvard Business School Press, 1996.

5

THE ROOTS OF FAME

We judge ourselves by what we feel capable of doing, while others judge us by what we have already done.

—HENRY WADSWORTH LONGFELLOW

Johnson & Johnson is well known as a U.S.-based global consumer healthcare products company. As Chapter 3, "Who's Tops and Who's Not? showed, the company had repeatedly topped RQ surveys conducted in the United States from 1999 to 2001. Similarly, in 2001 Lego won out in Denmark, Ferrari in Italy, Ahold in the Netherlands, and Microsoft in Australia. What do companies that are as highly regarded as these by consumers have in common? Do they do things differently than their rivals? Are they better at relating to consumers in those countries? If so, why? And better yet, *what do they differently*?

To explore these issues, in the remaining chapters of the book we examine the relative positioning of the best-regarded companies in the RQ Project. Specifically, to do so, we drew on four types of information: (1) their internal and external communications as displayed on their Web sites, in their advertising, and through their press releases; (2) the citizenship activities they carry out internationally; (3) the visibility of these companies in terms of awards received, media lists on which they appear, and media articles in which they are featured; and (4) interviews with selected executives from some of the companies.

The results are intriguing: Companies with high RQ scores appear to be substantially different from lesser rivals on five dimensions. This chapter summarizes our findings in terms of five principles derived from these observations that are represented in Figure 5–1—they describe key ingredients for building star-quality reputations. Chapters 6 to 10 deepen our understanding of these five principles. Chapter 11 describes the process that the FedEx Corporation went through over a three-year-period as it charged up the RQ ladder to take a top 10 position among consumers in the RQ rankings in 2001.

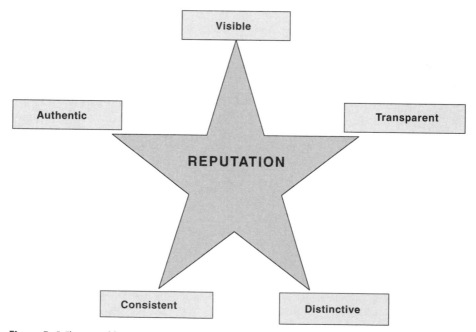

Figure 5–1 The roots of fame.

PRINCIPLE 1: BE VISIBLE

No matter how good a company is, there's no real reputation without visibility. Most of our RQ analyses confirm that familiarity with a company positively influences reputation with the public—most of the time. We should therefore expect companies with stronger reputations to be more visible across all media. It turns out to be true. In reviewing their communications and activities, top-rated companies tend to more readily disclose information about themselves than do lesser regarded companies and to be more willing to engage stakeholders in direct dialogue. Communications increase the probability that a company will be perceived as genuine and credible—and so attract support and advocacy from stakeholders.

Figure 5–2 shows a mid-1990s comparison of the communications budgets of companies with high and low ratings on *Fortune*'s measure of reputation. The results indicate that better-regarded companies tend to be more visible in all media than lower rated companies. They also have higher media spends, as the New York-based Council of Public Relations Firms showed from a survey of its members in 2000 (Figure 5–3).

There are a few exceptions to the rule that visibility helps reputation, most notably the tobacco companies. The data suggest that familiarity tends to hurt the reputations of companies

	Low Reputation	High Reputation
Magazine Articles	28%	57%
Magazine Advertising	20	48
Newspaper Articles	22	45
TV Advertising	5	26
TV Programs	5	21

Figure 5–2 Reputation and media visibility.

Source: Leslie Gaines-Ross, "Results of a Survey of 25,000 Fortune Readers," Presentation at the 1st Conference on Corporate Reputation, Image, and Identity, Stern School of Business, January 1997.

	HIGH Reputation	LOW Reputation
Media Relations	$1,096	$ 723
Executive Outreach	$ 227	$ 165
Investor Relations	$ 635	$ 367
Annual and Quarterly Reports	$ 920	$ 357
Industry Relations	$1,247	$ 329
Employee Comm.	$1,621	$ 545
Department Mgmt.	$ 256	$ 312
Total	$6,002	$2,797

Figure 5–3 Reputation and corporate spending on corporate communications in 2000.
Source: Council of Public Relations Firms, 2000

such as Philip Morris and RJR. The same has been true of AOL-Time Warner: In 2001, consumers who were more familiar with the company rated it *less* favorably.

Consistent with the idea that the media act as magnifiers, the benefits of visibility depend heavily on the *type* of exposure that a company achieves. Tobacco companies and AOL-Time Warner, like Enron, Arthur Andersen, Global Crossings, and World-Com, have become visible for all the wrong reasons. Naturally, their reputations suffered.

In Chapter 6, "Be Visible," we show that visibility is a two-edged sword: On one hand, it can be leveraged to achieve enhanced reputation. Most companies that topped national RQ surveys in 2001 benefited greatly from their national heritage. On the other hand, visibility can have enduring negative effects on reputation: ExxonMobil's reputation remains in the doldrums some 14 years after the Valdez oil spill despite settling claims, paying fines, and launching philanthropic initiatives. Consumers can demonstrate elephant-like memories when it comes to reputation-damaging crises.

PRINCIPLE 2: BE DISTINCTIVE

Reputations build when companies come to occupy a distinctive position in the minds of resource-holders. Take Intel and AMD, the two titans of microprocessors in the semiconductor industry. Both offer products of comparable quality, speed, and power. With a top-five RQ of 80.8 in 2001, however, Intel dominates AMD in the minds of computer buyers and other observers. Why? Because Intel owes its reputation not solely to the quality of its products, but to a wildly successful "Intel Inside®" marketing campaign launched in 1991 that virtually defined Intel as the only quality supplier of component parts and the guarantor of excellence to the end user. Since then, by licensing its name to over 1,000 PC manufacturers, Intel has participated in over $7 billion in advertising and promotions that used the "Intel Inside®" logo and produced an estimated 500 billion consumer impressions. Despite making no product sales directly to consumers, Intel thereby made itself central and distinctive to the public. Figure 5–4 shows a typical co-op ad that Intel ran and

Figure 5–4 Intel Inside: A popular co-op Web ad run in Sweden with Dell (December 2002).
Source: www.dell.com

that showcases its collaborative relationship with computer makers like Dell.

A similar process unfolds in all industries. Successful reputation building occurs when companies own an "empty niche." Companies competing in commoditized industries are powerful examples of this process. Oil companies, for example, grapple daily with negative stakeholder perceptions of their polluting potential. To counter these perceptions, most companies try to signal their concern for the environment with programs and initiatives. In doing so, they run into each other head on. In an effort to build distinctiveness in the environmental arena, for instance, in 2001 the former British Petroleum adopted a new identity as BP and unveiled a new corporate logo. The green and yellow symbols now blossom into a metaphorical flower to convey the company's new tagline "beyond petroleum" and its commitment to environmentally friendly technologies. A tongue-in-cheek ad campaign touted the company as being involved in all forms of energy production—things like solar energy, coal "...and, oh, oil"—clearly implying that oil is secondary to its strategy (even though oil still provides 90 percent of the company's revenues). BP's strategy is clearly to "own" perceptual space as the world's most environmentally friendly company. Its success will depend heavily on the credibility of that claim to stakeholders and on what rivals do in this hotly contested terrain.

The RQ Project shows that strong reputations arise when companies focus their actions and communications around a core theme. Consider again the U.S. medical products group Johnson & Johnson. The company invariably scores high in consumer rankings of trust. This is no accident: Trustworthiness is a focal point of all its communications. Its advertisements single-mindedly portray Johnson & Johnson as a nurturing and caring company, with babies and children invariably featured or mentioned (despite that the baby products division represents less than 10 percent of the company's portfolio).

Consider another top RQ company: Coca-Cola. All of Coke's communications portray a core "devotion to the product" and its seamless integration in the everyday lives of people. The Coca-Cola Company's dominance in carbonated beverages is a testament to the merits of establishing distinctiveness in the design of its reputation-building programs. Despite owning a broad portfolio of other beverage products, Coca-Cola remains dominated by Brand Coke and the distinctive personality attached to the bottle and the drink. Most Coca-Cola communications reflect this single-minded focus on the company's distinctive and most successful Coca-Cola brand, possibly to the detriment of secondary product brands like Fanta, Minute Maid orange juice, and Darsani water.

PRINCIPLE 3: BE AUTHENTIC

The public appreciates authenticity, and to be well regarded, you can't fake it for long—you've got to be real. Authenticity creates emotional appeal, and there's no reputation building without emotional appeal. Statistical analyses of RQ data in all countries confirm that the primary driver of reputation across all countries we've studied is the degree of emotional appeal that the company has to respondents. Being real pays off.

Johnson & Johnson is a good example. When asked to identify Johnson & Johnson's products, most consumers point to the company's line of baby products. There's no accident here. Johnson & Johnson heavily advertises its consumer products using emotional imagery about children and the nurturing role that parents play in their upbringing. This is so even though the baby products line accounts for no more than 5 percent of Johnson & Johnson's portfolio of products and services. Babies sell—and the authenticity of Johnson & Johnson is confirmed by its well-known credo, the statement of beliefs that everyone at Johnson & Johnson can recite almost verbatim and which is credited for having made the company "do the right thing" in the face of crises (like the 1982 and 1985 Tylenol poisonings that cost the company billions of dollars in product recalls, in the development of tamper-proof seals, and in postcrisis corporate advertising).

Rival healthcare products company Bristol-Myers Squibb (BMS) has had a relatively difficult time establishing authenticity with consumers. The maker of countless well-known over-the-counter medications arose from the merger of multiple businesses whose identities have remained relatively distinct. In 1999 BMS sought a common point for building its corporate brand. The company signed cyclist Lance Armstrong, winner of the Tour de France, to endorse the BMS brand. The theme? Cancer survival—Lance had defeated a severe case of testicular cancer through treatment with one of BMS's drugs. BMS communications sought to build emotional appeal with consumers through Lance's survival story and his subsequent parenting of a baby. The jury is out on whether consumers will react favourably to the "cancer survivor" theme that BMS has put out there as an anchor of its identity.

Ice-cream maker Ben & Jerry's is another case in point. In the 1999 survey we conducted with Harris Interactive, the small Vermont company took the fifth position behind Johnson & Johnson and Coca-Cola. The result was surprising because Ben & Jerry's is a considerably smaller company, one without the advertising presence and large revenue base of the other top RQ companies. What made it so appealing to the public? Without a doubt, Ben & Jerry's reputation rested heavily on perceptions of the company as an authentic, humane, socially caring, and community-minded business, whose bohemian leadership style (dress-down employee town meetings and gatherings) and egalitarian management practices (minimal pay differences among employees) was very appealing to the public.

However, when it comes to reputation management, no company can afford to rest on its laurels. Authenticity can dissipate. Ben & Jerry's demonstrated it in 2000 when the company was acquired by Dutch giant Unilever and the founders of the Vermont-based company left. To consumers, the spirit of the company departed with them. In our RQ survey of 2000, Ben & Jerry's was not nominated. When we invited the public to rate the company nonetheless, the company's RQ score had dropped from 78.4 to 76.

These findings confirm what we long suspected: In the long run, efforts to manipulate external images by relying purely on advertising and public relations fail if they are disconnected from the company's identity. A strong reputation is built from *authentic* representations by the company to its stakeholders.

This is a point frequently missed by advertisers and communications professionals—the spin-masters of old. *Influencing public opinion through orchestrated communications is doomed to failure in the long run if those programs are not rooted in core values that are articulated, believed, and lived by employees inside the company.*

In 1996 Royal Dutch/Shell embarked on an ambitious effort to rebuild a corporate reputation that was torn apart by the media following the company's mishandling of two major crises in 1995. The program it developed was rooted in a soul-searching process that required identifying the company's business principles and "core purpose"—the authentic values it supports and the behaviors it is willing to endorse. We worked with a team of Shell managers to unearth those values through focus groups held around the world. From these, Shell employees and leaders came to define Shell's core purpose as "helping to make the future a better place," a theme that has since become an anchor for many of the company's internal leadership initiatives and communications.

PRINCIPLE 4: BE TRANSPARENT

Strong corporate reputations develop when companies are transparent in the conduct of their affairs. Consumers ascribe stronger reputations to companies that communicate broadly about themselves. Conversely, companies that avoid communicating with the public—that provide minimal information about their inner workings, that avoid disclosing what they are doing, how they are doing it, and why—tend to lose ground in the court of public opinion.

Take Martha Stewart, the American home-style queen and the head of a very successful media empire. In mid-2002 charges of insider-trading were levelled against her for the advance sale of a small block of shares she held in a start-up company called Imclone just ahead of bad news. Although amounting to only a few hundred thousand dollars, the accusation of insider trading by Martha Stewart had a catastrophic effect on the corporate shares of Martha Stewart Living Omnimedia. A media maelstrom resulted that sent its shares plummeting by over 80 percent in an eight-week period and still threatens to engulf the company. Doubtlessly, the effect was reinforced by an ill-advised communications strategy that has refused media interviews, withdrawn her from the public eye, and generated a presumption of guilt in the court of public opinion.

Transparency helps build, maintain, and defend reputation. When companies make more and better information available about themselves, the public perceives them as more credible and accountable. Adequate disclosure is essential if investors and analysts are to make reliable assessments of corporate value. Financial markets depend heavily on the credibility of corporate financial statements and, indeed, on the credibility of the entire system of financial reporting and accountability.

The wave of corporate scandals that struck the financial markets in 2002 and that began with Enron had a strong, direct effect on the share prices of the companies in question. They also had enormous indirect effect on perceptions of the corporate sector as a whole due to the loss of public faith it occasioned. In September 2002 economists at the Brookings Institution, a Washington think-tank, released a study that estimated at over $35 billion the indirect cost of these corporate scandals. The report further judged that loss of faith in the transparency of the financial system would produce another 1 to 2.5 percent decline in the economy as a whole. Clearly, transparency is at the heart of public trust and represents the underbelly of corporate reputation.

PRINCIPLE 5: BE CONSISTENT

Top-rated companies are also consistent in their actions and communications to everyone. In a survey of senior managers of global companies, we found that better-regarded companies were more likely to orchestrate and integrate their initiatives cross-functionally. Companies with weaker reputations suffered from maintaining silos and from maintaining separate relationships with their constituents.[1]

Frequently, companies keep isolated staff in the community relations department (and sometimes in remote foundations) to manage relationships with local community groups; in investor relations departments to address financial analysts; in advertising departments and agencies to develop product-level promotional campaigns with occasional bursts of image-building thrown in; and in human resources departments to manage employee communications. Centripetal forces pulling these groups apart virtually guarantee inconsistency in what is said and done. At low-rated General Motors, for example, numerous overlapping and conflicting communications emanate from traditional brand-level silos, preventing loyalty from developing to the company as a whole. There are very few GM employees or customers—but there are countless Cadillac, Buick, and Saturn employees and customers.

Such structural silos damage a company's reputation-building efforts by proliferating images of the company to different stakeholders, many of which promote contradictory interpretations of the company's culture, core values, and strategic direction. By lowering consistency, they virtually guarantee that the company does not benefit from supportive behaviors from all of its stakeholders and so loses ground in the competition for reputational standing. Recent GM ads aired in mid-2003 appear to take a stab at this issue: For the first time, they present General Motors as the company behind the well-known brands.

SO, EXPRESS YOURSELF

When all is said and done, strong reputations result when companies build emotional appeal. It requires that companies "express" themselves convincingly, sincerely, authentically, and credibly to their stakeholder communities. By expressiveness, we mean a willingness by companies to put themselves out there, to convey who they are, what they do, and what they stand for. [2] As we've observed, companies vary significantly in the degree to which they actually achieve visibility, distinctiveness, authenticity, transparency, and consistency in their self-presentations. In the U.S., Johnson & Johnson and Coca-Cola are companies that have high expressiveness, as do Lego in Denmark and Ferrari, Barilla, and Ferrero in Italy. They express themselves –and the public identifies with them.

Figure 5–5 describes five core dimensions of expressiveness. It suggests that we can score companies on the degree to which they express themselves effectively to their stakeholder communities through targeted communications and initiatives. The greater a company's expressiveness, we find, the more likely it is to be emotionally appealing to stakeholders.

Expressiveness contributes to reputation building in two ways: On one hand, expressiveness helps consumers make critical decisions by reducing the amount of information processing they

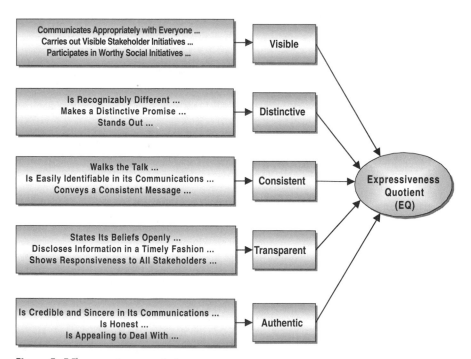

Figure 5–5 The expressiveness quotient.

have to carry out. Visibility reduces the need for search by making information about the company widely available. Authenticity is the "voice of the gut"—an authentic company is more likeable and trustworthy, and that may be enough to attract a consumer to its products, an investor to its stock, and an employee to its jobs. *Transparency* makes the company's statements and actions credible, reducing the need for vigilance and verification. *Distinctiveness* makes a company stand out and so reduces the efforts an investor or consumer has to go through to build a sophisticated understanding of the company. Finally, *consistency* clarifies the breadth of a company's activities and makes them interpretable. By being expressive, companies effectively "chunk" information about themselves and present them in attractive packages for stakeholders. By simplifying and predigesting information, expressiveness facilitates stakeholders' understanding of a company, reduces the need for additional time-consuming research, and increases the likelihood of obtaining supportive behaviors.

Expressiveness also helps corporate reputation building by promoting a shared understanding of the company among employees, customers, and investors. Visibility, distinctiveness, and transparency work together to reveal a company's core purpose, values, and beliefs. At the same time, consistency of messaging and initiatives helps to shape shared values among internal employees and external stakeholders that bind the company together. Internally, expressiveness creates predictability about the firm's key promises and enhances its credibility to employees; externally, expressiveness signals authenticity and facilitates a shared understanding of the company among investors, analysts, consumers, and the public at large.

What drives corporate expressiveness? Why do some companies achieve higher degrees of expressiveness, while others don't? There's evidence that expressiveness is itself a function of the degree to which companies are able to generate identification with the company by employees and customers. The more employees and customers identify with the company, the more likely they are to engage in supportive behaviors toward the company. Employees as well as customers act as ambassadors for the company.

Building reputation therefore involves generating identification. A recent in-depth analysis demonstrates that identification by a stakeholder group with the company is a function of four factors:[3]

Reputation builds identification—and vice versa: Employees are generally proud to belong to a company that they trust and respect—they bask in the company's reflected glory. The better the reputation that employees ascribe to their company, the more likely they are to identify with the company and so to act as good ambassadors in their dealings with other members and nonmembers of the company—to convey positive signals into their personal networks, whether at cocktail parties, dinner parties, or in informal settings.

Quality of communication improves identification—and vice versa: The quality of a company's communications with a specific stakeholder group affects identification with the company. Companies that communicate a great deal about strategic issues (such as goals and objectives, new developments, activities, and achievements) enable employees and other stakeholders to more easily uncover the company's more salient and distinctive features, thereby making it easier for them to identify with the company. Repeated exposure to information about the company increases its attractiveness and appeal, and reassures stakeholders about their participation in a worthwhile cause.

Companies that create a positive climate internally tend to strengthen employee identification. A positive climate invites employees to participate actively in discussions about the company and involves them more in decision making. In turn, openness in communications with supervisors and colleagues adds to feelings of self-worth—employees feel that they are taken seriously. Following the multiple crises that the company faced in the mid-1990s, Royal Dutch/Shell embarked on a complex organizational change process that brought together many layers of managers in a discussion and debate about the company's business principles. Open discussion facilitated healing and enhanced identification in a company whose external reputation had taken a heavy beating from repeated accusations of profiteering.

Personalized communications improve identification: In recent years companies such as Denmark's pharmaceutical giant Novo Nordisk and Germany's prestigious automaker DaimlerChrysler have invested in sophisticated computerized intranets designed to inform employees about the strategic pursuits of the company. That's also why they include elaborate feedback elements in those systems that are designed to facilitate the two-way flow of information and highlight the contributions that individuals have made to the company's success. Ulrike Becker, the Director of Internal Communications at DaimlerChrysler, put it this way: "Providing all employees and selected external target groups with all relevant company-related information at all times and at any location—that's the mission of Internal Communications, Web-based Media and Publications." They do so to promote employee identification.

Corporate messaging affects identification: Many leading companies rely on core strategic processes to promote identification. Royal Dutch/Shell created a scenario planning system to enhance crisis preparedness. The process involves all managerial staff in examining their assumptions about the future and debating the implications of selected scenarios across the company's diverse businesses. In promoting a common view of key strategic issues, the company enhances identification. In a comparable process, each year, Dutch consumer giant Philips identifies five to six core strategic issues that it organizes to address. The purpose of the process is to generate focus and consistency in how the company speaks to the media and in how managers present the company to employees. The more comprehensively a company invites participation by a stakeholder group in understanding its inner workings, the more likely that stakeholder group is to identify with the company. Following the September 11, 2001, bombings of the World Trade Center, many airlines initiated direct email messaging to customers to inform them about developments that affected the company. These personalized communications from American Airlines and United Airlines went a long way to creating sympathy, understanding, and trust in carriers whose reputations had been seriously tarnished by the terrorist attacks.

These four factors are the basis on which we created a measure of employee identification designed to examine how positively employees feel about a company and so the likelihood that they will demonstrate support for the company in their attitudes and behaviors. Figure 5–6 shows the components of corporate identification—and its link to employee perceptions of the company's reputation.

In chapters 6 to 10 we examine in detail the achievements and dilemmas that the best-regarded companies face as they strive to implement robust practices for reputation management across stakeholder groups. Chapter 6 takes a closer look at how *visibility* affects reputation—no company, we find, can develop and sustain

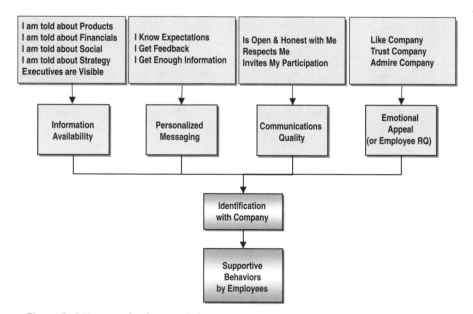

Figure 5–6 Measuring identification with the company.

a competitive advantage against its rivals without achieving visibility. Reputational advantage itself derives from achieving a position of *distinctiveness* in the minds of consumers—the subject we address in Chapter 7. With distinctiveness comes suspicion that companies may be cloaking themselves with disingenuous claims—requiring of companies what Chapter 8 describes as heightened *authenticity* in the claims they make, be they of product quality, concern for employees, corporate citizenship, or environmental sustainability. In Chapter 9, we show that claims of distinctiveness and authenticity are not enough. Increasingly, companies are expected to demonstrate them by opening up their operations to closer scrutiny—increasing their *transparency* to stakeholders. Chapter 10 concludes by showing how top companies achieve *consistency* across time and space—by systematically communicating coherent corporate stories to fragmented audiences. No small feat—and the weak of spirit need not apply.

ENDNOTES

1. C. J. Fombrun & V. Rindova, "Reputation Management in Global 1000 Firms: A Benchmarking Study", *Corporate Reputation Review, 1*(3), 1998: 205-214.

2. We were inspired to call this empirical measure the "expressiveness quotient" based on our work with M. J. Hatch and M. Schultz, editors of *The Expressive Organization,* Cambridge: Oxford University Press, 2000.

3. See the study reported by A. Smidts, A. Pruyn, & C. B.M. Van Riel, "The Impact of Employee Communication and Perceived External Prestige on Organizational Identification." *Academy of Management Journal, 44*(5), October 2001: 1051–1062.

6 BE VISIBLE

An old French saying about leading the good life goes as follows: *Pour vivre bien, il faut vivre caché*—to live well, live in hiding. Many companies act as if they believe it: They shun publicity, refuse media interviews, close ranks against what they perceive to be an inimical world, communicating minimally (particularly with the media) and only under duress. We call this the introvert posture, historically favored by companies guided by cautious investment bankers, and conservative politicians and lawyers.

That's actually bad advice. In today's globalized, mediatized, information-rich world, hiding is no longer an option. Stakeholders demand access, insist on knowing what you don't want to tell, and reporters are hell-bent on discovering and revealing it. In such a world, "Don't ask, don't tell"—the phrase popularized by the Clinton White House of the early 1990s as advice to gays and lesbians in the U.S. military —now seems hopelessly out of touch in suggesting that there might be things people actually don't want to know about.

It's simply not true. In fact, to paraphrase another bit of publicity made famous by a tabloid paper—it's more likely to be the case today that "inquiring minds want to know *everything*," and people eagerly seek out inside information to uncover in every realm of life, particularly if it's happening to the high and mighty— none more interesting than our largest companies and their senior executives. In a business-centered world, they have become the hottest subjects of gossip, innuendo, and scandal—and no one is more subjected to scrutiny and inquiry today than they are, whether from investors, institutions, individual stakeholders, or the media. The proliferation of corporate reports and newsletters describing mergers and acquisitions; the popularity of business news reports and dedicated outlets like CNBC, *Fortune* magazine, and the *Financial Times*; the media frenzy over outsized executive pay packages, former GE Chairman Jack Welch's corporate perks, or scandal-ridden executive suites at Enron, Worldcom, Adelphia, and Tyco International—all testify to that fact.

In such a frenzied marketplace for information, the question is therefore whether visibility helps or hurts companies. Does publicity help? Do exposure and familiarity breed favor, or do they generate contempt? Are the best-regarded companies more likely to reveal themselves to their publics or to guard themselves from scrutiny?

Marketers like to refer to a company's visibility as "top-of-mind awareness"—the probability that a company comes to mind when a consumer is prompted on a specific topic. The evidence we've gathered from the RQ Project to date is very much that reputations are built on a foundation of high top-of-mind awareness. *Simply put, the more familiar you are to the public, the better the public rates you.*

That said, although familiarity and reputation are always strongly correlated, reputation itself is considerably more than just being visible or well known to the public. For instance, among the top 10 rated companies in our U.S. study, only Coca-Cola and Microsoft were actually "very" familiar to more than

60 percent of consumers. Top-regarded companies are more than simply familiar—but they are definitely visible.

This chapter examines visibility as a strategic weapon. Why, we ask, does Coca-Cola earn 2 percent of all public nominations whereas archrival Pepsi, only gets 0.3 percent? How does tiny Vermont-based ice-cream maker Ben & Jerry's get to be so well-known compared to far larger rivals selling food products to consumers? What makes them top-of-mind? At the opposite extreme, how is it possible that the Swedish household goods company IKEA, whose products are in nearly every Dutch household, gets no nominations from Dutch consumers at all? Or that top fashion companies like Gucci or LVMH earn no visibility or favor from French and Italian consumers?

In exploring why some companies are more familiar than others to consumers, we extract five major factors that predict a company's visibility and familiarity. In the process, we inquire whether and how companies benefit from heightened exposure and indicate the conditions under which companies can leverage familiarity to build reputation.

Ultimately, a key finding of this chapter is that advertising is not nearly as powerful a tool for creating visibility as it once was. A company's name recognition is more credibly built through earned media coverage than through paid promotion. Think of all the visibility that Body Shop, Amazon, and Starbucks have amassed. Most of it did not come from advertising but from mentions in major media the world over.[1] The findings of the RQ Project suggest that positive visibility and reputation are more credibly and cheaply built from earned media coverage than from advertising.

Another key finding is that consumers lack information about a company's social initiatives—but welcome it when they get it. Perceptions of social responsibility enhance reputation and can be a positive source of visibility. Consumer data obtained from the RQ Project demonstrate that companies benefit reputationally from being known to persue social initiatives, but also indicate that care should be taken in self-promotions. Consumers are ambivalent about the degree to which companies should actively promote their social initiatives—less is probably better than more, and earned media from social initiatives is likely to be best of all.

UNDERSTANDING CORPORATE VISIBILITY

How visible are companies to consumers? The results of the RQ Project to date show that very few companies attract public attention, and the maximum visibility any single company attains is 19 percent—that is, one in five people spontaneously name the company. Table 6–1 compares the results in five countries, with Telstra, A.P. Moller, Fiat, KPN, and Microsoft hogging the most visible company status in Australia, Denmark, Italy, the Netherlands, and the United States respectively.

TABLE 6–1 The Visibility of Top-Nominated Companies in Australia, Italy, the Netherlands, and the United States

COUNTRY	HIGHEST PERCENT OF TOTAL COUNTRY NOMINATIONS	MOST VISIBLE COMPANY
Australia	19	Telstra
Denmark	14	A.P. Moller
Italy	16	Fiat
Netherlands	16	KPN
United States	12	Microsoft

Moreover, the most visible companies accounted for 80 to 90 percent of all nominations made by consumers in each country. It confirms that the threshold for visibility is extremely high indeed. Very few firms have high visibility, and those that do share similar characteristics.

Global Visibility: The most visible companies are often recognized by consumers because they are among *Business-Week*'s "10 Most Valuable Global Brands," a list regularly topped by Coca-Cola, Microsoft, IBM, GE, Intel, Nokia, Disney, McDonald's, Philip Morris (with Marlboro), and DaimlerChrysler (with its Mercedes brand).[2] Nominated companies in the 12 countries we studied generally included six of the following brands with high *global visibility*: Coca-Cola, Microsoft, IBM, Nokia, Disney, and Mercedes.

National Visibility: Consumers demonstrate a strong nationalistic bias and tend heavily to nominate brands from their own countries. Danes are more likely to nominate A.P. Moller and Novo Nordisk; Italians tend to nominate Fiat and Barilla; the Dutch turn to Philips or Ahold; and U.S. consumers think first of Microsoft or Wal-Mart. They have strong *national visibility*.

Negative Visibility: A third theme is the prominence the public gives to media coverage, particularly negative coverage. In 2001, high visibility was attached to companies like KPN in the Netherlands, to Firestone in the United States, to Cheminova in Denmark, and to Fiat in Italy—not least for the highly publicized financial, technological, or product crises they experienced.[3] They have high levels of *negative visibility*.

In an Internet-connected, media-saturated world, developing high negative visibility can happen overnight—witness the Enron-Worldcom executive scandals and the Ford-Firestone tire debacle. In the Netherlands, the negative visibility of the Dutch Railways exploded in 2001 following widely reported internal quarrels between top management, unions, and employees. In Denmark, TDC's bad reputation derives from disappointing experiences by consumers with its dizzying array of new service offerings under its previous Tele Danmark name.[4]

Negative visibility can also prove "sticky"—and companies that become known as "bad" companies sometimes retain lasting negative associations with consumer audiences; witness Exxon's enduring nominations among the companies with the worst reputations due largely to its mishandling of the Valdez crisis in 1989.

Figure 6–1 explores the link between visibility and RQ. Although few companies are nominated solely from perceptions as being best or worst, they do earn reputation from being visible. In Denmark, Novo Nordisk and A.P. Moller are nominated almost entirely for positive visibility. In the United States, Cisco and Johnson & Johnson score nearly 100 percent of their nominations for positive visibility, whereas Firestone, ExxonMobil, and Philip Morris are nominated entirely for their negative visibility. The results confirm that strong reputations result only

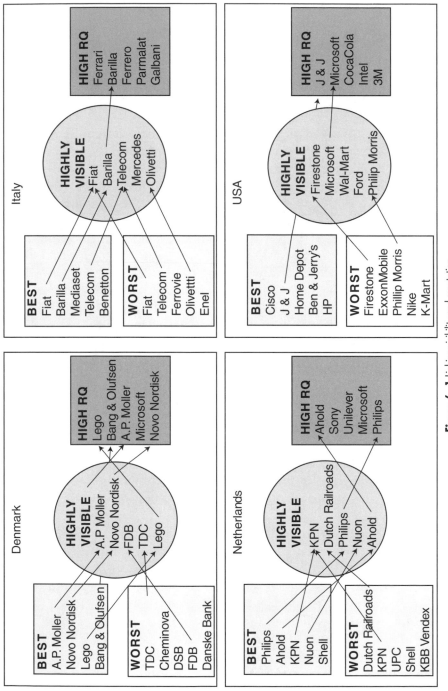

Figure 6–1 Linking visibility and reputation.

from positive visibility and that there are no reputational benefits to be had from negative visibility.

Figure 6–2 diagrams the results of a statistical regression of positive visibility and negative visibility on the RQ ratings for Denmark, Italy, and the Netherlands. It shows the supportive effect that positive visibility has on corporate reputations and the strong dampening effect of negative visibility. It helps explain why companies with splintered images—those nominated for both positive and negative visibility—have a hard time developing strong reputations with consumers.

WHEN SHOULD COMPANIES WORRY ABOUT NEGATIVE VISIBILITY?

To be known as being among the worst companies is never a good thing. However, a better question involves asking, When is it *really* a problem the company must address?

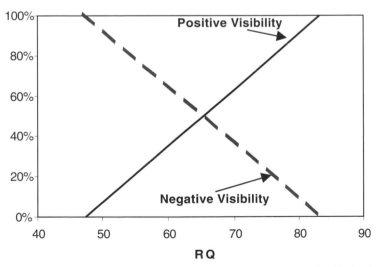

Trendlines are based on nominations data obtained from the Netherlands, Italy and Denmark in August 2001.

Figure 6–2 The relationship between reputation and visibility.

Figure 6–3 shows the results of a statistical analysis that focuses strictly on the relationship between negative visibility and reputation. The findings indicate that companies with more than 50 percent negative visibility develop substantially lower RQ ratings. It suggests that regularly tracking positive and negative visibility rates can help companies anticipate problems. Negative visibility creates reputational risk; when companies experience rising negative visibility, they are increasingly at risk of suffering reputational decline, and the threat of negative financial results looms ever larger.

THE DRIVERS OF VISIBILITY

How do the most highly nominated companies earn their public visibility? The 85 distinct companies that were examined in the RQ Project across five countries are, for the most part, large companies in terms of total revenues, market capitalization, number of employees, and advertising budgets. They also tend to be high performers, having high rates of return on total assets, equity, and in net margins.

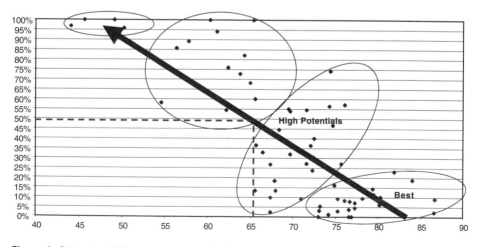

Figure 6–3 Negative visibility creates reputational risk.

However, not all large or high-performing companies get nominated. Based on their size and performance, companies like GE or Nokia should earn higher nomination rates than they do in the United States. Nor are nominated companies even the largest firms in their industries or the best financial performers.

Figure 6–4 summarizes the drivers of visibility. It suggests that visibility results from prominence in the minds of consumers:

- Public prominence occurs when companies (a) have high public exposure "on the street"; (b) proclaim their national heritage; and (c) have a strong presence in the media.
- Market prominence occurs when companies (a) have a powerful corporate brand or brand portfolio; (b) are listed on a public stock exchange; and (c) pursue high-profile corporate citizenship practices.

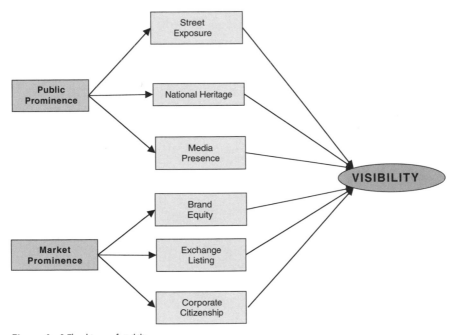

Figure 6–4 The drivers of visibility.

THE EFFECT OF STREET EXPOSURE

In the United Kingdom, 60 percent of all nominated companies are retailers or banks. They are the companies that consumers are most likely to think of because they have what our colleague Keith MacMillan at Henley Management College refers to as a high "street presence"[5]—broad exposure to the public who come into daily and direct contact with them.

Having A-locations in shopping centers and business areas, for instance, often helps them achieve heightened awareness. It's no coincidence that Carrefour and El Corte Ingles dominate the nominations in Spain, Spar in Austria, or Marks & Spencer, Sainsbury, and Tesco in the United Kingdom. In the Netherlands, three retailers are also among the 30 most visible companies (Ahold, KBB Vendex, and Laurus), and numerous financial intermediaries like ING, ABN-AMRO, RABO and Fortis are nominated. Italy has only one major food retailer among its top nominees—Coop Italia. But in the United States, consumers nominate Wal-Mart, K-mart, and Home Depot. As Majken Schultz of Copenhagen Business School points out, in Denmark, 18 out of the 25 most visible companies are business-to-consumer companies in retail (FDB, Dansk Supermarked, and Arla Foods), in financial services (Danske Bank and insurer PFA), and in telecommunications (TDC and Sonofon).[6]

THE INFLUENCE
OF NATIONAL HERITAGE

In 14 of the 15 countries we studied, the majority of the most visible companies were those whose headquarters were in the consumer's home country—with Italy the only exception. In the United States, for instance, only four of the 30 most highly nominated companies were non-U.S. companies. In France, the French car companies Renault and Peugeot-Citroen top the list, followed closely by food distributors Carrefour, Leclerc, and Auchan. In Denmark, A.P. Moller (best known for its MAERSK named subsidiaries), pharmaceutical products maker Novo Nordisk, and components manufacturer Danfoss are rooted in their Danish heritage too. Even in Italy, the top-nominated companies are themselves pillars of Italian capitalism, namely Fiat, Ferrari, and Pirelli.[7] Although well known nationally, few of these companies are ever nominated *outside* their home countries, confirming the nationalistic bias of consumers.

MEDIA PRESENCE EFFECTS

The media have powerful effects on corporate visibility. On one hand, companies regularly advertise their products and activities, thereby projecting attractive self-concepts and images to consumers. On the other, the media interpret, amplify, and shape news stories through commentaries that affect how consumers think about companies.

Negative media coverage virtually ensures high negative visibility. In 2001 Firestone, Microsoft, and Ford were all nominated in the United States because of extensive media coverage, most of it negative. So were KPN and the Dutch Railroads (NS) in the Netherlands and Fiat in Italy. In all countries high levels of negative visibility corresponded closely with intense and negatively toned media coverage about these companies. Not coincidentally, these companies earned low RQ ratings from consumers. In the United States, for instance, the four companies with the highest media recall by consumers (Bridgestone, Ford, AMR, and UAL) were ranked in the bottom 10 on overall RQ.

At the same time, companies regularly advertise to increase top-of-mind awareness with the public. The results of our analyses suggest that advertising may not always pay off: In 2000, Ford spent four times as much on advertising as did Marks & Spencer in the United Kingdom, yet earned a meager 10th place on visibility compared to the number one position of Marks & Spencer. McDonald's spent twice as much while Dixons spent three times as much as Marks & Spencer—only to earn 16th and 17th place respectively. Ford's advertising budget was likely drowned out by the Firestone-Ford crisis communications. Similarly, KPN was the biggest spender among the top-nominated firms in the Netherlands. However, although KPN's advertising may have earned the company top billing on overall visibility, sadly its advertising only amplified the negative media coverage it was getting, a result that was clearly accounted for by the low ratings KPN obtained RQ surveys since 2001.

Table 6–2 compares the advertising budgets of the top Dutch nominees with their visibility and RQ rankings. As Table 6–2 suggests, KPN's huge advertising budget perversely accentuated the negative media coverage the company was receiving, much of it related to financial problems brought about by the market downturn in 2000. Ahold, on the other hand benefited handsomely from the positive interaction between its paid advertising and a steady stream of positive media in 2001.

If companies make claims they can't deliver, boomerang effects can result that damage corporate reputation. Italy is a case in point. As Davide Ravasi, a colleague at Bocconi University in Milan points out, Telecom Italia, Enel, Tim, and Wind are among the largest advertisers in Italy. Enel's recent stock sale was supported by a massive communications campaign. Like Enel, Telecom Italia has been working hard to change from a private monopoly to a customer-oriented, service provider. The claims in both of their communication campaigns, however, may have created expectations that were not always supported by the quality of the service.[8] It may explain the negative visibility that these telecommunications companies earned in our Italian study.

The same results hold elsewhere. Despite huge ad spends and street presence, financial service companies, railroads, and telecommunications companies tend to receive relatively few nominations in all countries—and then, mostly for negative visibility, much of it the result of negative media coverage about failed expectations.

TABLE 6–2 Relating Advertising and Visibility to Reputation in the Netherlands

COMPANY	ADVERTISING SPEND (2000)	VISIBILITY RANKING	RQ RANKING
KPN	19.7	1	29
KBB Vendex	8.2	9	19
Laurus	9.1	18	25
Ahold	5.4	5	1
Sony	3.6	20	2

BRAND EQUITY UPS THE ANTE

The most visible companies are often those with strong corporate brands or strong brand portfolios. Table 6-3 lists the world's top brands based on estimates by consultants at Interbrand. As you might expect, a number of the most visible companies in Australia, Europe, and the United States are among them—none more so, perhaps, than Coca-Cola, whose logo turns up everywhere. The ubiquity of Coca-Cola at sporting events, on restaurant door fronts, airplane menus, soda machines, fast-food outlets, on umbrellas, posters, and television sitcoms is remarkable indeed. Microsoft's logo appears on virtually everyone's computer as consumers boot up their machines at work, at home, or in Internet cafés. Consumers are also cued by Intel's clever "Intel Inside" label on their computers, securing visibility for a B2B company that would otherwise have no consumer touchpoints. Similarly, GE's light bulbs and appliances, Nokia's cell phones, Disney's theme parks, McDonald's arches, Philip

TABLE 6–3 The Most Valuable Global Brands (2002) and Their Consumer Visibility

| | | VISIBILITY RANK IN MID 2001 | | |
COMPANY (COUNTRY)	2002 BRAND VALUE ($ BILLIONS)	US	EUROPE	AUSTRALIA
1. Coca-Cola (U.S.)	69.6	18	8	15
2. Microsoft (U.S.)	64.1	1	14	13
3. IBM (U.S.)	51.2	9	23	18
4. General Electric (U.S.)	41.3	5	–	-
5. Intel (U.S.)	30.9	30	–	-
6. Nokia (Finland)	30.0	119	26	-
7. Disney (U.S.)	29.3	17	–	-
8. McDonald's (U.S.)	26.4	20	7	5
9. Marlboro (Philip Morris, U.S.)	24.2	8	25	-
10. Mercedes (Daimler-Chrysler, Germany)	21.0	12	4	-

Source: *Business Week* survey with Interbrand, 5 August 2002.

Morris's Marlboro man, and DaimlerChrysler's Mercedes all create visibility.

Having strong brands, however, is no guarantee of prominence
and visibility. Table 6–3 indicates that some major brands have relatively low levels of global visibility, whereas some companies are
getting greater global payoff from their brand equity than others.
Microsoft, Coca-Cola, IBM, and McDonald's are the only brands to
achieve global visibility—all for different reasons, none of which
consistently rank among the top 10 cross-nationally. Philip Morris and DaimlerChrysler are highly visible to consumers in two of
three regions; Disney, GE, and Intel, only in the United States;
and Nokia, only in Europe. Clearly, having strong brands is a necessary but not sufficient reason for visibility.

A STOCK EXCHANGE LISTING INVITES SCRUTINY

Companies pursue a stock exchange listing in order to access the
capital markets. In doing so, they increase the level of scrutiny
to which they are subject by regulatory bodies, as well as by a
global network of analysts, reporters, and investors. Listing on
a stock exchange therefore generates higher media coverage
and public involvement with the activities of a company.

Most European firms are unaccustomed to the levels of public
scrutiny that listing generates. Often, they are family owned and
resist visibility and transparency. Of the companies nominated in
the United States 97 percent were publicly listed in 2001, with the
sole exception of Vermont ice-cream maker Ben & Jerry's, the legendary clothing retailer L.L. Bean based in Maine, and the giant
privately held maker of household products Amway. Across Europe, most are also publicly traded, although often shares are closely held in family trusts.

A stock exchange listing means that consumers quickly learn
about bad news. When KPN, the leading Dutch telecommunications company, suffered financial setbacks, the negative media
coverage it received precipitated a dramatic drop in its share
price. It also generated a threefold surge in negative visibility
for the company in 2001. The negative portion of the reputation

cycle clearly operates here: Heightened negative visibility leads to withdrawal of support from journalists and analysts, reduced interest by investors in the company's shares, and a price collapse—fueling a downward spiral in the company's stock and reputation.

CORPORATE CITIZENSHIP
RAISES PUBLIC PROFILES

Countries vary in the relative emphasis consumers place on the positive or negative visibility of the companies they nominate. In the United States negative visibility outweighed positives in 2001. In total, seven companies earned more than 60 percent of their nominations from negative visibility: Of these, Bridgestone/Firestone, Ford, ExxonMobil, and Philip Morris earned it for their involvements with significant consumer crises—Bridgestone/Firestone and Ford for the tire explosions on Ford Explorers in summer 2000, ExxonMobil for the public's continued association of the company with the 1989 Valdez oil spill, and Philip Morris for its legal battles over the cancer inducing effects of tobacco. Moreover, the U.S. public clearly blames Bridgestone/Firestone more than Ford. Ninety-nine percent of Firestone's were negative, compared to Ford's 62 percent. Clearly, Ford's immediate out-front apologies, CEO-led explanatory ads, and posture as public custodian were far more effective than Bridgestone/Firestone's slow response, bumbling denials, and reluctance to accept blame.

In Europe, positive visibility outweighed negatives, with Carrefour, Philips, Volvo (Ford), and Mercedes (DaimlerChrysler) earning the vast majority of their nominations for positive visibility. The companies nominated for highest negative visibility were Shell and Total-Fina-Elf, both of which suffered from perceived deficiencies in social responsibility—Shell for its involvements in 1995 with the sinking of the Brent Spar oil platform in the North Sea and Total-Fina-Elf for the vast oil spill by the *Erika* that polluted the coastline of Brittany in 2000.

In Australia, most of the nominated companies earn splintered visibility—led by telecom giant Telstra, most were nominated for both positive and negative reasons. After Telstra, McDonald's earned the highest negative nominations, with Australia's mining concern BHP and Australia's major banks and insurance companies close behind.

Corporate citizenship is a label that is increasingly attached to companies that take public positions as "good citizens"—and claim to behave responsibly, to safeguard communities and the environment, and to serve the best interests of consumers. A number of the most visible companies made it to the visibility lists for making credible commitments to corporate citizenship. In the United States Ben & Jerry's was among the top nominees, principally for its perceived citizenship initiatives. In Denmark Novo Nordisk's core business of insulin production has involved the company in countless social initiatives that project caring for consumers as patients. Much the same can be said of A.P. Moller and Lego, top Danish nominees with high positive visibility. A.P. Moller's founders have strong philanthropic involvements that benefit the Danish public. In the Netherlands, top nominee (and top-rated) retailer Ahold stood out in 2001 for being among the first companies in Europe to emphasize sustainable food production and maintain a strong involvement in local communities in which the company operates its numerous retail brands.

CAPITALIZING ON VISIBILITY

The best-regarded companies seek to take advantage of visibility by leveraging the visibility drivers in different ways. Some seek to leverage their national heritage, others to de-emphasize it. Some build up a more effective media presence by strengthening their corporate brands; others create decentralized brand portfolios to capitalize on local identification. The best of them develop combinations of local and global citizenship involvements that are designed to reduce perceptions of the company as "foreign" to local consumers. Clearly, the best companies pursue distinct strategies—but all of them are designed to capitalize on visibility.

LEVERAGING NATIONALISM
OR EMPHASIZING GLOBALITY?

Many companies build up their visibility by emphasizing national heritage. Companies like Coca-Cola, McDonald's, IBM, and Microsoft are emblematic of U.S. market capitalism and are heavily identified as such. They project an aggressively American ethos. Renault is French to the core, Fiat is Italian, and Volkswagen is German.

Although General Motors is heavily identified with the United States, the company de-emphasizes its American roots by creating autonomous local brands (e.g., Opel in France, viewed by many as a French car). Consumer goods makers like Unilever and Procter & Gamble do much the same by relying on portfolios of local brands emblazoned with local country identities to capitalize on national identification.

Others blur the line by seeking to adopt non-national identities. Many consumers are hard put to tell you where consumer electronics giant Sony is headquartered (Japan) and would be surprised to hear that Nokia is Finnish, that Addidas Salomon is French, or that Philips is Dutch. These companies actively seek to downplay their national heritage in order to minimize their liability of foreignness and capitalize on favorable local perceptions.[9]

At some point, however, companies with powerful global aspirations find themselves forced to de-emphasize their national roots. That's because consumer perceptions about foreign companies are a significant barrier to the mobility of companies into new markets. Since the early forays by American companies into European markets in the 1960s, multinationals have been looked upon with suspicion and often viewed as imperialist extensions of their home governments. Japanese and other Asian car producers and consumer electronic products companies experienced it themselves when they sought to establish manufacturing beachheads in the United States in the 1980s. They consequently sought ways to denationalize their identities and project their embeddedness in the local fabrics of countries by hiring local managers, involving themselves in local communities, and de-emphasizing the foreign nature of their operations.

Most recently, consider DaimlerChrysler, a company with a strong German heritage. Since its merger with Chrysler in 1998, Daimler executives have worked hard to overcome parochial perceptions of DaimlerChrysler as either German or American. Instead, the company now stresses the global nature of its involvements with consumers and its role as an integral participant in all of the nations in which the company produces and sells its cars. The advertisement shown in Figure 6–5 illustrates the global claim appealingly.

To capitalize on the advantages of both national heritage and globality, some companies claim explicitly to pursue a global-local, or so-called "glocal" strategy. Coca-Cola is among its top exponents, and the strategy enables the company to simultaneously build on its national presence in each of the countries in which it operates while capitalizing on global scope. In reality, it's doubtful anyone thinks of Coke as anything but American. The same is true for Sony and other multinationals who claim glocal pursuits. They remain firmly anchored in their

Figure 6–5 An advertisement by DaimlerChrysler demonstrating its globality.
Source: DaimlerChrysler

countries of origin. What they do well is develop strong local ties that are designed to reduce their perceived foreignness in local communities, principally by recruiting and benefiting local staff in their operations (often through jointly owned ventures or franchises) by adapting communications to local conditions (e.g., advertising and PR that accommodate local tastes) and by supporting local citizenship activities. Global economies are maintained through rationalized purchasing, production, and coordination of the company's network.

INCREASING YOUR MEDIA PRESENCE

The media clearly affect a company's visibility to consumers. The MRi (Media Reputation Index) is a measure of media reputation developed by the Reputation Institute with the market research firm Delahaye-Medialink. The index describes the degree of positive media reputation earned by the largest U.S. companies after content coding of all electronically available media coverage. The MRi calculates media reputation by weighting the quality of the media coverage by various factors, including the circulation of the specific media outlet and the prominence of the company's coverage in each article in terms of headlines, graphics, and positioning in the issue. Figure 6–6 shows the companies that earned the highest MRi ratings in the first half of 2001. Remarkably, the results confirm that many of the most visible companies that were among the top-rated companies in the RQ Project (e.g., Microsoft, Walt Disney, IBM, and General Electric) also earned top scores in the media. In other words, the public tends to notice the companies that are put "on the agenda" by the media and also tends to give higher ratings to those companies that get more favorable press coverage.[10]

The net positive effect of earned visibility in Figure 6–6 suggests that companies can indeed capitalize on their interactions with the media to build reputation. The strongest brands were more favorably covered, feeding a virtuous spiral of supportive impressions that energized positive attitudes from consumers, which in turn encouraged more favorable media. On balance, Microsoft appears to have gained most from media support during its antitrust battles with the Justice Department since 2000.

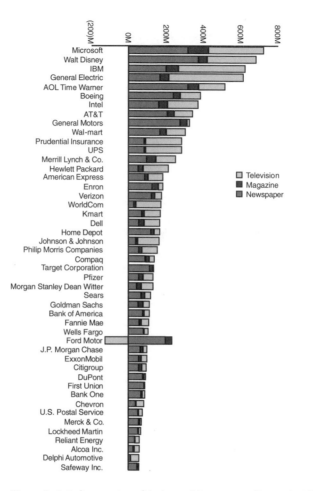

Figure 6–6 Media reputations of the largest U.S. companies (January 1–July 1, 2001).

Source: Delahaye-Medialink/Reputation Institute, 2001

Although advertising increases visibility, in contrast to earned media, advertising doesn't pay. Table 6–4 shows the relationship between advertising expenditures and the RQ scores of rated companies. Top advertiser Philip Morris does not earn brownie points from the public, whereas Sony's higher RQ score justifies its advertising spend. The same is true for KPN, whose

TABLE 6–4 Advertising and Reputation: US and the Netherlands

COMPANY	ADVERTISING (2000) $MILLIONS	REPUTATION QUOTIENT (2001)
US Companies		
General Motors Corp.	$3,935	76.03
Philip Morris Cos.	2,603	58.96
Procter & Gamble Co.	2,364	78.24
Ford Motor Co.	2,345	68.27
DaimlerChrysler	1,802	77.74
AOL Time Warner	1,770	67.56
Walt Disney Co.	1,757	78.52
Johnson & Johnson	1,601	81.59
Sears, Roebuck & Co.	1,455	71.08
Unilever	1,454	63.95
AT&T Corp.	1,416	69.49
General Electric Co.	1,310	77.22
Toyota Motor Corp.	1,274	75.56
McDonald's Corp.	1,274	74.17
IBM Corp.	1,189	78.58
Honda Motor Co.	1,035	75.58
Sony Corp.	1,030	80.49
Merck & Co.	984	72.25
The Netherlands	**Millions Dutch Guilders**	
KPN	19.7	54.6
Laurus	9.1	57.8
KBB Vendex	8.2	67.4
Ahold	5.4	78.2
Sony	3.6	77.3
NS	3.3	44
Rabobank	3.0	68
ABN Amro	2.9	66.5
Philips	2.7	67.9
ING	1.9	71
KLM	1.2	74.9

astronomical ad budget dwarfs that of Ahold but creates no rep-utational gains. It clearly indicates that high advertising does not mean a high RQ, and advertising has little to do with creat-ing distinctiveness with consumers. Companies like personal-care products maker The Body Shop and the Vermont ice-cream maker Ben & Jerry's (who earned a high RQ in 1999 before being bought by Unilever) are the stuff of legend for having built their reputations on media, not advertising.[11]

PROJECTING YOUR CORPORATE CITIZENSHIP

The mounting stakeholder pressures on companies have in-duced increased involvement by companies in citizenship ac-tivities to both respond and manage the demands they make. Figure 6–7 shows the growth rate in the number of companies issuing social reports in the last decade. It indicates the height-ened concern managers have with establishing supportive stake-holder relationships through citizenship programs.

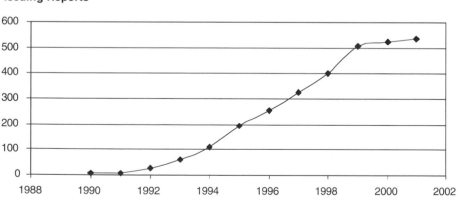

Figure 6–7 Growth in social reporting by Fortune 500 companies.
Source: Corporate Register.

Our research with Harris Interactive suggests that most consumers welcome corporate philanthropy and other citizenship initiatives, but are relatively uninformed about them. Over 54 percent of the U.S. public surveyed in 2001 recognize that companies have a role to play that goes beyond narrow profit-making, and 44 percent think they have broad social responsibilities that include treatment of employees and personal health and safety—as Figure 6–8 further indicates. But across countries, more than one-third of respondents (36 percent) consistently report feeling that they don't have enough information to rate companies on whether they support good causes.

More problematic is the fact that consumers are relatively ambivalent about whether and to what extent companies should advertise or promote their do-good involvements. Most U.S. respondents believe that companies should publicize their good deeds in some way—but disagree how much. Some 51 percent would like companies to publicize their good deeds through corporate advertising and press releases, whereas only 40 percent believe that publicizing good deeds should be done through minimal releases such as annual reports and on company Web sites.

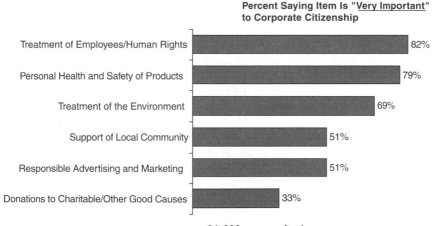

Percent Saying Item Is "Very Important" to Corporate Citizenship

Treatment of Employees/Human Rights	82%
Personal Health and Safety of Products	79%
Treatment of the Environment	69%
Support of Local Community	51%
Responsible Advertising and Marketing	51%
Donations to Charitable/Other Good Causes	33%

n=21,630 respondents
Representative Sample of U.S. General Public

Figure 6–8 The growing importance of corporate citizenship.
Source: Harris Interactive/Reputation Institute, 2001

A surprising 9 percent feel that companies should do good deeds but should not publicize them at all.

On the question of publicity, Figure 6–9 compares the attitudes of the Danish public against those of the U.S. public. Consistent with other European results, Danes think companies should do minimal publicity about their citizenship initiatives. Indeed, 18 percent of the Danish public (twice as many as in the U.S.) think companies should do no publicity at all. An even greater 24 percent of Italian consumers thought companies should do no publicity at all.

The polarized results in these surveys explain why companies are uncertain about how much they should pursue social initiatives and the degree of visibility they should give to their initiatives; some companies do more but say relatively little, while others say

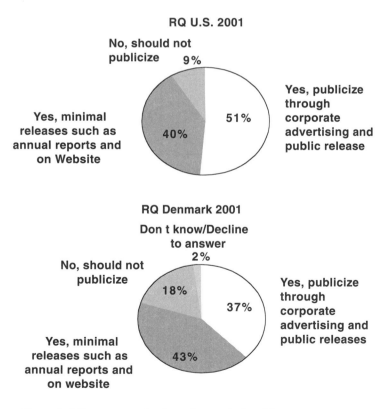

Figure 6–9 Corporate citizenship: Denmark versus the United States..
Source: Harris Interactive/Reputation Institute, 2001

a lot about what they're doing but do relatively little (to the consternation of many). Recent criticisms of BP's "Beyond Petroleum" campaign, for instance, have revolved around the company's self-promotion as an energy company with "...oh, yes, a little oil...," an environmentally friendly posture that is as yet undeserved given BP's extensive and continued reliance on fossil fuels.

Figure 6–10 captures a simplified representation of the kinds of images and positioning that Denmark's Novo Nordisk has adopted. The world's top insulin producer clearly seeks to project an aura of social responsibility around its operations, and care for its consumer patients that rely on its insulin for health maintenance. Comparable efforts typify the positioning of the most visible companies, Microsoft, General Electric, and Wal-Mart. Microsoft has benefited heavily from the media buzz that surrounded the colossal $19 billion philanthropic foundation created by founder Bill Gates in the late 1990s—and Microsoft's implied commitment to

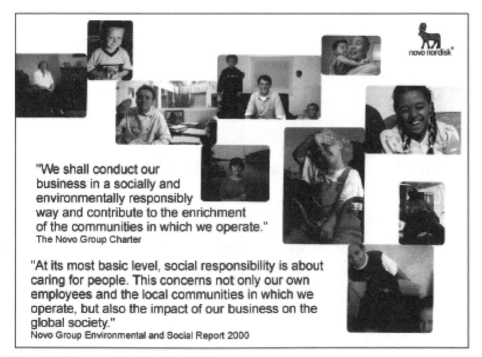

novo nordisk®

"We shall conduct our business in a socially and environmentally responsibly way and contribute to the enrichment of the communities in which we operate."
The Novo Group Charter

"At its most basic level, social responsibility is about caring for people. This concerns not only our own employees and the local communities in which we operate, but also the impact of our business on the global society."
Novo Group Environmental and Social Report 2000

Figure 6–10 Corporate citizenship at Novo Nordisk.
Source: Novo Nordisk, Novo Group Environmental and Social Report 2000

educational causes. General Electric's motto, "We bring good things to life," remains one of the most recognized slogans in the United States. Wal-Mart emphasizes a customer-centric and employee-centric positioning in its communications.

Others are clearly joining in. In April 2002, top Japanese automaker Toyota announced its "Global Vision 2010". As the company put it:

"Through Monozukuri—manufacturing of value-added products" and "technological innovation," Toyota is aiming to help create a more prosperous society. To realize this, we are challenging the below themes:

1. Be a driving force in global regeneration by implementing the most advanced environmental technologies.
2. Creating automobiles and a motorized society in which people can live safely, securely and comfortably.
3. Promote the appeal of cars throughout the world and realize a large increase in the number of Toyota fans.
4. Be a truly global company that is trusted and respected by all peoples around the world." [12]

Central to Toyota's vision are visibility, globality, and sustainability—increasing harmony between the company and society, and demonstrating responsiveness to stakeholders' concerns about the environment. It's confirmed in the following statement by Chairman Hiroshi Okida:

> Since its founding, our company has been aiming to enrich society through car making. Our goal is to be a "good corporate citizen," constantly winning the trust and respect of the international community. Continuing in the 21st century, we aim for stable long-term growth, while striving for harmony with people, society, and the environment. [13]

Consider fast-food giant McDonald's. In its communications, the company makes bold claims about its commitment to corporate citizenship: "The principle of giving back runs deep at McDonald's—instilled in us nearly fifty years ago by our founder, Ray Kroc. It is a part of our culture." As the company puts it:

"We are committed...
- To doing what is *right*.
- To being a *good neighbor* and partner in our community.
- To conducting our business with the *environment* in mind.

We are committed to making the world a better place and to providing socially responsible leadership in every community where we do business.

We are committed to greater transparency, continuous improvement, and dialogue on the issues." [14]

Like other leading companies, McDonald's also issued its first Social Responsibility Report in 2002, describing it as "...a beginning effort to compile and share information about our progress and plans in major areas of social responsibility."[15] The Ronald McDonald Children's House helps children in need of intensive hospital care and helps their parents as well. McDonald's uses the program to build visibility and reputation for the company through corporate citizenship:

> A strong mind. A strong body. And a safe, supportive place to grow. These are things that every child needs—and deserves—to have. Helping to provide these things is what we do. By creating, finding and supporting programs that directly improve the health and well being of children, Ronald McDonald House Charities is working to better the lives of children and their families around the world. To date, we've awarded more than $320 million dollars in grants worldwide towards our mission to make an immediate and positive impact on as many children as possible. And with support from a global network of 171 independent local Chapters in 44 countries—as well as hundreds of thousands of passionate and caring people—we've had plenty of success.

THE BOTTOM LINE?

Visibility is a double-edged sword: Consumers notice companies for both positive and negative reasons. Positive visibility tends to develop from projecting images of companies as caring and nurturing, while negative visibility tends to develop from corporate crises. The best-regarded companies are not always the most visible—for instance, though top-rated, Johnson & Johnson was considerably lower in visibility than Microsoft, Coca-Cola, Intel, and IBM. But it is the exception. The best-regarded companies capitalize on positive visibility by emphasizing their globalism, building a positive media presence, and conveying responsible involvement with their stakeholders. In Chapter 7 we show that the best-regarded companies are also *distinctive*— they build their visibility on a reputation platform that makes them stand out from the competition.

ENDNOTES

1. A. Ries & L. Ries, *The Fall of Advertising and the Rise of PR*, New York, HarperCollins, 2002.
2. *BusinessWeek*, August 5, 2002.
3. Research shows that consumers have a limited capability to store names in memory. On average, people can mention only five to seven company names spontaneously. High top-of-mind awareness indicates a high degree of cognitive elaboration by the public and suggests that the company is more likely to be evaluated by consumers on multiple criteria.
4. M. Schultz, K.U. Nielsen, & S. Boege, "Denmark: Nominations for the Most Visible Companies for the Danish RQ," *Corporate Reputation Review, 4*(4), Winter 2002: 327–336.
5. K. MacMillan, K. Money, & S. Downing, "United Kingdom: Best and Worst Corporate Reputations—Nominations by the General Public," *Corporate Reputation Review,* 4(4), Winter 2002: 374–384.
6. M. Schultz, K.U. Nielsen, & S. Boege, "Denmark: Nominations for the Most Visible Companies for the Danish RQ," *Corporate Reputation Review, 4*(4), Winter 2002: 327–336.
7. Italy seems to be an exception regarding the balance between national and international nominations. Forty percent of all nominated firms in Italy were non-Italian. As our colleague Davide Ravasi at Bocconi University suggests, a possible explanation is that many Italian firms are conglomerates that

are above all known for their products and not so much for the holding companies that link them together (see D. Ravasi, "Italy: Analyzing Reputation in a Cross-National Setting," *Corporate Reputation Review, 4*(4), Winter 2002: 354–361).

8. D. Ravasi, "Italy: Analyzing Reputation in a Cross-National Setting," *Corporate Reputation Review, 4*(4), Winter 2002: 354–361.

9. N. Gardberg & C. Fombrun, "Overcoming the Liability of Foreignness," *Academy of Management Review,* forthcoming, 2003.

10. The agenda-setting effect of the media was developed by Max McCombs and his colleagues, and has been well-documented in the political literature. Craig Carroll's doctoral dissertation relies on these data to test and confirm that this effect also holds in the corporate sector.

11. Note, however, that since reputations are cumulative buildups of attractiveness in the marketplace, a better analysis would involve examining the *cumulative advertising expenditures* of these companies over a longer time period—10 years, say. If we assume, however, that most of these companies make relatively stable advertising commitments year in and year out, then the past year budget is an adequate indicator, and we can indeed conclude a limited effect of advertising on consumer-based reputations.

12. H. Oshuda, Toyota, *http://www.toyota.co.jp/en/ci.html,* December 2002.

13. H. Oshuda, Toyota, *http://www.toyota.co.jp/en/ci.html,* December 2002.

14. McDonald's Corporation, *http://www.mcdonalds.com/corporate/social/index.html,* December 2002.

15. McDonald's Corporation, *http://www.mcdonalds.com/corporate/social/index.html,* December 2002.

7 BE DISTINCTIVE

A hallmark of the best-regarded companies is their distinctiveness. Whether viewed from inside or out, from top to bottom, across media channels, or comparing their actions and communications, the high RQ companies seem to distinguish themselves successfully from rivals: They stand for something. In large part, they do this by building their reputations around a "core reputation platform" —one that speaks to all stakeholders and tells them a story. Although, over time, a company may tell multiple stories to its stakeholders, the best-regarded companies tell stories that are rooted in a core reputation platform.

Sony is a company that has many stories to tell. Often the stories involve successful products like portable radios, the Walkman, or the Vega television. Sometimes they involve the entrepreneurial attitudes of Sony's founders in Japan. Mostly, however, they revolve around a common reputation platform built on the twin themes of innovation and miniaturization. In similar ways, the reputation platform of top-rated Swedish automaker Volvo (the car division is now a Ford subsidiary) is anchored firmly on the concepts of safety and security. The maker of healthcare products Johnson & Johnson builds reputation around a platform of care, nurturing, and motherhood. Its communications often display pictures of women with children and babies that crystallize the theme.

Not only do these highly-regarded companies present themselves to consumers with consistent communications built around such shared reputation platforms, they do so coherently through initiatives targeted to *all stakeholders*. This chapter examines some of the distinctive platforms that top-rated companies have adopted and the tools they rely on to communicate their platforms successfully to stakeholders in ways that attract attention and support. As we emphasize, distinctiveness does not develop by happenstance—it is managed. Competition often forces companies to look alike—rivalry forces them to imitate each other in order to stay abreast. What this chapter suggests is that companies can actually benefit tremendously from creating even *small* differences in perceptions by stakeholders. Often, these small differences are enough to produce an avalanche of recognition, support, and reputation from stakeholders.

WHAT ARE REPUTATION PLATFORMS?

Many of the more familiar companies rated in the United States as part of the RQ Project are listed in Table 7–1. The chart also describes the reputation platforms these companies use to give structure to their social initiatives and programs, as well as the taglines some of them use. A number of these companies are instantly recognizable on the basis of those slogans because they were widely and consistently popularized through print and broadcast ads over many years.

TABLE 7–1 Reputation Platforms and Slogans of Some of the Most Visible U.S. Companies (2001)

Company	RQ 2001	Reputation Platform	Slogan/ Tagline
Johnson & Johnson	82.5	Health and motherhood	The worldwide manufacturer of healthcare products
Microsoft	81.8	Integration	Your potential. Our passion.
Coca-Cola	80.8	Refreshment	To Benefit and Refresh (formerly "It's the Real Thing")
Intel	80.8	Innovation	Intel Inside
3M	80.2	Functionality	Innovation
Sony	79.4	Entertainment and design	Leading manufacturer of audio, video, communications and information technology products
Hewlett Packard	79.2	Invention	Invent
Kodak	78.2	Imaging	Take, share, enhance, preserve, print, and enjoy pictures
IBM	78.1	Technology solutions	Leader in creation, development and manufacture of advanced information technologies
Maytag	78.1	Performance and innovation	Intelligent innovation and superior performance
General Electric	78.0	Performance	Bringing good things to life
Walt Disney	78.0	Happiness	Making Magic
Charles Schwab	77.5	Cost and service	Creating a world of smarter investors
Dell	77.1	Distribution and value	Cost-cutting. Easy as Dell.
Procter & Gamble	76.6	Quality brands	Marketing. Make every day better for the consumer.
Sun Microsystems	76.6	Networking	We're the dot in .com
Home Depot	75.6	Value and service	Shop. Learn. Improve
Toyota	75.6	Future	Today Tomorrow
Nokia	74.3	Connections	Connecting People

TABLE 7–1 Reputation Platforms and Slogans of Some of the Most Visible U.S. Companies (2001) (cont.)

COMPANY	RQ 2001	REPUTATION PLATFORM	SLOGAN/ TAGLINE
Southwest Airlines	73.7	Service delivered with warmth, friendliness, individual pride, and company spirit.	A company of people
General Motors	73.6	Size and scale	People in motion
Pfizer	73.0	Life	Life is our life's work.
Nordstrom	72.9	Quality, value, selection, and service	
DuPont	72.1	Scientific research	Miracles of Science
Merck	71.8	Research	Bringing out the best in medicine
Oracle	71.8	Enterprise solutions	Software powers the Internet
Philips	71.7	Technological leadership	Let's Make Things Better
Nike	71.6	Marketing and design	Just do it
Xerox	71.3	Technology Innovation	The Document Company
McDonald's	71.1	Best quick service restaurant	A people company serving hamburgers
eBay	70.7	Facilitate trading objects	The world's online marketplace
Amazon	70.1	Personal service	Earth's Biggest Selection
Gateway	69.7	Personalized technology solutions	
Citigroup	69.3	Leadership in global financial services	
Sears	68.5	Low price retail	Where else?
K-Mart	66.4	Low price retail	The Stuff of Life
AT&T	65.2	Speed, flexibility, reliability, and security	

TABLE 7-1 Reputation Platforms and Slogans of Some of the Most Visible U.S. Companies (2001) (cont.)

COMPANY	RQ 2001	REPUTATION PLATFORM	SLOGAN/ TAGLINE
ExxonMobil	65.2	Scale and efficiency	The world's premier petroleum and petrochemical company
BP	65.0	Energy	Beyond Petroleum
Lucent Technologies	64.5	Global communications	Expect great things
Shell	64.3	Energy	To meet the energy needs of society, in ways that are economically, socially and environmentally viable, now and in the future.
Ford	63.9	Automotive	A global family of automotive brands and services
DaimlerChrysler	61.9	Transportation technology	Answers for questions to come
Philip Morris	56.4	Consumer packaged goods	Working to make a difference. The people of Philip Morris.
Bridgestone/Firestone	46.7	Tire performance	A Grip on the Future

Three themes seem to characterize the most popular reputation platforms:

- **Activity Theme:** Some companies try to build reputation around the key activities or businesses they are involved in. They convey the centrality of that activity to the company, be it online trading for eBay, transportation technology for DaimlerChrysler, or network computing for Sun Microsystems. Shell and ExxonMobil are in the energy business; Lucent is in the communications business.
- **Benefits Theme:** Others emphasize the attractive outcomes or benefits that stakeholders should expect from the company's activities as a way of inspiring allegiance. Sony en-

tertains. Dell cuts your costs. Disney makes you happy. K-Mart and Sears give you everyday low pricing. Bridgestone/Firestone makes high performance tires. Presumably, automaker GM believes that bigger is simply better.

■ **Emotional Theme:** Finally, companies differ in their reliance on an emotional theme to inspire support. Volvo's focus is on safety, Pfizer's on life, Johnson & Johnson's on motherhood, DuPont's on scientific miracles, Amazon's on personal service, and Southwest Airlines' on fun and friendliness—all try to establish an emotional bond with stakeholders to elicit a personal connection.

In the rest of this chapter, we examine three of the principal tools that companies use to convey the distinctiveness of their reputation platforms. They include customized slogans, unique trademarks and logos, and personalized corporate stories. As we will show, all of the themes succeed in varying degrees.

DISTINCTIVE SLOGANS

Some of the slogans and taglines used by the U.S. companies rated in the RQ Project and shown in Table 7–1 are more appealing than others. Many are enduring representations of the companies they characterize. GE's "We Bring Good Things to Life" is very familiar to most Americans. Coca-Cola's new tagline is now "To benefit and refresh," but far better remembered by consumers is the Coca-Cola slogan developed in 1942, "The Real Thing," which was also revived in 1971 and presents an enduring psychological barrier to rival cola-makers.

A surprising number of top companies—for instance Johnson & Johnson, AT&T, and Citigroup—don't use taglines at all to position themselves. Some use taglines, but only to describe their product or brand portfolios. Some use unevocative portfolio descriptions whenever they present themselves: Ford Motor Company offers the rather bland idea that the company is a global family of automotive brands and services; Sony is a leading manufacturer of audio, video, communications, and information technology products; IBM is a "leader in creation, development and manufacture of advanced information technologies."

It makes us wonder: Do top-rated companies have better more creative slogans? In reviewing Table 7–1, it's difficult to generalize about the effectiveness of the corporate slogans it documents. Some top-regarded companies do have strong taglines (GE's "We Bring Good Things to Life"), but so do some of the lesser regarded companies like Bridgestone/Firestone ("A Grip on the Future"). At any one point in time, it's not always the case that only the best-regarded companies will have the best taglines and communications. Even poorly regarded companies can still hire very good marketing consultants who can help them develop clever slogans and communications campaigns. Nonetheless, we suggest below some general propositions about the kinds of overall communications that better-regarded companies seem to make:

1. **Communications are *stakeholder-relevant*.** They anticipate the information needs of all their stakeholders and target specialized communications that are relevant to them. Take LEGO, the top-rated Danish company. Most of its messages include elements that are targeted to specific stakeholders—first children, then parents, retailers, the financial community, nongovernmental organizations, and the public.

2. **Communications are *realistic*.** They don't oversell. Highly rated Sony is a case in point. The giant Japanese maker of consumer products presents information about the impact of its business activities on the environment and publicly shares its stance on environmental sustainability. But it doesn't describe unrealistic objectives, allowing us to speculate on the possibility that it may someday provide measurable evidence of progress against the relatively vague objective of sustainability.

3. **Communications are *memorable*.** Consider 3M. Everything that is communicated by 3M is loaded with references to innovation—its reputation platform. The company recently published *A Century of Innovation, The 3M Story,* a book that celebrates the company's mining roots as the Minnesota Mining and Manufacturing Company.[1] At one point, a negative economy had

produced a downward spiral in its core mining activities, and the board decided to reconsider its core activities. Through innovative thinking, it decided to create sandpaper using the grit from its mine. Sandpaper, special cloths, and similar products became major successes of the company. Much later, 3M would again reinvent itself as the maker of Scotch Tape and Post-It Notes.

4. Communications *personalize the company's history*. Powerful historical elements increase employee pride in working for the company and stakeholder approval about the company. The official history of Hewlett-Packard makes nearly mythical reference to the garage where the two founders of the company started their global IT empire (see Figure 7–1). A large part of HP's communications references the way the company was launched from that garage and underscores the character of the company's founders and the remarkable and unique heritage the company can claim as its own. Such historical elements are resurrected in the reputation platforms and corporate stories of nearly all the top-rated companies. Ahold was the top-rated company in the Netherlands' RQ in 2001. The giant mega-grocery chain operator invariably recounts its cherished origins in a small, old retail shop in Zaandam, where Albert Heijn founded the company. Today, Ahold is in the number two position in the U.S. grocery market and is in third position worldwide despite a February 2003 accounting scandal that led to the ouster of its CEO and CFO and is likely to negatively impact its reputation.

Figure 7–1 Hewlett-Packard: Where it all began. "Stanford University classmates Bill Hewlett and Dave Packard founded HP in 1939. The company's first product, built in a Palo Alto garage, was an audio oscillator—an electronic test instrument used by sound engineers."
Source: http://www.hp.com/hpinfo/abouthp/histnfacts/

5. **Communications convey *leadership*.** Many of the top-rated companies hold leadership positions in their industries—or at least claim to do so, even in their slogans. Citigroup is the leader in financial services, IBM leads in information technology, eBay in online trading. Westpac proudly proclaims itself to be Australia's First Bank. Clearly, being first to do something or at least the leader in the marketplace conveys an aura of distinctiveness—even when it involves revealing dark secrets, as Figure 7–2 shows. The German

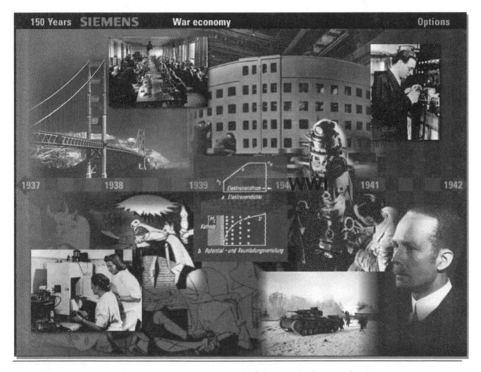

Figure 7–2 Siemens' Involvement in WWII: "The outbreak of WWII marks the start of a transition to a war economy. For Siemens this means management of raw materials, changes and reductions in quotas for raw and processed materials, and the regulation of manufacture. Orders from the Wehrmacht, the armaments industry and other institutions important to the war effort have priority. Manufacturing is banned in certain areas of electrical engineering to ensure that sufficient materials and capacity are available for war production. The manufacture of civilian commodities is likewise prohibited, or at least, radically reduced. Radios, gramophones, and other consumer goods are only produced in small quantities, as are electric light bulbs."
Source: Siemens, CD-ROM: Siemens, 150 years. Visions become reality.

technology giant Siemens recently celebrated the company's 150th birthday, in memory of which it created and distributed a CD-ROM that provided unprecedented detail about the company's involvements during World War II. It did so at a time when most German and Swiss companies have suffered reputationally from their collaboration with the Nazi regime. An excerpt is provided in Figure 7–2.

DISTINCTIVE TRADEMARKS AND LOGOS

A picture is worth a thousand words. Many of the companies in Table 7–1 use unique corporate logos to represent their portfolios of activities. Surprisingly, some of the best-regarded rely heavily on words (Johnson & Johnson, Coca-Cola). Some, however, are purely symbolic (such as KLM and Nike). Research shows that people are twice as likely to remember words when a picture is associated with them.[2] It probably explains why so many slogans and taglines are juxtaposed against other symbols or illustrations that express a specific look and feel for the company.

In 1992, the Royal Dutch Airline KLM set out to attract nonbusiness consumers to its flights. Consumer research showed that swans were associated with positive qualities such as trustworthiness, care, power, and style. Swans effortlessly and stylishly take off and land—they are also elegant and beloved (despite their natural aggressiveness—swans bite when you get close). KLM decided to build its campaign on television commercials showing a swan elegantly landing with airplane sounds and music in the background. It was an instant success and produced 80 percent recall with the Dutch public. Since then, the swan has become a KLM symbol that crystallizes and humanizes its "safe flying" reputation platform, and KLM integrates the swan in all of its printed materials, presentations, advertisements, and Web communications.

The umbrella plays a similar role for Citigroup—the company formed when Citibank merged with Traveler's in the late

1990s. The distinctive umbrella had been the corporate symbol of the Traveler's Group and was combined with the words and the red-blue color contrast to create a distinctive mark for the merged company. Metaphorically, the umbrella conveys protection, a useful metaphor for a diversified financial services company whose reputation platform is trust and safety.

citigroup

Nike's "swoosh" is among the most successful visual symbols of all time. Designed in 1971 as a stylized representation of the winged feet of the fleet-footed Olympian God Hermes, Nike has plastered it on all kinds of running shoes, sportswear, and equipment, but nowhere more visibly than on its startling print and broadcast ads featuring top sports celebrity endorsers like Michael Jordan and Andre Agassi, making it among the best known corporate symbols in the world. Figure 7–3 shows how the swoosh has evolved over the years, becoming infused with meaning of its own, devoid of verbal content.

Figure 7–3 Nike's swoosh over the years. Source: Nike (2003)

Following the merger of Akzo with Nobel, senior executives used the Akzo-Nobel logo to symbolize their newfound togetherness in numerous communications, internally and externally. Figure 7–4 shows examples of how Akzo-Nobel portrayed the CEO and key members of the board enacting the yoga-inspired logo.

Distinctiveness is deepened when, in addition to words and logos, a company creates a unique "look and feel." At Ferrari, the

Figure 7–4 Akzo-Nobel executives enacting the corporate logo.
Source: Akzo-Nobel (2003)

company that topped the RQ survey in Italy in 2001, the uniqueness of Ferrari is reinforced in the styling of its cars, its singular focus on professional racing, the consistent use of bold and primary colors in all of its communications, and its famous logo—the prancing horse. Figure 7–5 captures the essence of Ferrari's distinctive styling.

Style is also a critical differentiator, not only for Ferrari, but for top-rated airlines as well. In a study conducted by the Reputation Institute with Harris Interactive in 2000, we surveyed over 30,000 people in the United States to uncover the most popular airlines and the reasons that made them so. Although most airlines are disliked by the majority of consumers, Singapore Airlines and Southwest Airlines earned high marks from travelers.

When we examined why, both stood out from the rest of the industry with their distinctive focus on employees and the style with which they expect employees to interface with the traveling public. At Southwest Airlines, former CEO Herb Kehlerer was well known for acting like a cheerleader for his employees, constantly involving them in playful interactions that also extend

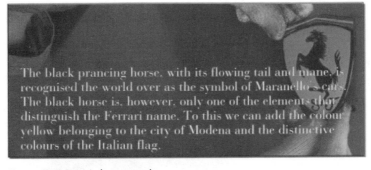

The black prancing horse, with its flowing tail and mane, is recognised the world over as the symbol of Maranello's cars. The black horse is, however, only one of the elements that distinguish the Ferrari name. To this we can add the colour yellow belonging to the city of Modena and the distinctive colours of the Italian flag.

Figure 7–5 Ferrari's distinctive style.
Source: www.ferari.com (2003)

to customer interactions. At Singapore Airlines, respect for employees prevails, and flight staff are treated with dignity, distinction, and respect—most visibly so in the company's dress code for flight attendants as well as in the company's ads. Figure 7–6 shows the signature welcome of the Singapore flight attendant and the company's focused investment in employee training.

DISTINCTIVE CORPORATE STORIES

A corporate story is a description that is designed to communicate the essence of the company to all stakeholders, to strengthen the bonds that bind employees to the company, and to successfully position the company against rivals. It is built up by identifying unique elements of a company, creating a plot that weaves them together, and presenting them in an appealing fashion. In our experience, a good corporate story should be no longer than 400 to 600 words.[3]

> **Unique Elements:** It's not easy to identify unique aspects of a company. Most companies today have a great deal in common because they are institutionalized by professional managers, most of whom have similar cultural and educational backgrounds, life experiences, and viewpoints. It should come as no surprise that researchers observe a striking similarity between

To maintain our position as a leading global corporation, Singapore Airlines is committed to recruiting and nurturing bright and dynamic individuals to meet our manpower needs. Throughout their careers, employees will be given opportunities for development and training to enhance their professional as well as personal competencies.

The SIA Group spends over $100 million on training each year and its training expenditure per employee far exceeds Singapore's national average per worker. In fact, our investment in employee training forms the largest component of the Airline's operating expenditure, clearly illustrating the emphasis we place on continual staff development.

Figure 7–6 Singapore Airlines: "Putting People First." The welcoming smile of a well-dressed Singapore Airlines flight attendant serves as a cultural signature of friendliness and hospitality. *Source: www.singaporeair.com*

the different value systems expressed by companies in credo-like statements reminiscent of the famous U.S. Declaration of Independence that begins "We the people...."[4] The challenge is to uncover and identify the elements that make a company uniquely itself. Often these unique elements are drawn from each company's personal history, its founders' backgrounds, and so on.

Unique Plots: Much like a good novel creates connections among characters that breathe life into a story, the unique features of a company have to be connected through a plot. Take a core element for a bank expressed as "customer focus." As a core element, it is hardly unique. Expressed through an active plot with actors and actions, it can take on distinct meaning. Consider how the Dutch Rabobank developed a unique plot for its customer-focused reputation platform:

> The Rabobank does not have shareholders who are mainly interested in a high return on their investments. The only thing that counts is to have satisfied customers, now and in the future. The Rabobank chooses to build a long-term relationship with its customers. That means that the advice fits the wishes of the customers and that these are not the advice with which the bank earns the most. But it also means that, in bad times, the Rabobank will remain supportive to its customers.

[Source: www.rabobank.nl, 2003]

A good story has to have a plot line. Folk tales, fairy tales, epic journeys, and romantic sagas are four typical plots. In the epic form, for instance, a heroic company finds itself confronting enemies or obstacles. As soon as everyone in the company pulls together, the company emerges victorious with growing market shares, profits, and job security. In its romantic form, the plot involves portraying a company as recovering from a bad fall or crisis, stemming perhaps from excessive growth, scandal, or the death of the founder. The company pulls together to overcome the emotionally taxing downturn and revive positive sentiment.

Unique Presentation: It's also important to develop unique presentation styles in telling a corporate story. Like other communications, after a period of ferment in which chaos reigned, most corporate web sites now demonstrate remarkable standardization and homogeneity in what they communicate and how. The challenge for a company competing against close rivals is to develop an expressive style that conforms to prevailing standards while making it stand out from the competition.

Achieving distinctiveness through corporate story-telling is therefore difficult. Nonetheless, we believe it to be worthwhile, not least because of bandwagon processes from which even *small differences* in how companies present themselves can have large effects on perceptions and reputation.

The more unique a company's reputation platform, the easier it will be to create strong and distinctive corporate stories. Many of the companies listed in Table 7–1 not only rely on unique slogans and logos, but tell a distinctive story about themselves that helps consumers and other stakeholders understand them better and distinguish them in the reputation marketplace.

For instance, consider LEGO, the company that topped the RQ in Denmark in 2001. Its core product, the LEGO brick, uses primary colors to evoke a unique set of associations in stakeholders' minds that involve childhood memories, the ambitions of youth, and their manifestations in construction projects. The LEGO brick appears in all sorts of formats, including giant creations in front of toy stores at prominent locations (e.g., the high-end FAO Schwartz toy store in New York) and the Legoland theme parks around the world that are built entirely out of LEGO bricks. Figure 7–7 shows how the company uses the LEGO brick as a corporate symbol to crystallize a reputation platform that is focused on the themes of construction, imagination, play, and learning. As Figure 7–7 indicates, the company also tells its corporate story very appealingly.

Close inspection of LEGO's corporate story shows that it has distinctive elements that are common to all good corporate stories. Its corporate story

- introduces *unique words* to describe the company.
- refers to the company's *unique history*.
- describes the company's *core strengths*.
- *personalizes and humanizes* the company.
- provides a *plot line*.
- addresses possible concerns of *multiple stakeholders*.

Figure 7–8 summarizes the basic structure that many good corporate stories provide for readers and viewers. We call it the Triple-A model of storytelling: (1) It describes the company's

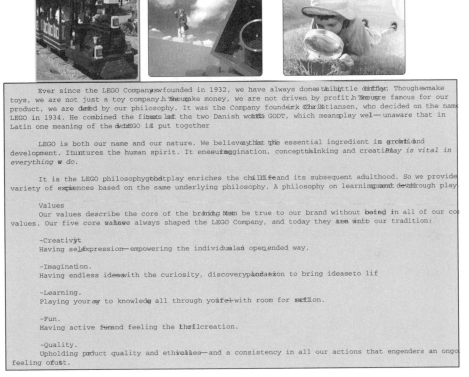

Ever since the LEGO Company was founded in 1932, we have always done things a little differently. Though we make toys, we are not just a toy company. Though we make money, we are not driven by profit. Though we are famous for our product, we are defined by our philosophy. It was the Company founder, Kirk Christiansen, who decided on the name LEGO in 1934. He combined the first two letters of the two Danish words LEG GODT, which means play well—unaware that in Latin one meaning of the word LEGO is put together

LEGO is both our name and our nature. We believe that play is the essential ingredient in growth and development. It nurtures the human spirit. It encourages imagination, conceptual thinking and creation. Play is vital in everything we do.

It is the LEGO philosophy that play enriches the child's life and its subsequent adulthood. So we provide a variety of experiences based on the same underlying philosophy. A philosophy on learning and development through play

Values
Our values describe the core of the brand. You can't be true to our brand without being true to all of our core values. Our five core values have always shaped the LEGO Company, and today they are built into our tradition:

-Creativity
Having self-expression—empowering the individual in an open-ended way.

-Imagination.
Having endless ideas with the curiosity, discovery and passion to bring ideas to life

-Learning.
Playing your way to knowledge all through your life—with room for reflection.

-Fun.
Having active fun and feeling the thrill of creation.

-Quality.
Upholding product quality and ethical values—and a consistency in all our actions that engenders an ongoing feeling of trust.

Figure 7–7 Lego's reputation platform emphasizes creativity, imagination, learning, fun and quality.
Source: LEGO, 2003

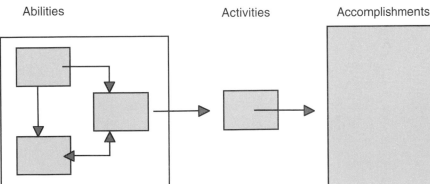

Abilities   Activities   Accomplishments

Figure 7–8 Corporate storytelling: The Triple-A model.
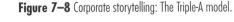

basic **abilities**—the core competencies that have enabled it be successful; (2) it summarizes the core **activities** the company is involved in; and (3) it provides readers and viewers with an overview of the company's **accomplishments**.

INVE is an interesting Belgian business-to-business company that provides feed and health ingredients for animal rearing. In 2002, we helped the company build a corporate story by aggregating and summarizing its abilities, activities, and accomplishments into the simplified chart of Figure 7–9.

After reviewing the basic story elements in Figure 7–9 and selecting a plot line, INVE's corporate story was told as follows:

> *INVE is a family holding of more than 30 companies that provides nutritional and health solutions in animal rearing. INVE is active in more than 70 countries and has production units in Asia, Europe and America.*

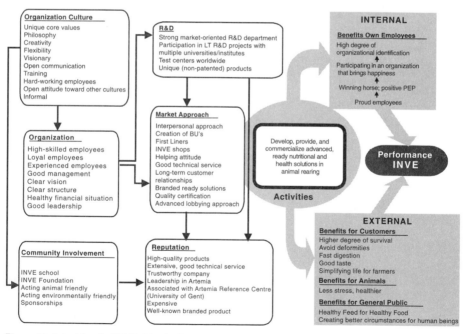

Figure 7–9 Applying the AAA Model to INVE

The company started out of the integration of poultry farms and slaughterhouses in the early 70s. A few years later the focus shifted to the basics in animal life: special ingredients and special application formulas. INVE's distinctive competence lays in its nutrition and health solutions for reared animals, especially young animals.

Today, the group focuses on solutions for aquaculture and agriculture, based on experience and research. For aquaculture the most reputable products are Artemia (of different sources and for various applications), the Selco®-range of enrichment products, the Frippak® and Lansy®-range of dry diets. In agriculture INVE provides feed additives such as Toxy-Nil, Ultracid, Salmo-Nil, Mold-Nil, feeding concepts like Lechonmix®, INVE NRJ Beef and INVE Boar Vital, herb applications and other advanced solutions such as specialities for conservation and treatment of raw materials and feeds.

INVE's high-quality products focus on the critical phases in animal rearing and offer crucial benefits such as increased survival rate, improved growth rate, reduced risk of deformities and diseases, early and high feed intake. The development of these unique, innovative, even pioneering products that have given INVE an established reputation in the markets is possible thanks to the continuous focus on research by highly-skilled specialists. INVE's backbone is its strong global Research and Development Departments organized by INVE TECHNOLOGIES NV. INVE has its own test centers worldwide, participates in long-term projects with renowned universities and institutes, and conducts market verification of experimental results with selected customers. With the help of specialized software, INVE's nutritional engineers apply their profound knowledge of raw materials, premixes, specialities and additives to formulate an optimal diet, taking into account the animal's needs according to age and gender. INVE has the necessary knowledge and responsibility to produce safe and sound feed.

By means of an extensive network of First Line sales people, Solution Managers, INVE Shops and local Service Centers, INVE adheres to a strong personal market approach focusing on long-term, partnering relationships with customers. INVE simplifies feed management for farmers and hatcheries, resulting in more efficient working procedures and high quality results, offering economic benefits to customers. INVE's ultimate goal is to contribute to better nutrition and health for people around the globe. Therefore INVE commits to enhance the total food chain, providing safe feed for cultured animals that end up as an important part of our daily food. INVE not only strives for sustaining health in humans but also works hard at promoting it. Two examples out of a long list may illustrate this. The Omega-3 eggs are the result of an INVE product resulting in a decrease of human cholesterol levels. And through its premixes INVE balances the profile of fatty acids and vitamins in beef, chicken and pork to help protect the heart of consumers.

INVE's philosophy is rooted in the strong belief of the company's founder, Mr. Flor Indigne, that people have to create positive things in harmony with nature. Happiness as a result, is what he wants to share with employees, customers, and all involved in the business activities of INVE. "Bringing Solutions," the main core value of INVE, therefore stands for "Bringing Happiness." The more than 600 employees of INVE take pride in being part of a company that emphasizes social responsibility that goes beyond pursuing "standard" business goals. Respect for different cultures is also strength of the company and is a substantial part of INVE's special reputation.

The current consolidated turnover of the company is _120M. The INVE Group is a financially healthy firm, with a yearly benefit of +/– 15% of the turnover in the last 5 years. The economic health of the company gives INVE employees, suppliers and customers' stability on a long-term base.

The corporate story of INVE was then used to develop a distinctive creative concept that resulted in advertising campaign in fall 2002, that is briefly captured in Figure 7–10.

WHAT MAKES A STRONG REPUTATION PLATFORM?

Across the five countries in which the RQ Project was carried out in 2001 (Australia, Denmark, Italy, the Netherlands, and the United States), the better-regarded companies often expressed themselves by relying on core reputation platforms. Close inspection

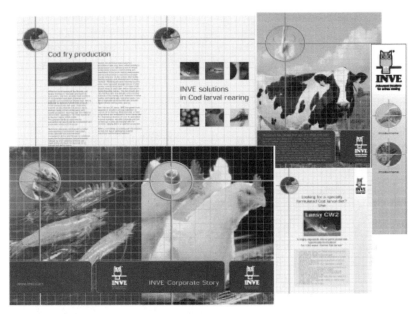

Figure 7–10 INVE advertising campaign (2002).

suggests that a possible difference between companies that are consistently top-rated and those that are less well-rated may lie in how well their reputation platforms—as well as slogans, logos, corporate stories, and communications—capture three key dimensions:

- **Strategic Alignment:** Strong reputation platforms convey aspects of the company's vision and strategy for business-building.
- **Emotional Appeal:** Strong reputation platforms convey features of the company that elicit emotional appeal.
- **Surprise:** Strong reputation platforms jolt peoples' awareness by creating unexpected juxtapositions.

STRATEGIC ALIGNMENT

A reputation platform—and the slogans, communications, and initiatives derived from them—should reflect the strategic positioning of the company. When Nokia tells us that it is busy "Connecting

People," we are instantly and accurately reminded of Nokia's core business—telephony. When Sun Microsystems tells us that it is "the dot in .com," we readily picture the networking technology that is the beating heart of the company. Only an upstart like Amazon would dare tell us that it is the world's biggest bookstore and put a trademark on it. When Xerox tells us it is "The Document Company"—we get it. 3M's "Innovation" and Hewlett-Packard's "Invent" both speak to the research activities central to their commercial success, as does Dell's strength in low-cost distribution with "Cost-cutting. Easy as Dell." eBay's "the world's online marketplace" works well too. The reputation platforms on which these companies root their initiatives and communications clearly do a good job of conveying the essence of their core business.

Less effective is Ford's "global family of automotive brands"—a bland description of Ford's extraordinary portfolio that includes Jaguar, Aston-Martin, Volvo, and Land-Rover. Nothing about Ford's reputation platform conveys an underlying unity of purpose and strategic direction, short of joint ownership of disconnected auto brands. More strategic coherence is implied by the description of General Motors as "People in Motion"—encompassing as it does all forms of movement and, presumably, the technologies behind all that motion. But it lacks alignment by not suggesting *how* GM conceives of motion itself. Among automakers, DaimlerChrysler's "Answers for Questions to Come" may be the most successful in conveying a reputation platform built around a strategic core of technology and invention.

Strategic alignment helps because it enables stakeholders to rely on the reputation platform and its derivative elements as a shorthand script, creating an improved ability for outsiders to understand and appreciate the company. In so doing, it provides stakeholders with a mental script for organizing any information they get about the company and an inclination to respond emotionally to whatever information cues come our way.

EMOTIONAL APPEAL

People resonate to the emotions conveyed by some of the stronger reputation platforms. Disney's desire to "Make Magic" for children and adults alike brings a smile to most people's lips—it makes them happy. The nonconforming individualists in us all resonate to the spiritedness of Nike's "Just Do It." DuPont reminds us of the awesome "Miracles of Science" that take a backstage to the products we use daily. Everyone likes the smiling babies that are so frequently portrayed in Johnson & Johnson's ads because of its reputation platform built on the theme of motherhood.

These are emotionally appealing positions. They draw from us an emotion-laden reaction—of wonder, excitement, resolve, joy, happiness, or passion. The reputation platforms reflected in their tag lines and campaigns manipulate us to experience a satisfying emotional connection with the company. Although surely top-rated Johnson & Johnson could do better here than to tell us it is simply a worldwide healthcare company, it does it very well visually, despite its lack of verbal fluency. IBM uses a very the low level of emotional imagery ("creating, development, and manufacture of advanced information technologies") that is clearly a remnant of the old Big Blue's white shirts of the past. Surely IBM could do better too.

Very workmanlike is Pfizer's "Life is our Life's Work." The research-based platform wants to imply passion and commitment, but conveys more pedestrian associations with day-to-day work, as does electronics giant Philips with "Let's Make Things Better"—the imagery is less descriptive of fundamental innovation (dreaming of "what could be") than it is of the tinkering technician involved in taking "what is" and making marginal improvements. Microsoft's "Your Potential. Our Passion" uses emotional terms but fails to convey the relationship between what the company actually does and how passion feeds into it.

Far less effective as reputation platforms are those created on the basis of false posturing. Philip Morris wants us to see the company as "Working to Make a Difference," a clearly disingenuous claim when it comes from a company accused of manipulating research and actively concealing information from the public about the cancer-inducing effects of tobacco. McDonald's wants us to see the fast-food business it operates as "A People Business Selling Hamburgers," but to many people that seems discrepant with the employment of low-wage youths in dead-end jobs selling unhealthy fat-filled foods to unsuspecting children. Coca-Cola may be "refreshing," but it's also a sugary, caffeine-filled, habit-forming drink that the company's detractors remind us does nothing good for the health of children around the world. The fact that Coke has very close ties to fast-food maker McDonald's for distribution of its product lines in soda fountains doesn't help those perceptions. The "refresh" imagery, however, does work well for Coca-Cola's other less-problematic product lines that piggyback on Coke's markets (Dasani water, fruit juices, energy drinks, coffees, and teas).

THE ELEMENT OF SURPRISE

Finally, we have a sense that reputation platforms—and the communications derived from them—are stronger insofar as they create surprise or delight as we read them. Communications that jolt us are more likely to be remembered:[5]

- Distinctiveness results from incongruous juxtapositions. People pay more attention to unexpected words. "Easy as Dell" offers an unexpected ending to the saying "easy as pie." Pfizer's "Life is our Life's Work" presents an alliterative use of the word life that forces our attention and delights us in its interpretation.
- Surprise is created when a reputation platform conveys something about the company that is original, rare, innovative, unusual, different, imaginative, typical and nonconformist.[6] When the Episcopal Church was faced with a downturn in attendance, it launched a media campaign to signal its youthfulness. In a series of print ads, the church showed Henry VIII in full regalia, with the surprise headline, "In a church started by a man with six wives, forgiveness goes without saying."[7]

Companies can clearly capitalize on these elements to forge attractive platforms for their corporate portfolios. The fact that most reputation platforms are neither unique, appealing, or surprising suggests that companies have a long way to go to capitalize on distinctiveness.

So, Distinguish Yourself

We've suggested in this chapter that reputation builds when companies adopt distinctive reputation platforms. Distinctiveness builds strength of association and comes from a company's success at building a reputation platform that is strategically aligned and emotionally appealing. The more distinctive its platform, the more likely a company is to get a disproportionate share of attention from consumers and stakeholders.

A reputation platform that is more successful at conveying strategic alignment and emotional appeal—even if it is only *slightly* better—can produce a "tipping point," a bandwagon process through which those who are perceived as more distinctive win a disproportionate share of visibility and reputation from observers.[8]

In a seminal paper, economist Seymour Rosen identified the skewed distribution of rewards that accrue to performers in different sectors, including sports and the arts.[9] He argued that disproportionate returns occur because of the human tendency to exaggerate small differences and to reward on the basis of *relative* performance rather than absolute performance. Differences are further exacerbated by intensified communications that converge on the few who are most noticeable (the "headliners") and largely ignore the rest.

The market for corporate reputation shares similar characteristics. Reputational markets are in fact winner-take-all environments in which a few companies come out on top, and most others lose. Disproportionate visibility and attention accrue to the winners because bandwagons develop as slight differences between companies induce companies to advertise their superiority, increase their familiarity, build reputation, and in turn fuel the company's attractiveness to resource holders as well as imitation by rivals.

Professor Rosen's observation appears to hold in many areas, from sports (where differences in performance are typically measured in one-tenth of a percent) to retail stores—where if you're only slightly better or cheaper than the competition, you can quickly dominate the market. In *The Winner Take All Society*, authors Robert Frank and Philip Cook note that across a variety of markets, the number one player regularly leaves its rivals in the dust and reaps outsized market valuations, often giving it the means to consolidate its position further through acquisitions.[10] Cisco Systems trounced Bay Networks, and General Electric did the same to both United Technologies and CBS/Westinghouse. Consultants at Mercer Management Consulting have called it the plight of the silver medalist. It suggests that achieving even small levels of *relative distinctiveness* can create huge rewards for companies.

In the next chapter, we suggest that descriptions of a company's distinctiveness will pay off, but only if increasingly skeptical audiences are convinced that they are *genuine* representations of the company. Being distinctive therefore calls for a second core characteristic of successful reputation-building—*authenticity,* the subject to which we now turn.

ENDNOTES

1. *A Century of Innovation, The 3M Story,* http://www.3m.com/about3m/century/3M_COI_Book.pdf.
2. J. A. Edell & R. Staelin, "The information processing of pictures in print advertisements," *Journal of Consumer Research,* 10(1), 1983: 45–61.
3. C. B. M. Van Riel, (2000), "Corporate Communication. Orchestrated by a Sustainable Corporate Story." In M. Schultz, M. J. Hatch, & M. H. Larsen, *The Expressive Organization: Linking Identity, Reputation and the Corporate Brand,* Oxford University Press: 157–182.
4. P. O. Berg & P. Gagliardi, "Corporate Images: A Symbolic Perspective of the Organization-Environment Interface," Paper presented at SCOS Conference on Corporate Images, Antibe, France, June 16–29, 1985.
5. Y. H. Lee & C. Mason (1999), "Responses to Information Incongruency in Advertising: The Role of Expectancy, Relevancy, and Humor," *Journal of Consumer Research, 26* (2): 156–169.

6. A. W. & B. L. Smith (2001), "Assessing Advertising Creativity Using the Creative Product Semantic Scale," *Journal of Advertising Research, 41* (6): 27–34.

7. S. A. Cone (1996), "How KeyCorp Competes with Breakthrough Marketing," *Journal of Retail Banking Services, 18* (2): 11–15.

8. Malcolm Gladwell, *The Tipping Point: How Little Things Can Make a Big Difference,* Boston: Little Brown & Co., 2000.

9. S. Rosen, "The Economics of Superstars," *American Economic Review*, 1981.

10. R. Frank & P. Cook, *The Winner Take All Society*. Upper Saddle River, NJ: Prentice-Hall, 1996.

BE AUTHENTIC

☐ n March 24, 1989 the Valdez oil spill washed onto the Alaskan shoreline and did damage not only to Alaska's pristine environment, but to the reputation of the oil company responsible for it—Exxon. In the 2001 Annual RQ survey we conducted in the United States, Exxon remained among the lowest rated companies despite 12 years of post-Valdez cleanup, new top managers, costly court settlements, and countless contributions to wildlife funds, save-the-tiger initiatives, local and national charities, foundations, and other social causes—not to mention a merger with Mobil that changed the corporate name to Exxon-Mobil. Why? Because of a lingering perception that the company that stands behind all these initiatives is not really a good citizen—that it is not authentic—a perception that has lingered in the minds of consumers years after the Valdez oil spill.

The French oil company Total has a similar credibility problem. Following an oil spill by the vessel Erika off the coast of Normandy in 1999, the company whose name was then Total-Fina-Elf was heavily blamed. Despite retribution, fines, contributions, and countless communications in support of stricter environmental regulation, changes in senior management, and advertising, in our 2001 survey the company was again nominated as the company with the worst reputation in France. Buoyed by popular accounts of the corporate slush funds paid to top French politicians, of lavish spending on Total-Fina's fleet of planes, of lavish parties and perks billed to the company by senior executives, the average French consumer has a strong sense that the company has been less than righteous, perhaps even disingenuous –that it's *not authentic.*

Contrast that to the example set by Johnson & Johnson following the two waves of tampering with the company's best-selling Tylenol products in 1982 and 1985. The poisonings generated abundant media. In both cases the company expressed its dismay and concern for the public and instantly initiated costly recall of all of its Tylenol in-store inventory. Abundant communications followed to reassure the public before reintroducing the product with enhanced safety features. The communications were so well handled that—dire predictions notwithstanding—in both cases Johnson & Johnson's market share returned to pre-tampering levels. Why? Johnson & Johnson conveyed to the public a clear sense that it handled the crisis appropriately, that it was *authentic* in its expressions of concern.

Doubtless, Johnson & Johnson benefited enormously from the fact that the company was not to blame for the tampering—that it was victim rather than culprit. But its speedy recall and out-front handling of the crisis remain a lesson for corporate communicators and legal staffs who often advise careful and measured response rather than speedy and vocal handling of the crisis.

Others have learned and applied valuable lessons from Johnson & Johnson's experience. Take Perrier, the French maker of bottled water. In the early 1990s chemical tests revealed small traces of benzene in Perrier bottles. Although these trace amounts were not hazardous, perceptions of tainting created uncertainty in the minds of consumers about the safety and purity of the water. To avoid any suspicion of danger that could damage the brand, the company immediately instituted a full and costly product recall followed by extensive messaging designed to appease public concern and explain the actions taken. In the aftermath, Perrier was perceived to have handled the problem well—to have been *authentic* in its actions—and consumers flocked back to the brand when it was reintroduced.

Perceptions of a company's authenticity have much to do with reputation management. To earn the benefit of the doubt, companies have to convey absolute honesty in all of their interactions with stakeholders—otherwise, any discredit by one stakeholder will instantly be communicated to all of them, reducing the degree of support they feel for the company.

Authenticity drives reputation. Authentic firms are seen as real, genuine, accurate, reliable and trustworthy. The common thread among many of the companies rated in the RQ Project is that they all have made commitments that are core to their business out of a sense of principle—and they live by it. The reason Johnson & Johnson tops the RQ rankings in the United States, whereas ExxonMobil and Philip Morris linger toward the bottom, has much to do with how they have handled past crises.

An event study conducted at Oxford University charted the impact of man-made catastrophes on the market values of 15 companies. They ranged from the first Tylenol tampering in 1982, to Source Perrier's recall of its carbonated, green-bottled water because of benzene contamination in 1990, to a Heineken recall due to rumors of broken glass in its beer bottles in 1993. As the authors put it, catastrophes "provide a unique opportunity to evaluate how financial markets respond when major risks become reality." On average, all 15 stocks they studied took an initial hit of 8 percent of their market value. However, the companies quickly sorted themselves into two distinct groups that the Oxford professors labeled the recoverers and the non-recoverers.[1]

The recoverers' stock sagged only 5 percent in the first weeks, while the non-recoverers' stock lost 11 percent. After 10 weeks, the recoverers' stock actually rose 5 percent and stayed comfortably in positive territory for the balance of the year. In contrast, the non-recoverers' stock stayed down and finished the year off by a sobering 15 percent. The conclusion: All catastrophes have an initial negative impact on price, but paradoxically, "they offer an opportunity for management to demonstrate their talent in dealing with difficult circumstances." Figure 8–1 compares the two groups of companies and shows how they differ.

Event studies like these support the thesis that reputations have considerable hidden value as a form of insurance—they act like a reservoir of goodwill. The insurance value derives from an ability to buffer better-regarded companies from taking as large a fall as companies with lesser reputations. Consider a study conducted by Jim Gregory, the founder of CoreBrand, a Connecticut-based consultancy, that examined the stock prices of companies on the New York Stock Exchange following the market crash of 1997. Consistent with the reservoir hypothesis, he argued that better-regarded companies would be cushioned from the crisis. His results confirmed that the market values of high-reputation companies were less affected by the market crash than were those of a comparable sample of companies with weaker reputations.[2] It suggests that the financial losses due to crises are likely to be lower for better-regarded companies because they are perceived as authentic.

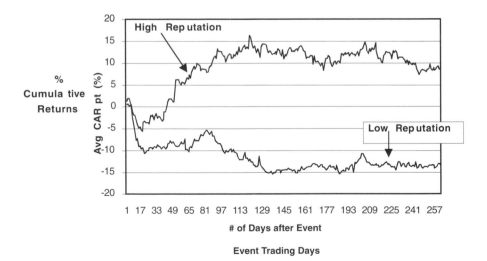

Figure 8–1 Crisis costs are higher for lower reputation companies.
Source: Adapted from Knight and Pretty, 1999.

Being authentic means narrowing the gap between claims and deeds, between who you are, what you say, and what you do. This is not simple to achieve, and the road to authenticity is littered with good intentions. Unfortunately, consumers are well aware of it, and to them, good intentions aren't enough –companies should be judged on their actions and behaviors.

Authenticity must therefore come from within. It begins with a *process of discovery* designed to unearth the "beating heart" of the company—what it stands for at its core, what it really is. Discovery is a bottom-up process initiated at the top, facilitated by the middle, and involving all employees in a dialogue about the company's core purpose, its reason for being. It is followed by a *process of internal expression* aimed at gaining acceptance of shared values among employees. A company cannot be authentic if its employees don't express the company's shared values in their day-to-day interactions with customers and suppliers, investors, and the public. They don't have to "speak with one voice," but surely they must "sing in harmony." Finally, being recognized externally as authentic will happen only if the company initiates a *process of external expression* designed to convey its core essence to all stakeholders in appealing ways. External expression generally involves crafting messages and launching initiatives that evoke emotional appeal—feelings of trust, respect, and liking among observers. External expression is also about demonstrating accountability: When promises of service are not kept, when stakeholder expectations are not met, does the company come down hard on the culprits or ignore the mishaps? Ignoring them virtually guarantees decline in reputation; shouldering responsibility conveys authenticity. The three processes are captured in Figure 8–2.

THE PROCESS OF DISCOVERY

Like people, companies have identities: A corporate identity consists of (a) features that employees consider *central* to the company, (b) features that make the company *distinctive* from other companies (in the eyes of employees), and (c) features

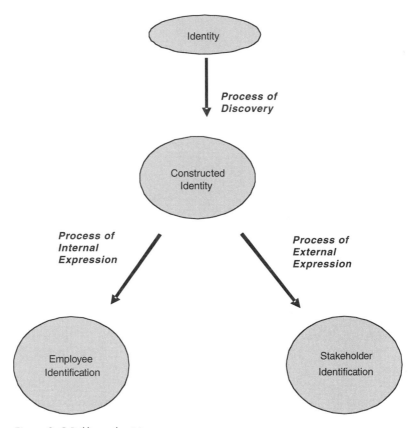

Figure 8–2 Building authenticity.

that are *enduring* or continuing, linking the present and the past to the future.[3]

Although all companies have identities, to uncover them involves a process of discovery—an active search for the ties that bind employees to the company, for the values the company holds dear and that are shared by most. Often these identity elements derive from beliefs and attitudes brought into the company by its founders. As we saw in Chapter 7, "Be Distinctive," developing a corporate story, for instance, often begins with research to uncover enduring features of the company—and pinpoint their origins. Many of the top-rated companies in the RQ Project express their distinctiveness through stories that refer to the company's historical roots.

The process of discovery sets out to reveal the company's inner core. As such, it juxtaposes elements uncovered from different sources in and about the company.[4] *Archival analysis* of the company's existing brochures, web site, press releases, and past communications provides information about how the company sees and presents itself. *Interviews and focus groups* with a representative cross-section of employees provides insight into identity features that employees see as typical of the company. Finally, *quantitative analysis* can be used to test the degree of agreement among employees about the apparent features of the company.

As Figure 8–2 suggests, a company benefits from having a fully constructed identity: It facilitates identification by employees and reputation-building with stakeholders. Customers, investors, and suppliers are more likely to support a company that they understand and like. Even the wider public is more likely to approve of a company whose identity it comprehends and finds attractive. Hence the growing importance of expressive messaging by companies: Internally, companies need to generate *employee identification*. Externally, companies need to engage and stimulate *stakeholder identification*.

Take the recent series of advertisements by Shell, labeled as "Profits & Principles. Is there a choice?" One of these ads focused on the strategic issue of global warming:

> *The issue of global warming has given rise to heated debate. Is the burning of fossil fuels and increased concentration of carbon dioxide in the air a serious threat or just a lot of hot air? Shell believes action needs to be taken now. We are delivering on our commitments to reduce greenhouse gas emissions from our operations. We are working to increase the provision of cleaner burning natural gas and encouraging the use of lower-carbon fuels for homes and transport. It's all part of our commitment to sustainable development, balancing economic progress with environmental care and social responsibility. Solutions to the future won't come easily. Particularly in today's business climate, but you can't find them if you don't keep looking.* [5]

This is an astonishing statement. It identifies Shell as a company concerned with a very public and emotional issue. In addition to this, Shell invites people to comment on the statements made by the company by sending an e-mail and participating in the "Profit and Principles debate".It speaks of a company that is actively addressing the issue through costly scientific research. It puts a stake in the ground for Shell on the question of sustainable development. Most importantly, it invites stakeholder dialogue about it. These are radical departures from Shell's traditional focus on the straight and narrow business of energy. It speaks of a Shell reborn. Why these communications from Shell? And how did they come about?

SHELL: A CASE STUDY IN IDENTITY CREATION AND EXPRESSION

In 1995 the Royal Dutch Shell Company was hit with two major crises. The first involved the proposed maritime sinking of an aging offshore drilling platform—the Brent Spar. Careful research conducted by Shell had supported sinking as the least environmentally damaging alternative for disposal of the rig. Nonetheless, Shell became the target of a Greenpeace action that portrayed Shell as a greedy and irresponsible company whose support for sinking was motivated by purely economic reasoning. Physical boarding of the inoperative Brent Spar by Greenpeace militants drew worldwide media coverage that sullied the Shell image, provoked massive boycotts of Shell stations in Germany, and ultimately forced the publicly humiliated company to back down in June 1995.

The second crisis of Shell's *annis horibilis* blossomed in the media in 1995 and involved Shell's operations in Nigeria. Under a joint-venture contract with the Nigerian government, Shell extracted oil from reserves located in the Ogonilands. Throughout 1995 Shell was accused of profiteering and political expediency for dealing with the ruling military junta of Nigeria that had taken power by force and of forsaking the rights of the Ogoni people to a fair share of the oil profits.

The two crises hit Shell hard. Shell's management realized that the company's performance depended heavily on its reputation, not only with the investment community but also with its own employees, with the general public, with the media, and even with activists. Shell decided to rebuild its reputational capital systematically through the three processes of discovery, internal expression, and external expression.[6]

Shell has always seen itself as technical, scientific, and analytical—a can-do company. However, the media regularly described Shell as patrician, slow moving, fat, rich, bureaucratic, and closed.[7] The two crises of 1995 therefore confronted the company with an incongruity between its self-concept and external perceptions of the company, a sense that it had lost touch with its inner soul—what some called its beating heart. Lacking this, the firm appeared opaque, mythical, and inimical to its observers. As a long-time executive at Shell put it, "It all added up to an image of Shell as a sort of giant phantom in a forest—difficult to see, with no specific contours, but with enormous, uncontrolled, undefined parts that might well do us harm. Moreover, it was a silent phantom. The multinational entity told no story about itself. Outsiders could only guess why it existed, what it did for a living, and how the world would be different if the company did not exist at all."[8]

As part of a larger company-wide change program, Shell created a team of specialists and charged it to develop a process aimed at changing Shell's reputation to become the World's Most Admired Corporation—abbreviated as the WoMAC-team, and guided by Charles Fombrun.

To uncover Shell's identity, the WoMAC-team relied on focus groups of Shell managers in different subsidiaries around the world who came together to discuss the company's core purpose, based on a common guide.[9] The output of each workshop was the group's view of Shell's core purpose. To guide their creativity, participants were shown short prototypical statements of core purpose at top firms like Hewlett-Packard, 3M, and Disney. Throughout 1997 and into 1998, a total of 32 workshops were held in 24 locations, involving 770 Shell participants from 48 countries. The following statements were typical of those generated by the groups to the question, What is Shell's core purpose?':

- Working to make a difference in people's lives (Canada)
- To keep people moving, improving the world (Malaysia)
- To make people's lives easier now and in the future (China)
- To unleash the world's energy resources to make the world run better (Nigeria)
- Enhancing peoples, companies, cultures, and countries (Australia)

Core purpose statements were pooled and presented to a meeting of Shell top managers from around the world. From close examination of those statements, introspection, and personal belief, Shell's top management team crystallized Shell's core purpose as "Helping People Build a Better World."

Internal Expression: To express the theme to employees around the world, Shell commissioned a short film that would bring the theme to life. Developed by the firm of Maurice Saatchi, thematically the short film highlighted the evolving wonders of technological change throughout the 20th century. It was shown on the first broadcast of the company's newly created internal network—Shell TV—in March 1997. The company then created a training center in the Netherlands where middle managers from around the world could come for leadership training, which involved in-depth exposure to Shell's culture through team-building exercises and exploration of Shell's identity.

External Expression: In addition to these internal initiatives, throughout 1998 Shell set in motion various external initiatives that were designed to demonstrate a growing sense of accountability to the company's nonfinancial stakeholders. In support of authenticity, Shell released a report in fall 1998 entitled "Profits & Principles—Does There Have to Be a Choice?" The report highlighted various steps Shell was taking to respond to stakeholder concerns about sustainable development and human rights. It also presented a road map of management systems under development for institutionalizing transparency and responsiveness, including accounting systems, standards-setting, external verification, and continuous improvement. Figure 8–3 summarizes these initiatives.

Shell's process of discovery is a good prototype of the sequence necessary to unearth and reveal a company's identity to the world. It creates the kind of authenticity that stakeholders want and that help the company build reputation. As Shell's story indicates, however, it has to be followed by credible processes of internal and external expression. We address these in turn.

Growing Awareness, Commitment, Understanding, and Exploration of Social Issues

1996	1997	1998
Roundtables/Open Dialogue On Society's Changing Expectations	Updated Statement of General Principles	First Presentation to Financial Analysts on non-financial aspects of Group performance
Public Statement of Support for Precautionary Principle on Climate Change	Group HSE Policy, Commitment and Procedure	Dialogue with Network of Experts on corporate ethics & social accountability
	MORI Poll on Global Opinions of Shell	
	Form Social Responsibility Committee	Workshops with Shell staff on social accountability and Business Principles
		Integrated verification of Group HSE

Figure 8–3 Expressing Shell's new identity.

THE PROCESS OF INTERNAL EXPRESSION

Once discovered and crystallized, a company's internal identity becomes the basis for the design of a constructed identity that is given shape through communications and initiatives targeted to employees. These messaging efforts are designed principally to generate collective endorsement, acceptance, and internalization of the company's constructed identity.

Experience shows that a company can apply four strategies to gain acceptance of its constructed identity:

Strategy 1: Crafting and Projecting Top-Down Persuasive Messages

Strategy 2: Creating Mid-Level Consensus

Strategy 3: Building Coalitions

Strategy 4: Allowing Chaos to Stimulate Dialogue and Consensus

These four change strategies are more or less appropriate, and the choice of strategy depends very much on the situation the company is in. Top-down persuasion is often more effective when radical changes in identity are necessary and the company has to move quickly due to market or competitive pressures. A mid-level consensus-seeking strategy is better suited to evolutionary changes that require stronger bonds among employees. A coalition strategy is more suited to diversified companies in which shared identities are problematic, and the company needs to mobilize coalitional support for its constructed identity across product lines, businesses, and divisions, and so must stimulate collaboration. Finally, chaotic strategies take even more time and are suited to more extreme situations in which companies face a great deal of variety due to the existence of highly diversified subcultures, with distinct identity elements and the need to adapt to local circumstances. Global companies and those operating highly diversified businesses often combine the four strategies to involve and express the company's internal identity to employees.[10]

Gaining acceptance of the constructed identity is vital in helping the company build authenticity.[11] Managers and employees are likely to differ in their perceptions of the company's identity, often resulting in a gap between the constructed identity and the identity that employees perceive—hence lowering their degree of identification with the company.[12] If identification is low, employees are less motivated to work and to participate in company life, and are less likely to act as ambassadors of the company to outsiders.

Throughout the 1990s, the U.S. based regional carrier Southwest Airlines provided an excellent example of the process of internal expression.[13] Under the leadership of Herb Kelleher, the top-rated airline regularly demonstrated regularly demonstrated how internal expression could affect three important levels of organizational outcomes: employees, customers, and profits. The airline's strong ratings on service quality derived from the commitment and skills of frontline employees who interfaced constantly with the customer. The company achieved it by treating employees like internal clients in order to encourage them to provide comparable service to passengers. Consistent with the reputation value cycle described in Chapter 2, "What Are Reputations Worth?" identity expression built employee capabilities and motivation that led to higher levels of customer service, thereby improving customer satisfaction and retention and increasing sales revenues and profits.

Internal expression always requires on strong leadership and vision. People want to know how their work fits into the broader business context and want to understand and believe in the goal that they're working toward.[14] Southwest Airlines had a strong mission and vision that shaped its corporate culture, how it implemented its business strategy, and how it treated its employees. The airline put employees first, ahead of the customer. Its core vision was that the better people were treated, the better they performed. Through the years, teamwork, serving others, and acting in the best interests of the company have been central aspects of Southwest Airlines' spirited and communal expression of its identity.

Another cultural theme at Southwest Airlines was its emphasis on humor. Part of the airline's mission statement states that customer service will be "...delivered with a sense of warmth, friendliness, individual pride, and Company Spirit." While this may sound simplistic, Southwest Airlines appears to live this idea actively. It makes extensive use of customer success stories detailing how far the company has gone to please its customers. One of these is that legendary chairman Herb Kelleher personally served drinks to customers on Another is that he regularly performed skits and sang rap songs at company events. To this day, Southwest Airlines is still renowned for the humor its employees display.

Clearly, Southwest Airlines' high RQ from consumers, good press, and financial success are based in large part on a powerful corporate identity rooted in employee involvement and commitment, identification between company and employee, and a strong customer orientation. Companies like Southwest Airlines that consistently earn top consumer ratings express an identity that first engages not just the minds, but the hearts of employees.

THE PROCESS OF EXTERNAL EXPRESSION

Whereas internal expression involves generating employee identification with the company, external expression is designed to promote stakeholder identification and build corporate reputation. As Chapter 3, "Who's Tops—and Who's Not?" indicated, stakeholder identification results from emotional appeal—a company's ability to induce perceptions of trust, liking, and respect—of *authenticity*.

Expressing the company's authenticity in an emotionally appealing way to stakeholders can be achieved by emphasizing either "profits, people, or planet"—to paraphrase a Shell report. To dwell on *profits* is to try to convey authenticity on the basis of consistency in the company's results and accomplishments. To dwell on *people* is to stress the company's broad responsibility to serve human interests by introducing and supporting socially responsible practices. Finally, companies also project authenticity by acting and communicating about the company's efforts to sustain the natural world—the *planet*. We highlight three companies from the RQ Project below—each of which expresses its authenticity differently in these areas.

SHELL'S EXPRESSIVENESS

What did Shell learn from the 1995 crisis events and ensuing losses of reputation and market value that precipitated a period of scrutiny? It forced Shell to reexamine its business model and historical values. In the process, Shell reevaluated its business model in ways that incorporate stakeholder expectations. As a result of its revised understanding of the changing expectations of stakeholders, Shell developed a set of internal principles about its way of being and acting. Finally, Shell conveyed these changes to its stakeholders using a variety of communication devices. Figure 8–4 presents the model of reputation management that emerged from the various initiatives of the WoMAC team. The model suggests a general process for others to follow.

Shell's experience suggests that well-targeted reputation management begins with a careful understanding of stakeholder expectations—the filters through which stakeholders process information about the company. Understanding stakeholders' filters is important because stakeholders use the filtered

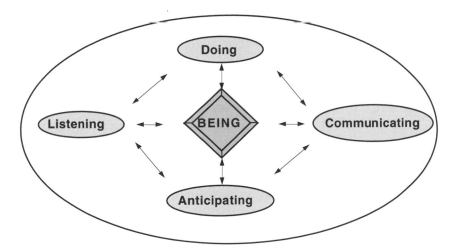

Figure 8–4 A learning model for generating authenticity.

information to form evaluative companies. We label this phase *listening*. Listening involves attentive interacting with stakeholders that enables the company to understand the standards against which their actions will be evaluated. Through listening, the company can also assemble the cognitive map of the worldviews espoused by its stakeholders and use the map as a guide in selecting its strategic positioning. Relying on focus groups and surveys in multiple countries and of multiple stakeholder groups, Shell made a sincere effort to really hear a variety of voices and to assemble as realistic map of the expectations of its stakeholders as possible.

A company that is serious about building a strong reputation takes the input from the listening phase literally to heart—to the very heart and core of the company's business activities. Shell reexamined both its business framework and core purpose. A company's business framework incorporates its traditions, identity, and aspirations for the future (such as strategic performance objectives). We call this stage *being* because here the company relies on its history and strategy to define its distinctive way of conducting business. We also call it being because it reflects concerted efforts to manage the company's culture and identity, interweaving the company's history, strategic goals, and relations with others. Both the revision of the statement of the group's business principles and its efforts to develop an identity statement are excellent examples of the sincere engagement in the being phase of reputation management.

Anticipating extends listening and being into a plan of action: It involves selecting those stakeholder expectations that call for a change in fundamental practices. This phase also addresses how practices will change so that the company's actions are consistent with stakeholder expectations. In that sense, it involves activating a new way of "doing." The principles of being helped managers define a set of relationships between Shell and its various stakeholders, including what set of expectations the group would strive to meet and address.

Finally, Shell created a number of communication items designed to convey its principles to stakeholders. We call this phase *communicating*—it involves expressive interaction with stakeholders through which a company conveys its position and the principles on which it will rely. Companys also take actions in accordance with these principles—actions that validate the content of their communications. The communications reflect the company's identity, its way of being, while addressing the concerns of stakeholders. Communications address concerns by informing, explaining, framing, embellishing, or otherwise symbolically representing the company's actions. Careful management of expectations and interpretations ensures that routine events in the life of large corporations do not turn into controversies and crisis.

We argue that by engaging in these processes a company achieves authenticity— a state in which the internal identity of the company reflects positively the expectations of key stakeholders and the beliefs of these stakeholders about the company reflect accurately the internally held identity. A primary mechanism for achieving authenticity is expressive communication with stakeholders: Expressive communications seek to represent the organization's identity rather than to grab attention and manipulate impressions. When a company's interactions with stakeholders are based on the principles of authenticity and expressiveness, the favorability of stakeholders' impressions result from genuine meeting of interests and commonality of values. Absent this foundation, a company's favorable reputation is likely to remain a temporary illusion that may crumble down under much lesser storms than the crises that hit Shell in 1995. Alternatively, acting from a foundation of mutual understanding based on transparency, a company is likely to receive support from committed stakeholders and to preserve its reputational capital in the rougher seas of inevitable controversies.[15]

Shell's experience shows that the environment can be represented by stakeholders' expectations. Therefore, stakeholders' expectations should be routinely monitored to ensure that shifting expectations do not jeopardize performance results. A corollary of this idea is that reputation management should be a cornerstone of strategic analysis, since it addresses how companies position themselves in changing environments. It also follows that changes in strategy should be conceived and evaluated in terms of their possible reputational consequences.

The model of reputation management that Shell derived from its experience shows that the management of corporate reputation is inextricably linked to the management of organizational identity. In order to influence how a company wants to be perceived, the company must change who it believes itself to be. In doing so, it also shifts from impression management to expressive communication, which stakeholders are likely to reward with deeper trust and commitment. Thus, the sustainability of a company's reputation as an asset is also better ensured.

NOVO NORDISK'S EXPRESSIVENESS

The Danish pharmaceutical maker Novo Nordisk is among the best-known and respected companies in Denmark, however, the company has the widest diabetes product portfolio and the most advanced insulin delivery systems in the world. In addition, Novo Nordisk has a leading position in haemostasis management, growth disorders, and hormone replacement therapy. The company's mission includes making contributions to scientific, humanitarian, and social progress. There's irony in the company's claim to want to rid the world of diabetes. After all, a company thriving mainly on the production and sale of insulin should hardly want see a reduction in the demand for insulin! Yet the company's actions suggest that the claim is authentic and that it describes exactly what Novo Nordisk is doing: searching for better methods of diabetes prevention, detection, and treatment. The company has responded to the alarming growth in diabetes with increased funding for diabetes research, development, and disease management programs visible from the diversity of diabetes discovery and development projects the company funds. Its investments in this area exceed those of any other pharmaceutical company.

As another example of the company's authenticity, Novo Nordisk helped raise consumer awareness of diabetes by launching the Diabetes Infoline in Bangalore (India), a call center aimed at providing information on diabetes and practical advice on managing it to people with diabetes and their families. It raises awareness about the disease in a country where the vast majority of people with diabetes are not diagnosed, let alone treated. Specially trained nurses and dieticians take calls 12 hours a day, 7 days a week. They answer frequently asked questions and provide qualified information on diet, nutrition, and the options for diabetes care that Bangalore has to offer.

With a reputation platform that promises "being there," Novo Nordisk has an obligation to contribute to better access to proper diabetes care in the poorest nations. The company has therefore developed the LEAD initiative—Leadership in Education and Access to Diabetes care—which aims to improve diabetes care in developing countries. This involves a four-pronged strategy for improved global healthcare, which includes developing national diabetes strategies, building national healthcare capacity, ensuring the best possible pricing, and providing additional funding.

The development of national diabetes strategies is the first of the four key issues in the Novo Nordisk model for addressing access to health, a model inspired by the World Health Organization (WHO). Through its national diabetes strategies project, Novo Nordisk is identifying best practices from around the world and encouraging national governments to adopt these in their countries with the company's support.

The company has also long recognized the value of partnerships as a means to sustainable solutions. Working actively to promote collaboration between all parties in the healthcare system in order to achieve common goals is part of Novo Nordisk's vision. In 2001 the company published a compendium of its initiatives in developing countries. The compendium describes more than 100 examples of partnerships, capacity building, educational programs, grants for diabetes research, and donations at times of crisis in Asia, Africa and the Middle East, and Latin America.

No matter how substantial the commitment of those engaged in improving access to diabetes care, the cost of insulin will always be a crucial factor. It explains why Novo Nordisk established a policy to make insulin available to the 50 poorest countries designated by the United Nations at prices not to exceed 20 percent of the average price of North America, Europe, and Japan.

WESTPAC'S EXPRESSIVENESS

Westpac was the first bank established in Australia. Originally known as the Bank of New South Wales, it was founded in 1817 and was incorporated in 1850 by an act of the New South Wales Parliament.

As Australia's first bank, Westpac has been involved with local communities from its inception. The company recognizes how vital it is for companies to play a greater role in supporting and contributing to the communities in which it operates. Westpac was established as Governor Macquarie's Great Colonial Undertaking and continues to embody the values and traditions that have served it so well throughout its history: integrity, trust and confidence, commitment to customers, employees and the community, and leadership through innovation. In June 2001 Westpac released a statement of its social responsibility practices. It is an important step in ensuring constructive dialogue with customers, governments, communities, and employees.

Westpac involves its employees in contributing to the community. Matching Gifts is a familiar community support program in which Westpac encourages the generosity of its staff by matching, dollar for dollar, employees' contributions to any tax-deductible charity of their choice. In addition, many employees volunteer time to local community programs. Management supports their efforts by providing them with paid leave and flexible working arrangements as a small way of helping them with the community work they do.

Every Westpac employee is entitled to a Community Volunteering Day of leave each year. This is a day of paid leave provided by the bank so its employees can easily participate in volunteering efforts.

Each year, the CEO acknowledges and rewards the volunteering efforts of Westpac staff through the company's Community Volunteering awards, which recognize individual and team excellence in providing financial support to local community groups.

As confirmation of its expressiveness in social responsibility, Westpac was recognized in Australia's Good Reputation Index, released by *The Age/Sydney Morning Herald*—an index created from ratings by specialized activist groups who rate companies on specific criteria in their own sector of activity. Although the ratings process has been extensively contested by Australian observers, it provides a measure of recognition of Westpac's community involvement. In a seperate comparison of Australian companies named in the BRW top 100 list, the bank placed second overall and fourth for social impact.

Despite its apparent community focus, however, Westpac's initiatives are not well known to the wider public. In the Australia RQ of 2001, Westpac was rated 20th by the public, well behind Coles-Myer and the far smaller Bendigo Bank. A stronger reputation platform and targeted communications designed to convey the bank's authenticity would doubtless help the bank's strengths gain public recognition.

THE CHALLENGE OF AUTHENTICITY

Authenticity builds reputation. At heart it comes from consistently doing the right thing over a long period of time. We indicated in this chapter that top RQ companies in different parts of the world achieve a high degree of authenticity by adopting identity features that are reputationally relevant. Other companies can and should be inspired by the examples they set and particularly by four lessons they teach:

- **Lesson 1:** *Clarify who you are* by taking the time to uncover your corporate identity.
- **Lesson 2:** *Develop a broad consensus* about your corporate identity through a systematic change process of internal expression that encourages identification with the company.
- **Lesson 3:** *Express your identity* through a broad messaging strategy designed to evoke stakeholder identification with the company.
- **Lesson 4:** *Remain true to yourself!* Don't compromise your core purpose and core values in order to more quickly respond to pressures put on the company by short-sighted groups of investors, activists, or consumers.

Jointly, these four lessons, when combined with visibility and distinctiveness, have helped many top companies build reputation and suggest ways that lower-reputation companies can work to catch up. In the next chapter, we discuss how transparency adds fuel to a company's credibility and reinforces stakeholder perceptions that the company is truly authentic.

ENDNOTES

1. R. F. Knight & D. J. Pretty, "Corporate Catastrophes, Stock Returns, and Trading Volume," *Corporate Reputation Review,2*(4), Fall 1999: 363–378.

2. J. R. Gregory, "Does Corporate Reputation Provide a Cushion to Companies Facing Market Volatility? Some Supportive Evidence," *Corporate Reputation Review, 1*(3), Spring 1998: 288–290.

3. S. Albert & D. A. Whetten (1985), "Organizational Identity." In L. L. Cummings & B. I. M. Staw (eds.), *Research in Organizational Behavior, 7,* 263–295.

4. C. Caroll & C. B. M. van Riel, "We who are many form one body: Organizational identification and the impact of multiple perceptions of identity and image in a global policy setting organization." Paper presented at the Academy of Management Conference in Washington DC, USA, August 2000.

5. www.shell.com.

6. C. J. Fombrun & V. Rindova, "The Road to Transparency: Reputation Management at Royal Dutch Shell." In M. Schultz, M. J. Hatch, & M. Larsen (eds.), *The Expressive Organization,* Oxford, 2001, 77–96.

7. *Investors Chronicle, 24,* October 1997.

8. A. De Geus, *The Living Company: Habits for Survival in a Turbulent Business Environment,* Boston: Harvard Business School Press, 1997.

9. J. C. Collins & J. L. Porras, *Built to Last: Successful Habits of Visionary Companies,* New York: Harper Business, 1994.

10. C. van Riel & J. J. van Hasselt (2002), "Conversion of Organizational Identity Research Findings into Actions," In

Bertrand Moingeon & Guillaume Soenen (eds.), *Corporate and Organizational Identities,* London: Routledge, 156–174.

11. M. W. Eysenck & M. T. Keane, *Cognitive Psychology,* East Sussex: Lawrence Erlbaum Associates, 1990.

12. D. Tjosvold, "Participation: A Close Look at Its Dynamics." *Journal of Management, 13*(4), 1987: 739–50.

13. A. J. Czaplewski, J. M. Ferguson, & J. F. Milliman, "Southwest Airlines: How Internal Marketing Pilots Success," *Marketing Management, 10*(3), 200, 14–17.

14. As William Pollard of ServiceMaster says, "In this new world of work we have found that people want to contribute to a cause, not just earn a living. When we create alignment between the mission of the firm and the cause of its people, we unleash a creative power that results in quality service to the customer and the growth and development of the people who do the serving. People find meaning in their work. The mission becomes an organizing principle of effectiveness." C. W. Pollard, "Mission as an Organizing Principle," *Leader to Leader, 16,* Spring 2000. Available: *http://www.pfdf.org/leaderbooks/l2l/spring2000/pollard.html.*

15. C. J. Fombrun, *Reputation: Realizing Value from the Corporate Image,* Cambridge, MA: Harvard Business School Press. 1996.

9 BE TRANSPARENT

A transparent object is one that allows light to pass through so that others behind it can be seen. By analogy, a transparent company is one that allows stakeholders to see right through it— the company is visible for all to see; it operates in the bright light of day. Figure 9–1 shows the new corporate headquarters of ING Group, the Dutch financial services giant with a growing global presence. Its see-through architecture suggests subliminally and metaphorically that the financial services giant intends to be transparent to its stakeholders.

In concrete terms, a transparent company allows stakeholders to gain access to all pertinent information needed to make an accurate assessment of the company's current operations and future prospects. More formally, Standards & Poor defines transparency as "the timely disclosure of adequate

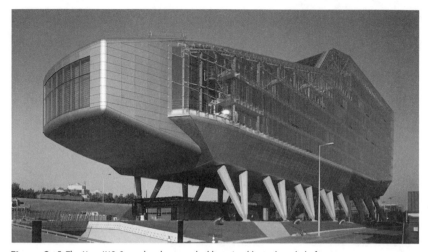

Figure 9–1 The New ING Group headquarters building: A subliminal symbol of corporate transparency near Amsterdam.

information concerning a company's operating and financial condition and its corporate governance practices." In a recently released study, S&P examined the disclosure practices of over 1,500 companies in the United States, Europe, Latin America, and Asia. They began with a list of 98 transparency and disclosure (T&D) practices and focused primarily on how these were carried out in corporate annual reports and other official documents. Their analysis uncovered dramatic differences in how much companies disclose within regions and among countries, with the United States and the United Kingdom demonstrating the highest levels of disclosure, and Latin American and Asia the least. Even where disclosure was mandated by law, they observed that implementation varied widely.

Significantly, they also found that the amount of information disclosed in annual reports was highly correlated with market risk and valuations. As they put it,

> ...companies with higher T&D rankings...have lower market risk. In addition, companies with higher T&D rankings based on annual reports alone tend to have higher price-to-book ratios. Our preliminary empirical findings indicate that companies can lower the cost of equity capital by providing higher transparency and disclosure.[1]

The findings suggest that the more transparent a company is, the more likely stakeholders are to rely on their disclosures and to have faith in the company's prospects. Consistent with the reputation value cycle discussed in Chapter 2, "What Are Reputations Worth?" companies clearly benefit from transparency. Moreover, the S&P study finds that nonfinancial disclosure also gets implemented erratically.

> Disclosure levels are lowest in the areas of ownership structure, investor rights, and management and board structures and processes. Those companies that ranked highest in this study practice a greater level of nonfinancial disclosure along with full financial disclosure.

At first glance, most firms seem to release a great deal of information about their operations. Companies communicate abundantly through press releases, advertisements, articles, books, and newsletters. Web sites provide access to a wide range of presentations, reports, speeches, and statements that reveal in nearly intimate detail the inner workings of companies and their operations. Enabling technologies like the Internet have quickened the pace at which corporate activities become known through chat rooms, news groups, online newsletters, and op-eds.

On second glance, however, companies and their operations can prove quite opaque and elusive. Direct physical contact with managers (beyond the front lines) can prove difficult indeed, requiring considerable patience and the "right contact" in the company who can open doors. Appointments have to be made in advance, and even then a cumbersome set of procedures requiring registration, badges, and escorts limits access to the inner chambers of the corporate elite. Clearly, not everyone is welcome, and direct contact with a company is limited to the privileged few that a senior stratum considers relevant. True and complete transparency, then, may be merely an illusion— but it is one that external observers are increasingly insisting on and which many companies are actively learning to address. It's evident in the growing number of resolutions that activist shareholders have introduced at corporate annual meetings in recent years.

Consider GlaxoSmithKline. In May 2003, the company became the first company in British corporate history to lose a shareholder vote on its executive compensation package. The resolution was introduced following a contentious confrontation between outraged shareholders and Glaxo's board over CEO Jean-Pierre Garnier's seemingly outsized pay package. As one shareholder put it: "Glaxo will no doubt say it made strenuous efforts before the annual meeting but there was nothing concrete. Given that Garnier's pay package had caused such an uproar, one would have thought they would have been more sensitive."[2]

This chapter examines how well-regarded companies manage their transparency. Our findings suggest that the better-regarded companies are adopting more transparent practices than their counterparts, not only in making more accurate disclosure of their financial position, but in making more visible and accessible the inner workings of their operations. As we demonstrate, transparency is not a goal in itself, but a means to an end—the need to increase trust and reduce stakeholder uncertainty about the company. We describe corporate transparency in terms of its expression in the five central reputation domains: products and services, vision and leadership, financial performance, social responsibility and workplace environment. As we indicate, the degree of disclosure depends heavily on how intensely companies are pressured to disclose by powerful stakeholders.

DEGREES OF TRANSPARENCY

The Bank for International Settlement lists four specific criteria for transparency:[3]

- *Comprehensiveness* means enabling users of information to make a meaningful evaluation of the organization, because the information is provided in an aggregated, consolidated format.
- *Relevance and timeliness* means enabling users of information to assess the expected risks and returns of using

products or services of the company at a relevant stage of their decision-making process.

- *Reliability* means faithful representation of that which it purports to represent. It must be verifiable, neutral, prudent, and complete in all material respects.
- *Comparability* is information that enables a user to compare across institutions and countries (if relevant) and over time.

Disclosure is crucial for maintaining public trust because it enables people to verify a company's claims. The demand for transparency reflects a human desire to reduce risk in decision making. Just as people's desire to reduce risk in product consumption led to labeling laws intended to protect consumers, so are investors asking for transparency of financial information in order to reduce the investment risks they face.

As the Standard & Poor study cited earlier indicates, better-regarded companies are more transparent. They provide more information about themselves than do others, and they invite stakeholders to dialogue with them about contentious issues. In a world that increasingly operates online, a preliminary indicator of transparency is the degree to which a company maintains an elaborated website that includes information targeted to the concerns of each of its stakeholders as well clarity about share ownership, board and management structure, and full financial disclosure—including contact names and access points. Sites with no contact information are generally opaque companies. The most transparent ones provide direct access to annual reports, press releases, employee surveys, product reviews, and assessments by the financial community.

Transparency produces trust: It enables interested stakeholders to verify the company's claims—thereby guarding against puffery and self-aggrandizement. The transparency cycle shown in Figure 9–2 operates as follows: A company offers products and services to consumers and interested stakeholders about all relevant processes involved in creating those offerings. Governments, the press, and NGOs evaluate corporate actions. Positive appraisals of actions taken by the company increase stakeholder satisfaction, which in turn improves trust, maintaining the company's license to operate.

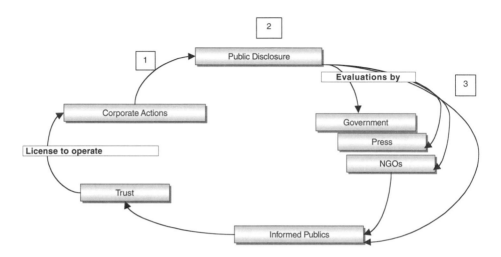

Figure 9–2 The transparency cycle.

Recent corporate scandals in the United States at Enron, WorldCom, and Adelphia and in Europe at Vivendi, LVMH, and Ahold have given us food for thought: clearly, transparency cannot be taken for granted. As U.S. President George W. Bush put it in his widely heard July 2002 speech:

> ...High-profile acts of deception have shaken people's trust. Too many corporations seem disconnected from the values of our country. These scandals have hurt the reputations of many good and honest companies. They have hurt the stock market. And worst of all, they are hurting millions of people who depend on the integrity of businesses for their livelihood and their retirement, for their peace of mind and their financial well-being.

The speech set the tone for increased transparency and disclosure by launching various initiatives. The first is a Corporate Fraud Task Force designed to function as a financial crimes SWAT team, overseeing the investigation of corporate abusers and bringing them to account. A second is a 10-point "Accountability Plan for American Business" designed to provide better information to shareholders, to assign clear responsibilities to corporate officers, and to develop a stronger, more independent auditing system. Core elements of that accountability plan include enforcing reimbursement of fraudulently acquired executive compensation, bans on future leadership roles in other companies, and personal certification by the CEO of the company's annual financial statements.

THE DRIVERS OF TRANSPARENCY

Pride generally drives people and companies to reveal information about themselves that tends to make them look good. Companies rarely take initiatives to provide information to external audiences on their own volition. It simply takes too much time and money to provide information that is comprehensive, relevant and timely, reliable and comparable. The adoption of transparency and disclosure practices therefore derives largely from an array of external forces that magnify its importance. Figure 9–3 summarizes the principal drivers of transparency. We examine these external drivers in turn.

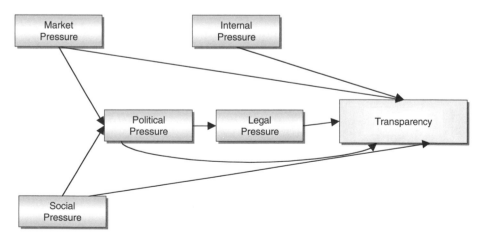

Figure 9–3 Five drivers of transparency.

MARKET PRESSURES

Companies regularly battle over intellectual property and often petition courts for access to internal company records. Pharmaceutical companies, for instance, are often asked by regulators to provide detailed records of their investment costs in the development of new drugs in order to justify their pricing strategies. Rivals carry out espionage tactics to uncover ingredients in competitors' products or to contend that their own products were unfairly copied and their property rights violated. Consumers often lament the high prices of drugs and energy, and contend that they are being gouged by greedy companies. These market pressures are encouraging companies to provide clearer depictions of their profit margins—to indicate their cost profiles and thereby justify the prices they charge.

Figure 9–4 shows how Shell, the giant Anglo-Dutch energy company, has responded to these demands by indicating in simplified form the breakdown of costs and revenues that produce its profits. An even more detailed breakdown would help, particularly if it addressed questions of current concern such as the relative size of executive compensation plans. These kinds of responses are increasingly expected of companies before they can earn transparency credits from the public.

SOCIAL PRESSURES

Skepticism about the corporate sector abounds. The process through which skepticism manifests itself includes boycotts and protests, often vented through specialized NGOs such as Greenpeace, World Wildlife Federation, consumer rights organizations, healthcare lobbies, and the so on.

Politicians and journalists are naturally attuned to the arguments that these pressure groups present. Defense of the public good, of human rights, and of the environment is hard to argue against—and companies that come under attack by consumer advocates are generally portrayed and perceived to be the "bad guys."

Journalist-author Naomi Klein is perhaps the most celebrated representative of the anti-corporate activist movement.

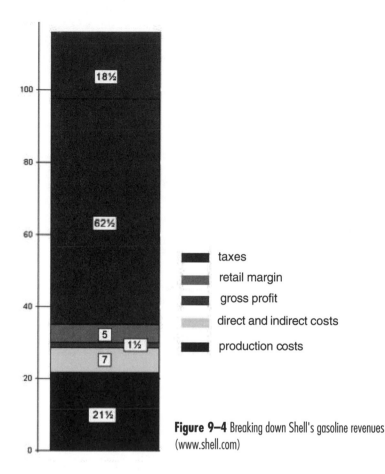

Figure 9–4 Breaking down Shell's gasoline revenues (www.shell.com)

Her best-selling book *No Logo* amassed praise and visibility for its vilification of large companies and their activities. It made sense of the otherwise anarchical demonstrations by disenchanted publics at annual World Economic Forum gatherings. As she put it in her follow-up book,

> The crisis respected no national boundaries. A booming global economy focused on the quest for short-term profits was proving itself incapable of responding to increasingly urgent ecological and human crises; unable, for instance, to make the shift away from fossil fuels and toward sustainable energy resources; incapable, despite all the pledges and hand-wringing, of devoting the resources necessary to reverse the spread of HIV in

Africa; unwilling to meet international commitments to reduce hunger or even address basic food security failures in Europe. It's difficult to say why the protest movement exploded when it did, since most of these social and environmental problems have been chronic for decades, but part of the credit, surely, has to go to globalization itself. When schools were under-funded or water supply was contaminated, it used to be blamed on the inept financial management or outright corruption of individual national governments. Now thanks to a surge in cross-border information swapping, such problems were being recognized as the local effects of a particular global ideology, one enforced by national politicians but conceived centrally by a handful of corporate interests and international institutions, including the World Trade Organization, the International Monetary Fund and the World Bank."[4]

As a result of the public discussion about the amounts of saturated fat in fast foods and its adverse effect on human health, McDonald's USA now communicates exact levels of each type of fatty compound in each of its products. In restaurants, the company displays detailed nutritional information about each of the items on the menu and has even decided to switch to a new type of cooking oil for making French fries in order to reduce fat levels. And, as Figure 9–5 indicates, the company also makes available on its website highly detailed nutritional information that specifies the fat content of each of its products. On September 16, 2002, the company announced a lower fat French fry that made headlines.[5] Clearly, the company is responding to social pressure for transparency of its product offerings.

Figure 9–5 McDonald's now offers detailed nutritional information on its Web site.

Source: http://www.mcdonalds.com/countries/usa/food/index.html.

POLITICAL PRESSURE

Political pressure clearly impacts disclosure of corporate information. In 1998, for instance, a political party in the Netherlands accused IKEA of allowing factories to use child labor to produce its products in order to minimize costs. Through brute monopoly power, the accusations said, it forced its suppliers to offer extreme discounts in the production of IKEA products. In order to survive, these suppliers had to cut labor costs and started hiring children. This type of political pressure forced IKEA to adopt codes of conduct. To convey product transparency, IKEA now even labels its carpets "child labor free."

In 2001 IKEA introduced a code of conduct governing working conditions and environmental awareness among suppliers. This deals with matters such as health and safety in the workplace and forbids the use of child labor. The practical work of implementing the code of conduct is carried out by coworkers in IKEA Trading Service Offices worldwide. Many suppliers already meet the threshold requirements of the code; others are working together with IKEA to carry out necessary improvements. IKEA also works closely with external quality control and audit companies who check that IKEA and its suppliers live up to the requirements of the code.

LEGAL PRESSURE

Political speeches like that of President Bush and the legislative initiatives he proposed in 2002 exert legal pressure on companies to ensure their transparency in order to protect consumers. A recent and powerful legislative initiative is the U.S.'s Sarbanes-Oxley Act, which, in the wake of the U.S. corporate scandals of 2002, proposed a complete overhaul of corporate disclosure and governance rules in America. It has greatly empowered the SEC, created a new Accounting Oversight Board (AOB), and increased penalties and sanctions. One of the overall principles around which all provisions in the Act were formulated is transparency. The Act is therefore a good example of how political pressure applies legal might to make firms more transparent by punishing

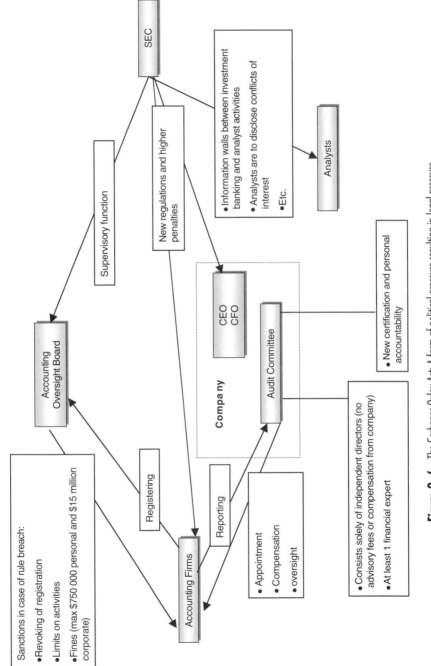

Figure 9–6 The Sarbanes-Oxley Act: A form of political pressure resulting in legal pressure.

them if they do not comply. Figure 9–6 portrays the inner workings of the Act. It proposes new forms of certification for corporate CEOs and CFOs, restrictions on directorships, rules on reporting and verification of financial statements, and strict walls between analysts and auditors in accounting and financial service firms to prevent conflicts of interest from arising.

PLATFORMS FOR CORPORATE TRANSPARENCY

Transparency is expressed in the behaviors and initiatives of companies. Historically, demand for disclosure first took place at the product level with package labeling. As capital markets grew larger and more sophisticated, demand for improved disclosure of financial information grew in visibility. More recently, demand for disclosure has extended to the workplace and to social programs. Increasingly, we see companies publishing results of employee satisfaction surveys and prominently displaying awards obtained from civic organizations and other recipients of philanthropic funds directly on their websites. For a time, these response strategies themselves became sources of distinctiveness for the first movers that initiated them. The Body Shop capitalized heavily on its early environmental posture in the personal care products industry. Benetton did it when it launched shock ads in the 1980s based on social issues like AIDS, furs, and other agendas with significant activist support. BP is trying hard to claim the "green label" in the energy industry.

From our analysis of the companies rated in the RQ Project, the best of them (and many seeking to leap ahead) increasingly rely on one or more of five platforms on which they demonstrate their transparency. Figure 9–7 describes them in terms of the five key dimensions of reputation that drive the emotional appeal of rated companies.

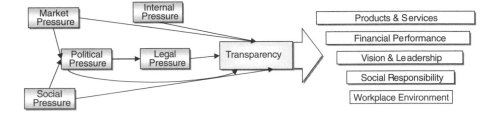

Figure 9–7 Five transparency platforms.

TRANSPARENCY ABOUT PRODUCTS AND SERVICES

The oldest platform of disclosure is labeling—it began when cow herders started branding their cattle to distinguish them in open fields. Later, wholesale coffee makers started packaging smaller individual packets with company labeling. Packaging and labeling were the first area from which companies benefited from being transparent.

Now, many companies are trying to improve consumer trust by increasing product transparency. Current issues surrounding genetically modified (GM) foods and livestock diseases have made consumers wary about the contents of food products. Recent consumer lawsuits have stimulated legislation that forced companies to specify nutritional values on their food products. Today, some companies are going beyond what is mandated. The European epidemic of mad cow in the late 1990s encouraged McDonald's also to adopt more detailed traceability than required. As Figure 9–8 indicates, Marks & Spencer, for example, uses selected farms and other suppliers to ensure the quality of its products—it can trace a specific piece of meat to the original cow, going beyond the traceability requirements of the European Community.

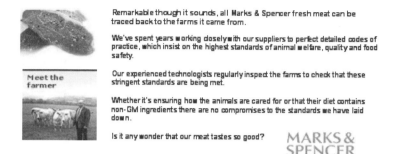

Remarkable though it sounds, all Marks & Spencer fresh meat can be traced back to the farms it came from.

We've spent years working closely with our suppliers to perfect detailed codes of practice, which insist on the highest standards of animal welfare, quality and food safety.

Our experienced technologists regularly inspect the farms to check that these stringent standards are being met.

Whether it's ensuring how the animals are cared for or that their diet contains non-GM ingredients there are no compromises to the standards we have laid down.

Is it any wonder that our meat tastes so good?   MARKS & SPENCER

Figure 9–8 Product transparency at Marks & Spencer. Source: Marks & Spencer, 2002

The Anglo-Dutch energy company Shell is highly transparent about its products and services, not only in the amount of information it provides, but in the way it communicates the information. For example, the website page shown on Figure 9–9 is structured to provide each stakeholder group direct access to information related to a specific query. Local product information is also highly detailed and easily accessible. In the Netherlands, for example, a new product (Shell Pura) was given its own website along with detailed product related information such as production processes as well as environmental impacts.

Figure 9–9 Product and service transparency at Shell. Source: www.shell.com.

TRANSPARENCY ABOUT FINANCIAL PERFORMANCE

In the aftermath of Enron's demise and Arthur Andersen's collapse, political forces are putting increased pressure on the legal and regulatory systems to institute stricter guidelines on disclosure of both financial and nonfinancial corporate information. They are reinforced by comparable demands from stock market investors and from financial rating agencies.

The top-rated company in the 2001 Dutch RQ was the giant Dutch food retailer Royal Ahold. The company has long been known for having investor relations group that is among the best organized in the world. In an assessment of Dutch annual reports by Rematch, Ahold's financial report scored best in terms of informational value, readability, and layout.

Figure 9–10 A cartoon on the cover of the Economist. Source: *The Economist,* 2002

The company has received numerous awards for its excellent approach to providing the financial community at large and its stockholders with timely and accurate financial information. Detailed information is easily accessible in the form of Webcasts, presentations, discussions, reports, road-show presentations, and so on. The company does not limit itself to providing raw financials, but goes further in satisfying the need for details. Background statistics and operational explanations bring Ahold's investor relations to life.

Ironically, in February 2003 financial irregularities in Ahold's U.S. food services operations indicated that that the company had misled investors by overstating earnings by as much as $500 million. Both the CEO and CFO resigned, and the company's shares plummeted by 61 percent. While details have not yet been brought to light, it seems clear that the company's apparent transparency was only surface-deep and lacked authenticity. Members of the public were sufficiently fooled in the short run to rate the company well in 2001, but lack of genuine transparency will have proven costly in the long run, and the company's reputation is bound to take a significant hit in future consumer polls.

Now consider the Australian bank Westpac. The company ranks high on Standard & Poor's Australian Financial Transparency Index. The company goes further than simply communicating standard financial data, however. For instance, it defines and reports details about the number of "valuable customers" it has had over time and links this to the success of its new customer relationship management platform. The bank also graphically illustrates the change in the proportion of customers across the different value segments over time. Westpac's annual report provides a clear description of the regulatory environment in which it operates and the relevant requirements that it has yet to meet. Furthermore, it offers specific information about the regulatory impact in each of its major geographical markets, including the relevant regulatory bodies and their roles in each area. By reporting in this way, the company clearly increases its financial transparency to stakeholders, a fact that can only benefit Westpac reputationally.

TRANSPARENCY ABOUT LEADERSHIP AND VISION

Transparency of leadership is conveyed by the degree to which a company's CEO and other top executives are visible to employees and stakeholders—the degree to which they perform in the limelight and take part in wider public debates. Years of studying CEO reputations, for instance, have convinced Leslie Gaines-Ross, Burson-Marsteller's Chief Knowledge Officer, that a good part of perception management for companies involves increasing public visibility and appreciation for the company's CEO. Her analyses indicate that star CEOs cast a significant halo over the companies they run—think of Jack Welch at GE, Andy Grove at Intel, and Richard Branson at Virgin. The danger, of course, is that the downfall of a CEO can mean the downfall of the company (witness the impact of Martha Stewart's indictment on insider trading charges in 2002 and 2003 and the scandal's effect on the shares of the company that bears her name). On the other hand, winner CEOs often take their reputational capital with them.[6]

As we showed in Chapter 7, "Be Distinctive," companies put a stake in the ground when they rely on core reputation platforms around which to anchor their initiatives and communications. They convey transparency about their visions that forces them to toe the line. Top rated companies, such as Novo Nordisk and 3M, are so heavily invested in their reputation platforms of diabetes care and innovation respectively that their communications are significantly more focused than the communications of many of their peers, and they convey consistency and the determination to hold true to their vision. They continually manage to reinvent themselves and their offerings to fulfill the demand that potential consumers do not yet know they have.

Even companies that are not highly innovative in terms of their products and services can be highly transparent in communicating their visions. The crucial factor that the public rewards is whether the vision is itself attractive and appealing. If it is, then the company may be rewarded with both fame and fortune. Transparency about leadership and vision can help maintain support from stakeholders that are otherwise dubious about the company's prospects. Internet bookstore Amazon earned the loyalty of its investors and consumers throughout the 1990s—and through the dissipation of the Internet bubble in 2000—due to its considerable transparency in vision and leadership and to a savvy Jeff Bezos and his vision of operating the "world's largest bookstore" online. What normal investor would stick to investing in a stock that hadn't earned a dime in profits since its inception?

Another reason Ahold had a top reputation rating in Holland in 2001 is that the Dutch retailer seemed consistently transparent about its vision, mission, strategy, and governance structure. Not only were the company and its leaders very visible participants in public debates and in the media, they were also trusted—not least because they constantly communicate what the company stands for and what its vision means concretely. On its corporate Web site, for instance, Ahold gave examples of how it had implemented its vision on various topics, including the direction of the company in the future. Webcasts spotlighting Ahold's CEO, Cees van der Hoeven, were available online to explain management's vision of Ahold's future, and Mr. van der Hoeven was constantly quoted in the Dutch press: He ranked third in the 2002 Intermediar Citation Index of press visibility. All of these factors contributed to Ahold's strong public reputation. It's disappointing indeed to witness the company's fall from grace in early 2003. The systems were good, but systems are only as good as the people implementing them. A number of people at Ahold forgot to keep their eye on the ball.

The way 3M communicates about its vision and about its leaders make it a powerful example of transparency in vision and leadership. For instance, 3M grants stakeholders access to innovation stories detailing the development of new products. Furthermore, its clear vision of the future is communicated openly. Not coincidentally, the NGO group Keep America Beautiful (KAB) has announced that 3M will be the 2002 recipient of its annual "Vision for America" Award. KAB is recognizing 3M's dedication to continuously improve products and manufacturing processes while minimizing its impact on the environment and developing strategies for sustainable development. As KAB president G. Raymond Empson put it,

> 3M is fostering and furthering the understanding of environmental progress. Their history and vision of sustainability and innovation has mirrored the sense of responsibility for the environment KAB works to impress upon citizens. 3M's farsighted accomplishments are truly worthy of KAB's highest honour.

In 1975, as the environmental movement was dawning in America, 3M adopted the 3M Environmental Policy, believed to be the first global environmental policy with measurable results from a major manufacturing company. That same year, 3M introduced the voluntary Pollution Prevention Pays (3P) program. By 2001, 3P had prevented the creation of 821,000 tons of pollutants and saved $857 million. More than 4,820 3P projects have been initiated by 3M employees worldwide.

The company's deep commitment continues today. 3M's process of moving toward long-term sustainable development is called eco-efficiency, as first defined by the World Business Council for Sustainable Development. The strategy to achieve this goal is advanced by 3M's Environmental, Health, and Safety Management System. This includes continuously improving compliance assurance systems to meet and exceed government and 3M standards. 3M's Environmental, Health, and Safety Management System also involves emphasis on Life Cycle Management, a systematic process applied to ensure appropriate consideration of environmental, health, and safety issues during the development of the hundreds of new 3M products each year.

TRANSPARENCY ABOUT CORPORATE CITIZENSHIP

Transparency in citizenship is increasingly viewed positively by both companies and stakeholders alike—and is probably due to pressure from the public. Citizenship refers to business decision making that links corporate practices to ethical values, legal compliance, and respect for people, communities, and the environment.[7] Our examination of top-rated companies suggests that they regard citizenship initiatives as more than a patch-work quilt of disparate practices, occasional gestures of goodwill, or initiatives motivated by marketing, public relations, or business benefits. Rather, a posture of corporate citizenship means a comprehensive set of policies, practices, and programs that are integrated throughout the company' operations and supported and rewarded by top management.

A growing number of companies not only acknowledge, but also communicate, the business benefits of corporate citizenship. Their experiences are bolstered by a growing body of empirical studies that demonstrate that citizenship has a positive impact on business economic performance and does not harm shareholder value. Companies also have been encouraged to adopt or expand their citizenship efforts as a result of pressures from customers, suppliers, employees, communities, investors, activist organizations, and other stakeholders. As a result, companies of all sizes and sectors are more inclined than ever to look for ways to demonstrate their authentic involvement in the social fabric of local communities and to talk about it—to make them visible and transparent to the world.

As Chapter 6, "Be Visible," demonstrated, customers, investors, regulators, community groups, environmental activists, trading partners, and others are asking companies for more and more detailed information about their social performance. In response, leading companies are responding with a variety of reports and/or social audits that describe and disclose their social performance on one or several fronts. As part of this move toward greater disclosure, many companies are putting increasingly detailed information about their social and environmental performance—even when it may be negative—directly onto their publicly accessible Web sites.

TRANSPARENCY ABOUT WORKPLACE ENVIRONMENT

A growing number of companies are also trying to capitalize on transparency about workplace issues. Companies that top surveys of the best places to work for, best employer for minorities, and other such lists often provide a wide range of information about their workplaces in an effort to attract employees. Indeed, some of those surveys are based on companies making their own case for being rated among the best—which requires them to prepare detailed descriptions of their internal practices and how they stack up against rivals.

It has become relatively commonplace at most major companies to make available information about what the company offers in terms of employee benefits, job opportunities, training programs, and career opportunities. McDonald's, for instance, tells employees exactly what steps to take to become a manager of their own McDonald's franchise—and what benefits and opportunities are likely to come their way. The company states boldly that it is governed by a "People Vision": "We're not just a hamburger company serving people; we're a people company serving hamburgers." The People Principles show the company's workplace transparency. They describe McDonald's values and the corporate culture they embrace. In turn, transparency about the corporate culture, salaries, benefits, and incentives allow potential employees to make an informed choice about where to apply for a job. It also helps the company address the difficult challenge of recruiting.

Given its workplace transparency, it's no coincidence that McDonald's regularly earns awards for its workplace practices. McDonald's Sweden was recently named Best Competence Company by a leading Swedish University, based on independent jurors rating over 100 companies' commitment to employee training and career development. Jurors cited McDonald's culture of enthusiasm and commitment to providing real opportunity to all employees as key factors in their unanimous vote.

The Australia National Training Association named McDonald's Australia 1999 Employer of the Year. It was the third consecutive year that McDonald's was so honored. In addition, McDonald's is certified by the government of Australia's National Training Authority, which allows McDonald's managers to receive University credit in management.

For the third year in a row, McDonald's was named Brazil's Best Employer in the retail industry by a leading business magazine. McDonald's focus on training, employee development, and opportunities for advancement were key factors in receiving this award, especially since McDonald's is a first job for 67 percent of its crew in Brazil. McDonald's is also the largest employer in the retail industry in Brazil.

Top-rated companies clearly go further than the commonplace in describing their workplaces. Novo Nordisk, for instance, is a company that also communicates very openly about its work atmosphere, corporate culture, and benefits. The company is highly transparent towards all stakeholder groups (as it demonstrates by using an explicit stakeholder map; see Figure 9–11) and continually invites dialogue with them. Indeed, so convinced is Novo of the importance of the workplace that it is one of the few companies to publish regular surveys of employee satisfaction—a very transparent process indeed, since it forces the company to reveal itself in good times and bad.

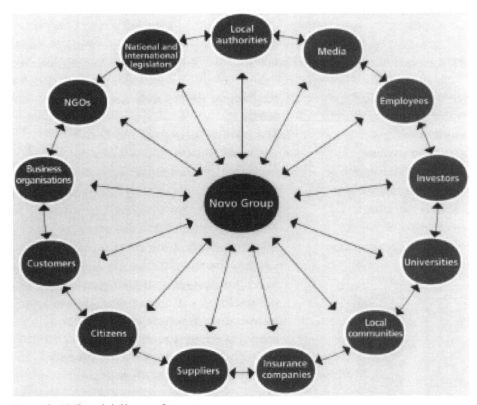

Figure 9–11 The stakeholder map of Novo Group.

THE CITIZENSHIP TRANSPARENCY INDEX

Below we describe 10 criteria with which to measure a company's transparency about corporate citizenship.

1. *Is corporate citizenship a prominent component of the company's mission, vision and values statements?* The mission or vision of a socially responsible business frequently refers to having a purpose beyond making a profit or being the best and specifies that it will engage in ethical businesses practices and will seek to create value for a variety of stakeholders, including shareholders/owners, employees, customers, vendors, communities, and the natural environment.

2. *Does the company say what it means by "corporate citizenship"? Does it mean what it says? are the company's stated values compatible with corporate citizenship?* Social responsibility cannot flourish in an environment where innovation and independent thinking are not welcome. If the stated values of a company are inconsistent with communitarian values, then it will be difficult for the company to be transparent. Goals and aspirations in this area can be ambitious, but the company must not only say what it means—it must show that it means what it says.

3. *Is the full board and/or committees involved in planning and progress reports on corporate citizenship?* Many companies establish social responsibility committees of their boards to review strategic plans, assess progress, and offer guidance about emerging issues of importance. Some boards that do not have these committees have the full board consider issues of corporate social responsibility. In addition to having committees and boards, some companies have adopted guidelines governing their own policies and practices around such issues as board diversity, terms, and compensation.

4. *Is there a special senior officer with direct responsibility for corporate citizenship?* Some companies have

a senior officer with responsibility for corporate citizenship. Participation of such individuals in critical company decisions ensures that citizenship considerations are taken into account.

5. *Is corporate citizenship included in the company's strategic planning?* A number of companies are beginning to incorporate CSR into their long-term planning processes, identifying specific goals and measures of progress or requiring CSR impact statements for any major company proposals.

6. *Is there direct accountability for meeting corporate citizenship goals?* In some companies, in addition to the efforts to establish corporate and divisional social responsibility goals, there are similar attempts to address these issues in the job descriptions and performance objectives of as many managers and employees as possible—for example, by incorporating diversity goals in managers' hiring practices. This helps everyone understand how each person can contribute to the company's overall efforts to be more socially responsible.

7. *Are the company's efforts in areas of corporate citizenship communicated to all employees?* Many companies now recognize that employees cannot be held accountable for responsible behavior if they are not aware of its importance and provided with the information and tools they need to act appropriately in carrying out their job requirements. These companies publicize the importance of corporate social responsibility internally, include it as a subject in management training programs, and provide managers and employees with decision-making processes that help them achieve responsible outcomes. Many companies use innovative Web-based training technologies to educate and train their workforce and suppliers.

8. *Are there employee recognition and rewards for employees who behave ethically and demonstrate appropriate corporate citizenship behaviors?* Most companies understand that employees tend to engage in behavior that is recognized and rewarded, and that

they avoid behavior that is penalized. The system of recruiting, hiring, promoting, compensating, and publicly honoring employees all can be designed to promote corporate social responsibility.

9. *Does the company conduct regular social and environmental audits and reporting? Are the company's initiatives independently audited?* A growing number of companies have come to understand the value of assessing their social and environmental performance on a regular basis. From the informal query "How are we doing?" to scheduled surveys to the formal audit process conducted by outside experts, companies are seeking information about how they are viewed and how they are progressing in meeting the expectations of investors, employees, customers, business partners, and community members on a range of corporate social responsibility issues.

10. *Does the company use its power to influence business partners and/or industry colleagues to have them adopt and implement corporate citizenship policies?* Some socially responsible companies recognize that they can play a leadership role in influencing the behavior of others, from business partners to industry colleagues to neighboring businesses. They understand that ultimately it is in everyone's best interests to have as many companies as possible honoring the requirements and expectations of corporate social responsibility.

We use these 10 criteria as the basis for constructing a Citizenship Transparency Index (CTI)—an instrument for measuring the degree of citizenship companies demonstrate. It consists of coding yes-or-no responses to each of the questions above. The CTI is represented in Figure 9–12.

We carried out a close inspection of the websites of the five top-rated companies and five worst-rated companies in each country in which the RQ Project was carried out in 2001. Each company's website was coded for its corporate transparency. Based on our qualitative analysis of the transparency of these companies in the RQ Project, U.S. companies led the way in

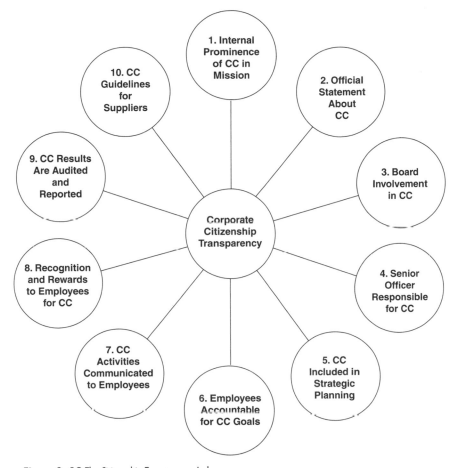

Figure 9–12 The Citizenship Transparency Index.

communicating about their citizenship, followed by the Netherlands, Australia, Denmark, and Italy. Across countries, Microsoft,
Ahold, Sony, Novo Nordisk, and Johnson & Johnson scored at
least 70 percent scores. All of them convey a high level of citizenship transparency. They report and communicate regularly
about their citizenship activities to all stakeholders.

In contrast, the worst performers on the Citizenship Trans-
parency Index were almost all Italian companies, most of the
Danish companies (except for Novo Nordisk and Bang &
Olufsen), as well as Nike, Nordstrom, NS (Dutch Railroads),
UPC, Baan, and Ben (currently T-Mobile).

These results highlight the existence of a gap between reality and perceptions. Some companies actually carry out a significant degree of citizenship activities—however, and for whatever reasons, they choose not to make it known. For instance, General Electric is among the world's highest donors and sponsors of corporate citizenship programs. As the RQ Project demonstrates, however, very few people are aware of the company's social initiatives, which leads to the recurrent finding that companies like GE can best improve their reputation with the general public by increasing the communications they make about what social initiatives they're already carrying out.

Despite its fall from grace in March 2003, it's clear that Ahold has been doing many things right. For years, the company has been an active participant in international organizations addressing topics of social responsibility. It's also a member of the Amnesty International Dutch Business Round Table and CSR Europe (since 2002). The company is on the Food Marketing Institute (FMI) and CIES executive boards. Eurocommerce and FMI are two of its primary lobby organizations. Ahold representatives also chair the Global Food Safety Initiative (GFSI), Eurocommerce Food Law Committee, and FMI Government Affairs Committee.

A good example of Ahold's social responsibility policy is the "low energy superstore" at their Stop & Shop chain in Massachusetts, which was the culmination of nearly three years of cooperation and innovation among Ahold companies. Another example of corporate citizenship at the company is its involvement following the September 11, 2001, terrorist attacks on the United States. Ahold's U.S. companies worked toward a common goal of raising funds to benefit the victims of the tragedy. Ahold has also taken a leadership role through projects such as the Global Food Safety Initiative—advancing the development of global standards to ultimately benefit consumers with safer food.

Top-rated Microsoft seems driven by the belief that amazing things happen when people get the resources they need. To that end, Microsoft has been using technology to "spark potential" of individuals and communities since 1983. No other technology company contributes more toward broadening access to technology and creating digital opportunities. Last year alone, Microsoft and its employees gave over $246.9 million to help people and communities realize their potential.

Microsoft's giving is based on four foundational pillars: expanding opportunities through technology access, strengthening nonprofits through technology, developing a diverse technology workforce, and building community.

In contrast, consider one of the companies that scored lowest on our Corporate Citizenship Transparency—apparel and footwear giant Nike. On May 12, 1998, Nike's CEO Philip Knight stood before the National Press Club and vowed to implement a six-pronged plan to improve labor conditions in his company's 600 contract factories. The speech didn't appear to be a palliative: Knight seemed genuinely concerned that activists and journalists had found Nike to be fostering sweatshops and lax safety standards abroad. Knight was brave: He described his company's product as "synonymous with slave wages, forced overtime, and arbitrary abuse," and announced a series of reforms that included new labor policies for health and safety, child labor, independent monitoring, and workers' education. "A sea change in company culture" is what he called the move.

As for the details, Knight promised to meet the U.S. Occupational Safety and Health Administration (OSHA) standards in indoor air quality. He said the minimum age for Nike factory workers would be raised to 18 years for full-time and 16 for part-time employees. He ensured Nike would include nongovernmental organizations in its factory monitoring. He vowed an expansion of Nike's worker education program, making available free high school equivalency courses, and an expansion of Nike's micro-enterprise loan program to benefit 4,000 families in Vietnam, Indonesia, Pakistan, and Thailand. Knight also promised to fund university research and open forums on responsible business practices.

Three years later, Global Exchange, an international human rights organization that has monitored Nike's labor practices since 1988, issued a report following up on Nike's promises. "Still Waiting for Nike To Do It" is a 115-page investigation, and the title pretty much says it all. According to Global Exchange's researchers, Nike has fallen short on all six areas of reform it had promised.

If Global Exchange is to be believed, Nike seems not to have made good on its promise to institute OSHA standards. Toluene, a chemical solvent known to cause central nervous system depression and liver and kidney damage, is apparently still being used in Nike sneaker manufacture. And although the amount of Toluene has been reduced, Nike seems to be providing factory managers advance notice of testing, "giving them considerable scope to change chemical use to minimize emissions on the day the test is conducted," according to the report.

Among the report's other claims are that only one nonprofit organization has been permitted to audit a Nike factory; that Nike's education program has expanded, but wages paid in Nike factories are not high enough for the majority of workers to give up overtime income to take courses; that Nike refused reputable academics access to Nike factories to conduct research; that Nike subcontractors continue to employ workers under age 16; and that the company continues to work with factories that demand 70-hour work weeks from employees.

Many media groups now praise Nike. The weekly magazine *Newsweek,* for example, reported in 1999 that Nike has "set the apparel-industry standard for reform of wages, hours and minimum working ages in its contract factories." The *Journal of Business Ethics* has called Nike an "ethical transnational," and *Business and Society* has applauded the company for cooperating with human rights groups and adopting a factory code of conduct.

Not coincidentally, Nike is said to have spent nearly $3 billion on a public relations campaign aimed at silencing its critics. Nike's PR has included sponsoring socially responsible business conferences and funding media projects. In October 2000, for example, attendees of one such meeting, the Natural Step Conference in Atlanta, Georgia, were shown a film describing Nike's newfound commitment to social justice. These inconsistent reports about Nike raise legitimate questions about the company's authenticity and transparency on corporate citizenship.

CONCLUSION

Transparency is proving increasingly important in maintaining reputation with ever more demanding stakeholders and an intrusive institutional environment made up of regulators, legislators, politicians, lobbyists, and activists. The two areas that traditionally received the greatest push were demands for greater transparency of products and transparency of products and financials.

They're still hot topics. But as institutional pressures mount, everyone is adopting increasingly comparable standards about their products and financials. Companies are finding growing opportunity to distinguish themselves by emphasizing new transparency platforms—especially those of leadership and vision, corporate citizenship, and workplace environment.

CEOs are fast becoming the flag-bearers (or pall-bearers) of corporate transparency. The best of them are vital interpreters of the company's direction for all stakeholders, and they participate in wide-ranging, highly visible social debates. At the same time, it's clear that the two domains where corporate reputations are being built and destroyed—and are most likely to continue being challenged in unprecedented ways in the 21st century—involve citizenship issues and the workplace. Top companies are recognizing these issues in spades, doing more about them, and opening themselves up to heightened scrutiny in these areas. It's no longer a question of *whether* a company should be transparent about its citizenship activities and its workplace—the question is *how*. As the next chapter tells us, the answer is *consistently*.

ENDNOTES

1. Sandeep Patel and George Dallas. "Transparency and Disclosure: Overview of Methodology and Study Results", Standard & Poor, proprietary evaluation of transparency and disclosure practices at over 1,500 companies, October 16 2002. All citations in this section are to this document.

2. "Bittter Pill for Glaxo," The Business, May 25-27, 2003, 9.

3. Risk Library, Committees at the Bank for International Settlements (BIS), http://newrisk.ifci.ch/145360.htm, November 2002.

4. N. Klein, *Fences and Windows: Dispatches from the Front Lines of the Globalization Debate,* New York: St. Martin's Press, 2002, 14–15.

5. "Wholesome Fries," *The New York Times,* September 16, 2002.

6. L. Gaines-Ross. See also J. Porac, J. Wade et al., "Hitch Your Wagon to a CEO-Star...," *Corporate Reputation Review, 1,* 1997.

7 C. Fombrun, "What is Corporate Citizenship." In N. M. Tichy and A. R. McGill, *Global Corporate Citizenship,* New York: Wiley & Sons, 1997.

10 BE CONSISTENT

As consumers, we are under assault. Numerous messages are constantly broadcast to us by companies and by the media, creating a cacophony of logos, sounds, and signals. Since we can't pay attention to all of their messages, we consciously and subconsciously select from the vast array only those that are relevant to us—and we screen out the rest.

Relevance is a judgement call we each make subjectively—in viewing an ad campaign, for instance, what's relevant to you may not be relevant to me. Some of us are drawn to humorous ads, while others are drawn to moody ads, others to representations of beauty, and others to high-tech displays of virtuosity. Research indicates that the messages most likely to get through to us are those that elicit emotional involvement and those that fit easily into pre-existing mental categories—personal "file folders" created from our past experiences. Since emotions—the experience of pleasure and pain—are among the earliest and most powerful imprints in our minds, it's no coincidence that the most important factor to explain why people feel more or less favorably toward a company is the company's emotional appeal—a dimension measured in the RQ Project with attributes that describe the degree to which consumers trust, like, and admire a company.

At the same time, research shows that we are more likely to notice messages that confirm our preexisting beliefs about a company. Once built, a reputation is inertial and difficult to change. The merged company ExxonMobil continues to be ascribed a very weak record on social responsibility despite large sums donated to charity and involvement in multiple philanthropic efforts. Arguably, this occurs because of the public's deep-seated memory of the Valdez spill. To alter public perception would require massive and consistent messaging and initiatives designed to drive out these inertial associations and create entirely new ones—something the Tiger-emblazoned company has so far avoided doing.

In the three previous chapters, we showed that well-regarded companies tend to adopt and implement reputation platforms that are distinctive, authentic, and transparent. In this chapter, we demonstrate that the company's reputation platform also has to be *consistently* enacted across all stakeholder groups and through all of the company's communications and initiatives. Building a strong reputation platform is central to the execution of a campaign of communications and initiatives designed to earn the company a favorable reputation. As Figure 10–1 illustrates, the best-regarded companies implement such campaigns in five steps:

Step 1. They *dialogue* with stakeholders.

Step 2. They enforce a *shared identity* throughout the company.

Step 3. They adopt service standards and *integrated communications systems* that facilitate coherence.

Step 4. They *coach employees and partners* to communicate harmonious messages that are consistent with the company's reputation platform and corporate

story, and that reflect the company's shared identity. Often, they are personally branded by the
company's CEO.

Step 5. They *measure progress* in implementation systematically.

These steps are actually modules that are not necessarily
sequential and can have some degree of simultaneity. For analytical purposes, however, they can be thought of as unfolding
linearly in time.

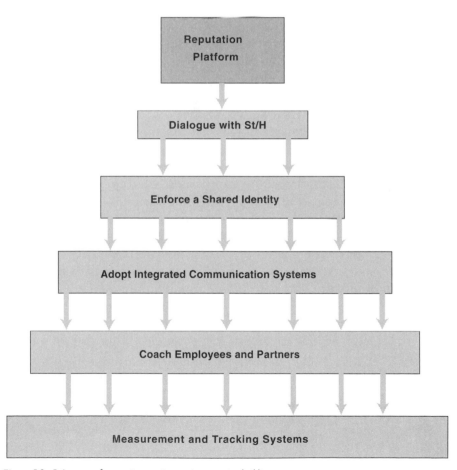

Figure 10–1 A process for creating consistency in reputation-building.

STEP 1: ESTABLISH A DIALOGUE WITH STAKEHOLDERS

Companies have to deal with the demands of three primary stakeholder groups—employees, customers, and investors. In addition, makers of consumer products are particularly pressured by two secondary stakeholder groups—activists and the general public. As Chapter 1, "Why Reputations Matter," showed, all of them are influenced to a degree by filter groups like financial analysts and the media.

In seeking to enact a reputation platform, a company needs to address the expectations of all of these stakeholder groups. That's a costly proposition, however. Most companies have numerous stakeholders, and large diversified companies can claim the whole world in their stakeholder set. Some are easily known and accessible; others operate below the radar screen and are invisible for the most part. To economize, consultants often suggest that a company prioritize its stakeholders, and concentrate its reputation-building activities on a limited set of stakeholders.

Doing so can be deceptive. Prioritizing stakeholders creates an *artificial sense of order*. It implies that some stakeholder groups are more important than others in carrying out reputation-building activities. Although some stakeholders have more visible power because they control key resources like financial capital (investors) or revenues (customers), in fact all stakeholders are now equally powerful in their ability to influence how a company is perceived. Intel learned this the hard way: The 1995 controversy surrounding its Pentium chip was started by an online letter circulated by one individual who indicated to a newsgroup that there was a tiny error embedded in calculations produced by Intel's branded chip. Others quickly joined the online conversation, inviting response from the company. When Intel turned a cold shoulder on their concerns, the topic blossomed even further. An avalanche resulted when the media picked up on it, forcing Intel to back down.

The point is that corporate reputations are vulnerable to attack from *all* stakeholder groups—be they individuals or companies, distant groups or powerful institutions. Reputation management is not a matter of selecting powerful stakeholders;

it's about interfacing with the broadest possible cross-section of stakeholders, particularly those that are seemingly weak or "off-the-radar screen," establishing a dialogue with them collectively and then selecting a reputation platform, corporate story, initiatives, and messaging strategies that can help address *all of their expectations,* consistently so.

That's no simple matter. Take the following example of a communication by Lufthansa:

> Lufthansa Cargo, like all other airlines, is looking under every nook and cranny to cut costs. In North America it decided to give its sales operations a big haircut, eliminating a dozen cargo sales positions in favour of farming the work out to a newly formed general sales agency.
>
> Lufthansa's corporate strategy has proved correct. Quality, flexibility and cost consciousness have lastingly strengthened our profitability," Jurgen Weber pointed out. Thus the Group managed to lift its operating result by EUR 227 million to EUR 332 million.

The communication was clearly targeted to please one key constituency: Investors. After all, cost-cutting always earns favor from investors. However, the message gives short shrift to employee interests. If Mr. Weber did what most CEOs are advised to do, he probably sent a letter to employees warning them of job cuts as a necessary cost-cutting measure—the "I'm sorry" letter; investors and analysts got the "efficiency and profits" letter; and the media got the sugar-coated press release describing the initiative as a necessary competitive action.

Unfortunately, in a transparent and interconnected world, all of these communications are read by *everyone*. It's impossible not to look like a greedy company when profits are made to go up by putting some people out of work. The customized model of communicating only to the most visible, powerful stakeholders with messages colored to their parochial interests ultimately results in backlash—often it alienates a critical constituency such as employees, depressing morale. It also gets picked up by reporters and activists who sympathize with the downsized employees and who mobilize marches, demonstrations, and boycotts.

Heaven forbid the company CEO receive a bonus from the board in that same year—a cynical employee population is likely to rebel and the media make an unflattering story of it that damages the company's credibility.

Good reputation management is about developing high sensitivity to the concerns and expectations of all stakeholders and establishing a mature dialogue with them so that actions taken that principally affect one stakeholder group recognize the concerns and expectations of all the others. When Intel puts its *Intel Inside*® logo on a computer, it is communicating with customers, surely. But it is also communicating with investors about the brand value it is creating; it's communicating with current and potential employees about the pride they should feel in seeing the corporate logo emblazoned on their friends' PCs. When Novo Nordisk publishes an employee satisfaction survey on its Web site, it speaks volumes not only to employees but to all stakeholders who are curious to know whether the company they're investing in has motivated employees or that the company they buy insulin shots from for their diabetic children *really cares.*

When speaking with one special interest group, the company must therefore be highly sensitive to the effects of any specialized initiatives or communications on all the other groups. The reputation platform a company adopts must be distinctive, authentic, and transparent to *every* stakeholder a company depends upon. And reputation management really means *risk management*: It involves anticipating the downside risks to the company's reputation from losing support from any stakeholder whose personal interests might diverge from those of the company as a whole.

Conducting reputational risk management requires the construction of stakeholder maps that capture the critical concerns and expectations of the company's stakeholder environment. It puts the onus on the company to create a reputation platform and a corporate story that is sustainable *across* stakeholder groups: The story has to succeed in finding and maintaining the right balance between the competing demands of all relevant stakeholders and the wishes of the organization itself.

Shell is a case in point. In 1995, after the company announced that it intended to sink its outdated Brent Spar platform in the

North Sea, it found itself completely unprepared to handle the backlash that ensued. An important reason for its lack of preparation was the internally focused mental model that Shell had long relied upon to make decisions. Often referred to as the DAD model (Decide, Announce, and Defend), it was the dominant approach that Shell took to decision making. It was an insider model, reflecting the self-referential character of Shell's executives:[1] (a) Shell claimed unique insider understanding of the rationale for its Brent Spar decision; and (b) Shell denied that such knowledge and contributions could be properly assessed in terms of universal criteria of effectiveness, efficiency, and fairness. The company also relied on expert assessments of ecological risk while refusing to speak to activists like Greenpeace who were intimately concerned about these issues.

The media fallout and subsequent soul-searching the company went through since 1995 has apparently paid off. Consider the company's innovative Web-based Tell Shell campaign—a coherent effort to build two-way dialogue and information exchange with stakeholders. Tell Shell is also based on the DAD model, but reverses the order of things: The model begins with dialogue, followed by decision making, and then do it (implementation). It's a singular contrast to the old version of the DAD model.

Developments in online technologies make it easier to invite and maintain an active and ongoing dialogue with multiples stakeholders. The challenge comes in being willing to change on the basis of that dialogue. It requires a different mental model of decision making, one that is not easy to develop in companies with institutionalized structures, cultures, and practices. But beware: To invite dialogue and not be prepared to listen and act on the messages received can damage authenticity.

STEP 2: ENFORCE A SHARED IDENTITY

As Chapter 7, "Be Distinctive," indicated, developing a reputation platform and rooting all of the company's communications around a shared corporate story can facilitate reputation-building. Stakeholders are more likely to be receptive to corporate messages when they perceive the contents to be coherent. To them, it implies that the company speaks harmoniously about its efforts—and so must be more authentic about what it is saying. Inconsistency in its communications and initiatives suggests the opposite—that the company may be disingenuous and less than authentic about its actions.

A good corporate story helps diverse stakeholders experience consistency in the company's messaging. To be credible, it has to be created in an open dialogue with a representative cross-section of the company's key stakeholders and should meet four criteria: First, the story should be *realistic*. All stakeholders should perceive the contents of the story as accurate depictions of the company. Second, the story should be *relevant*—stakeholders should perceive the key message of the story as addressing their interests and concerns. Third, the story should present the company as *responsive*. Fourth, the story should be *sustainable*—it must find and maintain a balance between the competing demands of all relevant stakeholders and the preferred options of the company itself.

The reputation platform—and the corporate story that derives from it—ensures that a minimal level of commonality of expression will result throughout the company. But it will still allow for too much variation. A key tool that companies use to enforce consistency further is visual identity. Much as the military uses flags and uniforms, and religious groups use rituals, music, uniforms, and scents, companies are finding it advisable to develop restrictive policies addressing the use of their names, logos, colors, and typeface so that stakeholders are exposed to a consistent set of visual cues that describe the company. These are clearly useful tools, and Web-based technologies increasingly facilitate the creation of libraries of approved images, styles, formats, and typefaces for corporate documents. Not only do these libraries provide ready access to the guidelines governing their use, but they often enable direct downloads of approved formats, enabling instant conformity by remote parts of the company.

Many of the high-ranked companies in our global RQ study use the same name at both product level and corporate level. Microsoft, Coca-Cola, Sony, Lego, Bang & Olufsen, Ferrari, and Microsoft benefit in this way from the transfer of brand value from product advertising investments to the corporate level.

But it's also true that many high-RQ companies maintain separate names for the company and its brands. The best known are probably consumer goods titans Procter & Gamble and Unilever, famous for ownership of a stable of powerful product brands and reticent about promoting the overarching corporate umbrellas that govern those brands. The same logic characterizes giant Ahold, owner of large supermarket chains around the world. Ahold uses its corporate name only in communications targeted to financial audiences and to potential hires. Nonetheless, the Dutch public nominated and rated Ahold as the company with the best reputation in the Netherlands in 2001. Apparently, Dutch consumers can make the link between Ahold, the company founded by Albert Heyn, and the brand-name retail stores they shop at.

The endorsement decision is a difficult one. Companies regularly face it when they are involved in mergers and acquisitions, when decisions have to be made about the rebranding of the joined entity. In a valiant effort to retain the historical identities of both partners to the fusion, many mergers have copped out entirely—fusing their previous names into lengthy, often unspeakable combinations. Auditor PriceWaterhouseCoopers is an example: a fusion of former rivals Price-Waterhouse and Coopers & Lybrand. The fusion of automakers Daimler-Benz and Chrysler produced DaimlerChrysler; Exxon and Mobil came together as ExxonMobil; and the marriage of Texaco and Chevron produced ChevronTexaco. But visit the Chrysler Web site, and you're hard put to know that it has a corporate parent. Apparently, the parent company assumes that separating the brands is advantageous—the link to the corporate name is not something that Web surfers need to know about.

Separate branding creates problems for companies seeking to build corporate reputations. It makes difficult a shared identity, visual projections, and the whole apparatus by which identification and personalization is created in the minds of stakeholders. If there are two (or more) companies under the umbrella, what unites them?

By contrast, fusions of pharmaceutical companies demonstrate a more deliberate vision of the need for a common reputation platform for the joined entities. When Sandoz and

Ciba-Geigy joined forces in March 1996 in the largest corporate merger in history, the two companies shed their pasts and were reborn under the name of Novartis. In 2000, Novartis and AstraZeneca merged their agricultural businesses to form Syngenta, the world leader in plant protection and the number three in the seeds business.

Clearly, the corporate name can be a useful tool for injecting shared identity elements internally and externally. It also makes possible a transfer of key corporate values from the company to its business-level brands. Top-rated Sony is a good example of a company that seeks to transfer a reputation platform built on innovation, quality, and miniaturization to its multiple business units. When Sony sought to enter the movie production business, it found itself overstretched—the reputation platform didn't apply well to those unrelated markets and may be among the reasons that explain Sony's inability to maintain credibility in that space. Swiss food giant Nestle is similar in its efforts to convey to consumers across its businesses the clear link between the corporate parent Nestle and the company's many product names (e.g., Nescafe, Nesquick). Beverage behemoth Coca-Cola vacillates: The Coca-Cola Company (TCCC) is the parent of multiple business units united around a reputation platform of refreshment, one that encompasses dozens of brands, including Dasani water, Minute Maid orange juice, and Fanta. Few consumers realize that they are all TCCC owned business units. The transfer of shared values is made more difficult across TCCC business units insofar as stakeholder allegiance to the parent company is weakened by parochial allegiance to the company's seemingly separate brands.

Figure10–2 contrasts four principal types of endorsement that ING has used for its subsidiaries. They constitute points along a continuum and their corresponding visual identities.

Corporate managers generally disagree with business-unit heads about the merits of strong and weak endorsement. Often rancorous, emotional debates occur around the question of how much intrusion to allow of the corporate brand over the business brands. Qualitative research we've conducted in four industries

	A. No Endorsement Standalone	B. Weak Endorsement	C. Medium Endorsement	D. Strong Endorsement
Visualization	'affiliate name'	'affiliate name' member of 'parent company name' (logo)	'parent company name' (logo) 'affiliate name'	'parent company name' (logo) 'specialization'
Example	Mercantile Mutual	Mercantile Mutual 'Member of ING (lion)'	ING (lion) Mercantile Mutual	ING (lion) Insurance
Corporate branding strategy	Stand-alones, low degree of parent visibility, high degree of autonomy at business unit level, avoiding spill-over effects.	Low degree of parent visibility, used by companies in a transition phase of complete autonomy towards integration into an integrated market approach.	High degree of parent visibility, no consistent fit with the key elements of the corporate message, applied in Greenfields or in more mature markets where competitors already have achieved a strong position.	High parent visibility, high degree of identification with corporate level, high degree of transparency, strict coordination of communication strategy, showing the strength of the group.

Stand Alone	
Weak Endorsement	
Medium Endorsement	
Strong Endorsement	

Figure 10–2 Forms of corporate endorsement at ING. Source: ING 2001

with diverse managerial participants demonstrates the standard arguments used on both sides:

Arguments favoring strong application of a reputation platform:

1. We want to create a sense of internal coherence in order to simplify internal cooperation.
2. We want to show outsiders the strength and size of our organization.
3. We want to express unity towards the outside world.
4. We are responsible, so we want to be in control; uniformity in branding simplifies this.
5. Cost reduction: uniformity is cheaper than having to support a range of different brands.

Arguments favoring weak application of a reputation platform:

1. Adding the corporate brand to our business unit communications implies that investments in our business unit–level brand have become useless.
2. We have a typical national brand name that fits well with our local situation; as soon as we replace this by the corporate brand, we will lose substantial market share.
3. Visualizing a formal link with the corporate name will limit our commercial freedom (e.g., our choice of distribution channels).
4. Size is nice for financial audiences and as a consequence for corporate headquarters, but not for our business unit in our markets.
5. Increased importance of the corporate brand implies increased power for corporate managers, which implies reduced freedom and power of business unit management.

Even after a decision is made to promote a shared reputation platform, acrimony often remains that prevents effective implementation of that platform and limits the synergies achieved. We therefore recommend careful analysis of the benefits to be gained from promoting a shared reputation platform across business units. It should be based on a shared understanding that a common reputation platform is best justified when:

- The company is pursuing a diversification strategy that puts it in closely related businesses. The Coca-Cola Company's diversification strategy into beverages is a related diversification strategy that would benefit from a shared reputation platform and closer application of a common identity in the management of its brands.
- The company relies on centrally coordinated systems and practices for fulfilling its major market functions. Ford Motor Company operates a wide range of auto businesses, including Ford, Jaguar, and Aston-Martin. So does General Motors, with Saturn, Chevrolet, and Cadillac. These businesses rely on decentralized structures for executing design, production, and marketing tasks, that have made a shared reputation platform difficult to implement.
- The company expects employees and consumers to identify more with the corporate parent than with the brands. Pharmaceutical products producer Johnson & Johnson clearly stimulates identification with the company rather than with its businesses despite strong brand names of their own (e.g., baby powder). Johnson & Johnson's consumer outreach is rooted in promoting identification with the corporate umbrella.

STEP 3: IMPLEMENT AN INTEGRATED COMMUNICATION SYSTEM

When a company opts to implement a shared reputation platform and project a common identity, that identity must then be controlled. Doing so requires integrated communications that harmonize the messages and initiatives conveyed by the company to its multiple stakeholder groups. To deliver integrated communications, companies increasingly rely on technological solutions that can enable coordination far more easily than centralized oversight and approvals.

The well-regarded Dutch electronics giant Philips provides an interesting example of a diversified company that has adopted a strong reputation platform and relies on an integrated system to orchestrate global communications from its Amsterdam headquarters. Consider the key elements of the corporate story it tells:

> Founders Anton and Gerard Philips were innovators and entrepreneurs who succeeded in business while improving the lives of customers and employees. Their founding belief was that by daring to make choices that improve the lives of people both inside and outside the company, they would be successful not by coincidence but by design.[2]

The company readily describes its rootedness in electronics and its evolution through a gamut of successive technological innovations that crystallized its business. Figure 10–3 shows the interrelated set of innovations from which Philips emerged with three principal lines of business: lighting, medical systems, and consumer electronics.

In 2001, the company embarked on a strategic reorganization to implement a "One Philips" strategy. The first task was to simplify Philips' complex portfolio of thirteen business units down to five. In parallel, the company recognized the need for

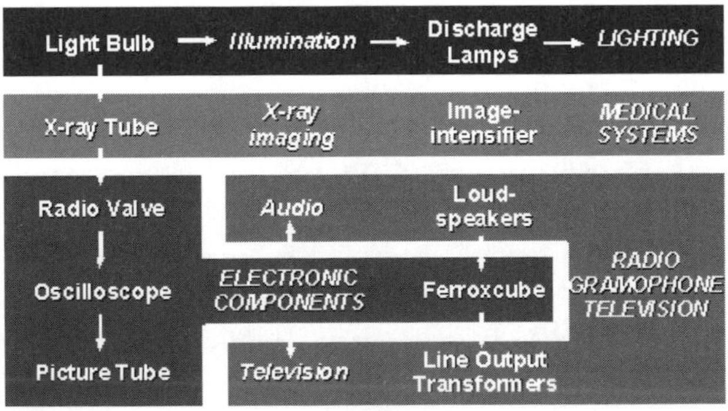

Figure 10–3 Philips and its technological trajectory.

Source: Philips, 2002

greater consistency in its communications across those business units. To do so, corporate communications was tasked with managing Philips' exposure to all internal and external stakeholders, developing messaging for communications issues, orchestrating an orderly and effective delivery of corporate and key divisional and product news, and setting guidelines to promote a "one voice" policy for Philips.

Figure 10–4 Philips logo and slogan.
Source: Philips, 2002

A slogan was selected to crystallize the innovation platform of the company and galvanize the attention of both employees and consumers—"Let's Make Things Better." The company then began the arduous task of revising decision-making processes and setting monthly planning meetings designed to construct a groupwide communications plan that could govern internal communications and the global messaging of the Philips brand, centered around the common reputation platform. Key elements of that platform include

- **Vision and Strategy:** One company with a digital electronics focus, partnering with others.
- **Brand and Marketing:** Investing in competence building.
- **Technology and Innovation:** Technology for people, a passion for innovation.
- **People and Values:** Creating a sustainable, rewarding environment.
- **Finance and Performance:** Return to growth, ongoing discipline, and quality focus.

The vision of One Philips and its implications for communications are shown in Figure 10–5.

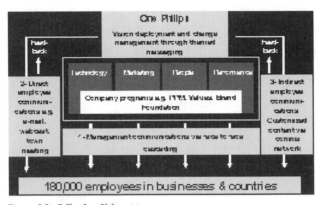

Figure10–5 The One Philips vision.
Source: Philips, 2002

To implement the One Philips platform required linked systems. Figure 10–6 shows some of the interrelated elements of Philips's communications system. It begins with common themes for communications throughout the company. Implementation of those themes is coordinated by a global steering group of some 15 communications professionals operating with a common editorial calendar and executing the plan through concerted media relations, PR support, speechwriting, speaker placements, and the deployment of common tools and templates across the business units.

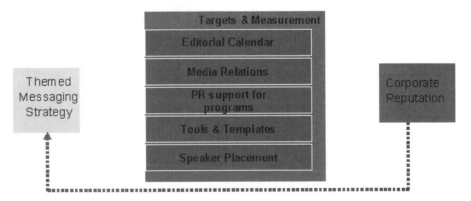

Figure10–6 Execution of communications at Philips.
Source: Philips, 2002

The communications structure is three-tiered and involves

- A centralized Corporate Communications Council with responsibility for global management of communications. The Council oversees all internal groupwide communications and concentrates on addressing strategic issues from the business sector and from special interest groups.
- Communications teams at the level of the company's core product divisions: They address global communications relevant to the product divisions and concentrate on consumer and industry issues. They also manage internal communications in the divisions.
- Local communications teams operating as a shared service across the group and divisions. They address issues relevant to the geography and coordinate internal and external communications that are relevant across Philips businesses at the local level.

All of these teams are supported by a global network of preferred suppliers of communications services.

To coordinate the activities of these geographically diverse communications professionals across the company, Philips relies on an extranet. Figure 10–7 shows the home page of the Philips GroupCom online community. It provides communications professionals with immediate access to the communications calendar, media content, and ongoing projects.

Extranets and intranets have become very popular tools for integration of corporate communications. During a company visit to DaimlerChrysler's headquarters in Germany, we were invited by senior managers to view the company's impressive intranet— a system that provides direct access to approved logos, typefaces, and images of the company for use in publications around the world. It also enables all employees to be instantly informed about media content and all press releases sent out around the world. Speaking in harmony is facilitated by the system: When DaimlerChrysler managers are tasked with preparing their own comments for a public forum, they can easily access top management speeches as well as prepared presentations and other

Figure 10–7 Philips' online community for communications.
Source: Philips, 2002

predigested communications content. They are therefore less likely to be caught off guard expressing opinions likely to create unappealing headlines for the company.

STEP 4: COACH EMPLOYEES AND PARTNERS

Ultimately, consistency depends on people's understanding, willingness, and commitment to singing the company song in harmony. An important tool for developing harmony is to involve senior managers in coaching their more junior colleagues about communications. Much as opera singers retain vocal coaches, so too are companies relying more systematically than before on formal coaching of executives by communications professionals, from formalized media training, speech-writing, and presentation skills training to more subtle one-on-one skill-building. In many companies, internal communications staff often act as personal consultants to executives in developing their personal brands.

When systematically applied, training and coaching are also a valuable mechanism for inducing widespread understanding and acceptance of the company's reputation platform and for diffusing it not only among employees but also among supply chain partners. Specialized extranets designed to link a company to its suppliers, dealers, customers, or employees all require complementary training and coaching in their effective implementation. They are also the means through which the company conveys its values and identity—its reputation platform.

Highly rated GE maintains a well-known training facility in Crotonville, New York. Former CEO Jack Welch relied heavily on Crotonville to spread the company's point of view to rotating managers attending the company's technical and managerial training programs. Similarly, when Shell embarked on its massive global transformation in the mid-1990s, it created an education center in the Netherlands where managers came for exposure, exchange, and training in the company's vision for the future.

In many companies, the CEO has become the head coach for personalizing the company to stakeholders. A favorable impression of a CEO enables people to put a face on the faceless and create meaning out of uncertainty. Ernst & Young's Center for Business Innovation reported that institutional investors give nonfinancial measures as much as 35 percent of the weight in their evaluations of companies. Topping these analysts' list of factors were management credibility and the ability to execute strategy, both of which emanate from the CEO suite.

Brand-name CEOs also act as powerful magnets to potential employees, helping to attract the best talent and keep turnover rates low. Universum, a consulting firm that regularly surveys MBA students about their job preferences, reports that many of the companies that are most attractive to MBA students have such brand-name CEOs.

Developing consistency across a company therefore requires visible leadership that systematically conveys the company's reputation platform. Stakeholders look to a CEO who clearly and credibly communicates the company's mission and direction.

They expect that a CEO inspires and motivates employees. Emerging from the dazzling new information economy is therefore a homespun image of the CEO as storyteller. In his book *Extraordinary Minds,* Howard Gardner notes that storytelling is a powerful way to influence constituencies.[3] He describes how powerful leaders build narratives that create a common bond with their followers by describing goals they seek in common, obstacles that lie in the way, ways of dealing with those obstacles, and the promise that utopia can be achieved. These stories, like legends, breathe life into otherwise impersonal companies and their products.

A CEO can also create reputational capital by focusing on local constituencies. Leonard Riggio, CEO of Barnes & Noble, has made a concerted effort to shape the personality of his bookstores so that they mirror the communities they inhabit. Manhattan's Union Square store, for example, reflects the funkiness of the neighborhood and plays host to writers' book signings and poetry readings. His company's attention to local constituencies and Riggio's own voice in these matters provide Barnes & Noble with permission to enter new markets and win over customers.

Many of the companies in the RQ studies in the five selected countries have visible CEOs with strong track records. The companies often dedicate significant parts of their Web sites to them. In the United States Bill Gates is probably the best-known corporate chief even though he's no longer Microsoft's CEO—John Balmer took his place in 2001. For one, Gates is the living example of someone who fulfilled the "American Dream," starting his own company from scratch and building it up to colossal status. For another, his symbolic and substantial gift of over $19 billion to create the Bill and Melinda Gates Foundation sent a powerful message about the fundamental good a company can do—casting a powerful shadow of goodwill on the Microsoft empire.

Johnson & Johnson is another American firm with consistently high reputation rankings and a powerful and highly competent CEO. Although not as celebrated or as well-known as Bill Gates, William Weldon is recognized as a solid leader who lives and breathes Johnson & Johnson. Having been with the company for a long time and climbed the corporate ladder, Weldon acts as a powerful mouthpiece for communicating the company's reputation platform and corporate story.

In the Netherlands CEOs are also visible to consumers, and their speeches and actions appear in the media. The top-reputation companies have highly recognizable and praised CEOs. Before the financial scandal that unfolded in early 2003, Ahold's then CEO Cees van der Hoeven had been one of the most cited CEOs in the Netherlands –he took third place in the 2001 Intermedia Citation Index, and was named "Mister Investor Relations Netherlands" in 2001 by Rematch, an investor relations research unit that praised his clear, consistent, and comprehensive approach to communicating the company's financial position. The subsequent scandal demonstrated how deceptive a company can be.

In Italy, Ferrari similarly showcases its key figures. The legacy of Enzo Ferrari, the founder, is central to the corporate culture. Key facts from his life are highlighted and celebrated. The current CEO, Luca Cordero di Montezemolo, is himself a colorful and decorated figurehead for Ferrari and personifies the company's heart and soul.

In Denmark, a prime example of the importance of a company's chairman is A.P. Møller's figurehead CEO Mærsk McKinney Møller. Mr. Møller is a highly visible leader who has accumulated much praise during his life through his role both within and outside the company, most recently for his involvement in funding Copenhagen's controversial new Opera house. He is well known both in Denmark and to the shipping community worldwide.

Clearly, CEO brands are valuable vehicles for carrying out the kind of formal training and coaching needed to execute corporate reputation platforms. CEO brands act as powerful focal points for shaping consistency throughout the companies they lead.

STEP 5: ADOPT A MEASUREMENT AND TRACKING SCORECARD

The endgame of all integrated communications systems like those of Philips or DaimlerChrysler is measurement. To maintain alignment between the corporate vision and the execution of communications and initiatives requires a credible scorecard. Most companies build their scorecards around the volume of external coverage, the favorability of that coverage in each region, and the reputational changes they expect from carrying out their communications. Having a credible scorecard, committing to targeted results based on that scorecard, and rewarding business unit managers as well as communications staff for achieving those results are they key ways companies can ensure successful implementation of integrated communications.

Throughout this book, we emphasized the importance of adopting metrics that can enable consistent monitoring of the company's actions and initiatives. In Chapter 3, "Who's Tops— and Who's Not?" we described the Harris-Fombrun Reputation Quotient[sm] or RQ developed by Charles Fombrun and Harris Interactive. The instrument is a standardized scorecard that enables cross-national comparisons of perceptions. Companies can create their own customized scorecards by adapting the standardized version of the RQ to their own operations. As we've shown, the six dimensions of the RQ are common to all companies, as are most of the 20 reputation attributes. However, companies may also want to track specific attributes that reflect strategic options they are pursuing. This should not be done at the expense of the standardized attributes but by enlarging the set and adapting the attributes to make them more specific to the company at hand. The resulting reputation scorecard can be used to track the perceptions of all stakeholder groups using various data collection strategies, including online surveys of the public and employees as well as standard telephone and in-person interviewing.

A second tracking tool we find extremely useful is the systematic rating of a company's media coverage. Most companies today rely on press and video clipping services. Unfortunately, most such services do not provide useful analysis of the coverage. Working with Delahaye-Medialink, the Reputation Institute developed the standardized MRi instrument to assess media coverage in terms of the same attributes and dimensions as a company's

reputation scorecard. In the standardized version of the MRi, companies are rated on the 20 attributes of the RQ, and the rating describes how favorable the company's media coverage is and how
it is positioned relative to other companies. This is done electronically for English-language coverage but has become increasingly feasible in other languages. It can also be done qualitatively
for media that are not yet electronically available. Tracking media
using the same metric is a valuable complement to the measurement of stakeholder perceptions.

A third tracking tool we recommend is to construct a coding system based on the reputation scorecard for all of the company's outgoing messaging, including press releases, website
content, annual reports, and executive speeches. Content analysis of outgoing messaging closes the loop: It reports what the
company is *saying* to its stakeholders. When juxtaposed against
media ratings and stakeholder ratings, it pinpoints the specific
areas the company is targeting and enables identifying the specific attributes and dimensions of reputation on which the company needs to do further work if it is to successfully shift media
coverage and stakeholder perceptions. Figure 10–8 describes
the integrated nature of a company's tracking system for reputation management.

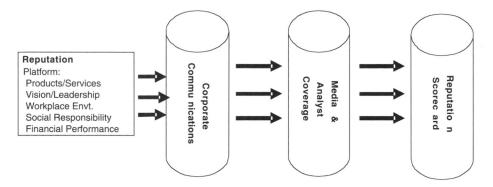

Reputation
Platform:
Products/Services
Vision/Leadership
Workplace Envt.
Social Responsibility
Financial Performance

Corporate Communications

Media & Analyst Coverage

Reputation Scorecard

Figure 10–8 Reputation measurement and tracking.

CONSISTENCY: TOP DOWN
AND ALL AROUND

Consistency is an important characteristic of the best-regarded companies. It is achieved by adopting a reputation platform, shaping an identity around it, delivering integrated communications, and infusing the company with the spirit of its reputation-enhancing themes.

For consistency to take hold, we suggest four key points:

- Create a platform that will be perceived as credible, relevant, and realistic by all stakeholders on which your company depends.
- Create a corporate story based on at least two emotional drivers that give the story appeal and above all make it easier to remember.
- Add attention-getting symbols to the media in which you express the corporate story; one picture says more than a thousand words.
- Develop appealing channels to express the story, whether through advertising, public relations, or social initiatives, including personal branding of top executives (in addition to the CEO).

Some of the tools with which companies build consistency are straightforward to implement: They involve developing strict guidelines, use of a common logo, adopting logical brand architecture, building a communications plan, creating intranets and extranets, and adopting standardized measurement and tracking. Others are more difficult and depend very much on the example set by the company's top managers: If a company really wants to be consistent, its leaders have to set an example every day.

Finally, as we suggested from the start, consistency involves "singing in harmony" with all stakeholder groups. It remains true that most companies are biased to consumers and tend to overemphasize the importance of marketing communications. Advertising budgets generally dwarf the budgets allocated to other forms of communication despite consistent evidence that earned media is a more cost-effective medium of building support. The challenge for would-be reputation managers is therefore to demonstrate a credible business case for reputation-building to companies heavily invested in a consumer- or investor-dominated worldview. That's the challenge to which FedEx rose in 2000, and we describe the company's reputation-building initiative of the last few years in the next chapter.

ENDNOTES

1. R. L. Dunbar & D. Ahlstrom, "Seeking the Institutional Balance of Power: Avoiding the Power of a Balanced View," *Academy of Management Review, 20*(1), 1995, 171–192.

2. Interview with Pieter Schaffels, vice president, Philips, January 23, 2003.

3. H. Gardner, *Extraordinary Minds*. New York: Perseus, 1998.

11

BECOMING A TOP COMPANY: THE CASE OF FEDEX

I n 2001 actor Tom Hanks was nominated for a third Academy Award for his role as a modern-day Robinson Crusoe in the popular film *Cast Away*. He played a FedEx manager passionately committed to the company's objectives of reliability and service. Obsessed with efficiency, he is shown sending a self-addressed FedEx package to Moscow, just before boarding a flight, in order to check the speed with which the package arrives.

On his return flight, the company plane Hanks is riding on crashes, and he endures five years on an isolated island, his only companions a Wilson basketball and a FedEx package addressed to someone in the Midwest. Hanks ultimately finds his way home on a raft, clinging to the package. The film closes with Hanks fulfilling FedEx's service commitment by personally delivering the package to its addressee.

At the 2002 Super Bowl FedEx showed an alternative ending for the film as a commercial that begins with a Tom Hanks look-alike ringing a farmhouse doorbell, and a woman coming to the door.

> "Hi," he says. "I was marooned on an island for five years with this package, and I swore that I would deliver it to you because I work for FedEx."

> "That's very thoughtful," replies the woman. "Thanks."

> "By the way, what's in the package?" asks the Hanks character.

> "Nothing really," she replies. "Just a satellite phone, GPS locator, fishing rod, water purifier, and some seeds. Just silly stuff."

The humorous ad was subsequently rated number one in polls conducted by CNBC, *New York Times,* and the *Los Angeles Times*. As James Watson, Corporate Vice-President of Strategic Planning and Control and Chief Accounting Officer for FedEx, put it, "The ad did a great job of communicating the commitment of the FedEx team to reliability and to service, in what we typically like to use, which is a humorous environment. We're proud of that one, and we think it signifies what all of the FedEx family is committed to, which is outstanding service and reliability."[1]

Over the 30 years since FedEx began operating in 1973, the company earned a privileged leadership position in global air transportation by forging a powerful brand built on the twin themes of service and reliability in the overnight package delivery business. By the mid-1990s, however, the company was faced with increasing competition and declining performance, not only from its long-established rival UPS, but from a bevy of other upstarts in the express carrier market. To address the challenge, FedEx launched a series of strategic initiatives that required fundamental changes in FedEx's global communications and reputation management practices. In the rest of this chapter, we outline the changes FedEx introduced, the communications structure that resulted from its efforts, and the success the company has enjoyed as a result of introducing a wider portfolio of services under an invigorated family of FedEx brands.[2]

INTRODUCING RADICAL CHANGE

The story begins in 1998 when FedEx made the decision to acquire Caliber Systems, a company that included various operating companies, including RPS (a small package ground service), Roberts Express (an expedited service), Viking Freight (an LTL carrier), and Caliber Logistics and Caliber Technology (integrated logistics and technology solutions). They were joined to Federal Express (the original express distribution service) to make up the group of companies operating under the FDX name. "This is a strong complementary fit; the whole can become greater than the sum of its parts," commented chairman and CEO Fred Smith about the acquisition.

Over the next two years, FDX oversaw the assimilation of these companies, and many of FedEx's trademark service and technology enhancements were introduced to the new services. For two years, FedEx maintained separate express and ground divisions from an operational and marketing perspective. But by late 1999, the landscape had changed: Customers wanted a "one-stop" transportation resource—one point of contact, one invoice, and FedEx's guarantee of reliability across all modes of transportation. Faced with more aggressive competition (made more visible by UPS's landmark IPO in November 1999—at the time the largest initial offering in corporate history), FedEx had to react. In January 2000 FedEx decided to extend its corporate brand across all of its operating companies in order to capitalize on the FedEx name. Although the express and ground networks would continue to operate independently, the new FedEx would compete collectively, offering express services through FedEx Express, ground services through FedEx Ground, less-than-truckload services through FedEx Freight, and unified sales, marketing, IT, and customer service through FedEx Services.

In January 2000 FedEx set out to capitalize on the power of its global brand. In a move to integrate the services provided in the company's portfolio, FDX Corporation was renamed FedEx Corporation. The subsidiary companies took their place as Federal Express became FedEx Express, RPS became FedEx Ground, Roberts Express became FedEx Custom Critical, and Caliber

Logistics and Caliber Technology were combined into FedEx Global Logistics.

To centralize the sales, marketing, customer service, and information technology functions for the subsidiaries, FedEx Corporate Services (FedEx Services) was formed to begin operations in June 2000. "It's time to leverage and extend one of our greatest assets, the FedEx brand, and to provide our customers an integrated set of business solutions," remarked Smith.

In the following year, a number of acquisitions and realignments changed the size and scope of various FedEx operating companies. The first initiative came just one month after the corporate rebranding announcement and produced a new subsidiary. In February 2000 FedEx Corporation announced the acquisition of Tower Group International, a leader in the business of international logistics and trade information technology. Tower Group would be the foundation for FedEx Trade Networks, a company whose purpose would be to assist customers with international trade and transportation. A month later, Trade Networks itself acquired Worldtariff, a customs duty and tax information company.

In January 2001 FedEx Logistics was streamlined to further improve customer service. The major subsidiaries under FedEx Global Logistics were moved to other operating companies. FedEx Supply Chain Services became part of FedEx Services, and Caribbean Transportation Services, a company brought in through the Caliber acquisition, became part of FedEx Trade Networks.

The following month, FedEx finalized the acquisition of American Freightways, a leading LTL carrier serving 40 U.S. states. American Freightways was then merged with Viking Freight, the only major FedEx subsidiary not to undergo a name change through the corporate rebranding, and was reborn as FedEx Freight in February 2001.

By 2003 the might of FedEx was evident in its configuration of operating companies: FedEx Express, FedEx Ground, FedEx Freight, FedEx Custom Critical, FedEx Trade Networks, and FedEx Services. In combination, they form the premier global provider of transportation, e-commerce, and supply chain management services, with annual revenues of $22 billion, second only to $30 billion rival UPS.

Under the new structure, the FedEx companies operate under a common internal motto: "Operate independently, compete collectively." By operating independently, each company can focus exclusively on delivering the best service for its specific market. As CEO Fred Smith stated in the announcement of the Caliber acquisition, "We've been studying the express and routine transportation markets for 25 years, and I'm convinced that they are distinctly different, each requiring complete focus and dedicated expertise to maximize productivity, customer service, and cost-competitiveness." By competing collectively under the FedEx banner, however, all of the operating companies benefit from being under one of the world's most recognized brands. Figure 11–1 shows the "new FedEx" as it revealed itself to the world.

Figure 11–1 The new FedEx (2000).

THE ROLE OF FEDEX COMMUNICATIONS

Although the launch of the FedEx family of brands in Figure 11–1 received substantial media coverage, it failed to convert long-standing skeptics into evangelists. Critics predicted a diluted

FedEx brand. Financial analysts derided the synergies that could be expected from the operational model. Media reporters mischaracterized the structure and questioned its long-term viability. Employees continued to operate and communicate in the original operating silos from which they came.

Led by Bill Margaritis, the head of the company's global corporate communications, FedEx Communications embarked on a strategic campaign to gain recognition of the company's new business model and to create internal and external ambassadors for the new FedEx family. The effort was supported by enthusiastic participation from the leadership team across the operating companies.

The process began with systematic quantitative and qualitative research and analysis conducted between September and November 2000, with support from the FedEx's lead PR agency Ketchum Communications:

- **Employee Surveys:** Results indicated minimal understanding and acceptance of the new FedEx structure, underscoring the need for change management communications.
- **Competitive Analysis:** A national opinion-leader survey demonstrated the need to illustrate the business model's synergies clearly and effectively.
- **Share of Voice" Study:** An analysis of media coverage between January and October 2000 identified ineffective reporting of new FedEx messages, underscoring the need for more aggressive, targeted media relations.
- **Journalist Survey:** A telephone survey of business journalists identified a lack of awareness of FedEx's new configuration and a continued perception of the company as "less integrated" than competitors, reaffirming the need to educate journalists and counteract inaccuracies.
- **Review of Financial Analyst Reports:** Financial reports issued by analysts post-January 2000 expressed skepticism about FedEx's business model, demonstrating the need to proactively communicate successes and provide substantive proof points to the financial community.

THE COMMUNICATIONS CAMPAIGN

The initial mandate was clear: It involved explaining the new FedEx configuration and its "one vision, one voice." To do so, FedEx Communicators developed a crossfunctional campaign. After securing senior officer involvement and approval early on, communications were intended to leverage support across functions and divisions and to establish processes and support for the campaign throughout FedEx. Figure 11–2 diagrams the workplace-to-marketplace strategy through which FedEx sought to reposition the FedEx brand from the inside-out.

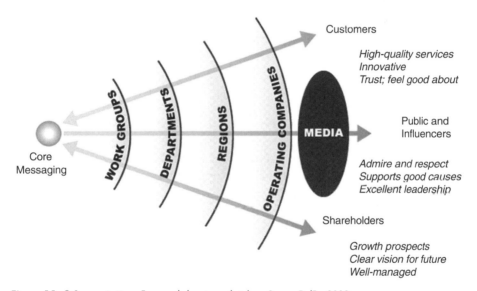

Figure 11–2 Communications: From workplace to marketplace. Source: FedEx, 2002

The formal objectives of the communications campaign were to increase understanding and support of the new FedEx among target audiences and to enhance FedEx's competitive positioning, brand equity, and stakeholder value. Target audiences included financial media, industry analysts, customers, and employees. The tactical goals of the communications campaign were:

- To construct an internal foundation for crossfunctional, collaborative communications that would be designed to:
- To educate media and dispel misperceptions about the New FedEx.
- To capitalize on blockbuster announcements and "moments in time" to communicate about the new FedEx family of operating companies.
- To initiate a corporatewide internal communications campaign about the new FedEx.

EXECUTING THE COMMUNICATIONS CAMPAIGN

The internal foundation for the communications campaign was set when the company created a crossfunctional communications board that would take charge of revitalized communications processes across the operating companies. The board took responsibility for developing the new FedEx messaging platform, infusing those messages and themes into all communications materials and channels throughout the company. Finally, to facilitate coordination, FedEx activated "InfoCentral," an electronic information repository accessible to all communicators that provided access to media content, contacts, a calendar, speeches, images, and guidelines for interpreting the new FedEx to stakeholders.

To address the second tactical goal, FedEx began a systematic process of media education. The communications group identified an "inner circle" of media contacts and conducted briefings about FedEx to forge or strengthen relationships with reporters and to reinforce messaging and reduce perception gaps. The company also launched a "FedEx Truth Squad" patterned after political campaign tactics in which coverage is monitored in real time and inaccuracies or misperceptions are immediately challenged and corrected. Finally, FedEx blanketed top-tier media by allocating media staff to build strength with targeted media contacts.

To complement its systematic outreach to employees and media, FedEx also made sure to capitalize on "blockbuster moments" to galvanize attention. Significant business events likely to get stakeholder attention were treated as opportunities to speak out about the company. This included the launch and expansion of FedEx Home Delivery, the alliance between FedEx and the U.S. Postal Service, the introduction of holiday shipping seasons, the acquisition of American Freightways, earnings announcements, and customer wins. Each event was treated as an opportunity to directly counter skepticism and to link the company's overall growth strategy to the announcement.

By far, the most important tasks of the campaign were to mobilize employees behind the changes and to explode the operating silos. Among the initiatives that were put in place, some stand out, including

- Launching "The Way Ahead" campaign to excite employees about the new FedEx and fuse operating company cultures into a unified whole.
- Conducting senior management "rallies" and town hall meetings with operating company employees.
- Distributing comprehensive employee communications, including information about cross-operating company successes.
- Streamlining channels of distribution and creating information-rich collateral to facilitate sales force communications.

EVALUATING THE PERFORMANCE OF FEDEX COMMUNICATIONS

The communications campaign had two objectives: To make the new FedEx more visible and more widely understood by all key stakeholder groups, and to improve the competitive positioning of FedEx in the marketplace. We examine some outcome measures of each objective.

Did the Communications Campaign increase the visibility of the new FedEx culture across operating companies?

Employee surveys conducted in fall 2002 suggest that customer-facing employees (e.g., FedEx Ground contractors, customer service representatives) embodied new FedEx value and brand attributes, improving customer perception of FedEx. In addition, all FedEx communications incorporated companywide content and messaging themes.

Media coverage has increasingly supported the FedEx vision. As Mark Tatge put it in *Forbes*, "[Fred] Smith's...revamp is the most radical redesign of FedEx in its 28-year history.... Ground shipping, accounting for a fourth of sales, is growing at 8% to 10%....." Writing in *Fortune,* Matt Boyle stated, "...FedEx has successfully transcended its image as simply an air express carrier...to become a one-stop shop for any shipping need.... FedEx's stock [is] up almost 30% for the year...while UPS's stock is up just 19%.... FedEx [has] won the hearts and minds of the broad business audience this year...." John Lippert put it this way in Bloomberg: "FedEx chairman Fred Smith says he's engaged in one of the greatest transformations in corporate history...."

For their part, the FedEx Truth Squad worked hard to set the record straight on numerous occasions, and FedEx responded aggressively to inaccurate or incomplete media coverage on an ongoing basis. For example, *Business Week*'s May 21, 2001, article "The Ground Wars" included erroneous coverage of FedEx. The Truth Squad deconstructed the inaccuracies in a series of briefings with the reporter and with senior editors of *Business Week*. A letter to the editor and full correction ran in *Business Week*'s June 11, 2001, issue.

Finally, employees demonstrated a somewhat improved understanding of the new FedEx structure and better customer-facing performance. Communications surveys revealed 88 percent of FedEx Services employees understood the "operate independently, compete collectively" strategy "clearly" or "fairly well," and 84 percent "agreed" or "somewhat agreed" that they contributed to the strategy. Armed with more comprehensive communications materials and improved understanding, the sales force increased cross-selling of services, securing multi-operating company customer contracts from such companies as Hyundai Motor America, Daisytek, and Wal-Mart.

Did the Communications Campaign Enhance FedEx's Competitive Position, Brand Equity, and Stakeholder Value?

The company delivered strong financial results in 2001–2002. For the full fiscal year, FedEx reported earnings before the cumulative effect of accounting changes of $2.39 per diluted share, up 20 percent from $1.99 per share the previous year. Net income for the year was $2.34 per diluted share, including a noncash charge from an accounting change of $0.05. Excluding the previous year's fourth quarter charges of $124 million, earnings for that year were $2.26 per diluted share. Additional consolidated results for the fiscal year were

- Revenues of $20.6 billion, up 5 percent from $19.6 billion in the previous year
- Operating income of $1.32 billion, up 23 percent from $1.07 billion the previous year
- Income before the effect of the accounting change of $725 million, up 24 percent from the previous year's $584 million
- Free cash flow of $616 million, compared to ($69) million the previous year

"FedEx achieved record earnings and generated significant free cash flow during the year," said CEO Fred Smith. "Our FedEx Ground and FedEx Freight units are operating at record profit and service reliability levels. FedEx Express has significantly reduced capital spending levels and has also been able to achieve record levels of service reliability, even as volume has declined during a difficult economic environment." The company's CFO, Alan Graf, Jr., echoed those remarks: "FedEx benefited in the quarter by offering customers a broad range of services in the express, ground, freight, and supply chain solution areas."[3]

As a result, analysts indicated increased acceptance of FedEx's strategy and market positioning. Scott Flower of Salomon Smith Barney put it this way: "Volume gains reflect [FedEx's] success in signing new customers…and point to nascent signs of possible…market share gains from an improving service perception."

Customer successes also reinforced the merits of the business model and the power of the integrated brand. Despite a general market slump, FedEx's overall business grew in 2002, particularly at newly branded FedEx Freight and FedEx Ground. The latter reported double-digit growth, with more than 25 percent growth in the FedEx Home Delivery unit. These results are evident and explain the strong market value of FedEx shares relative to the S&P 500 shown in Figure 11–3.

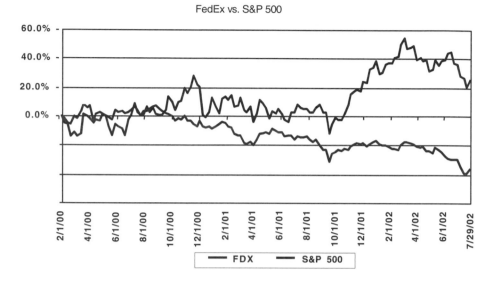

Figure 11–3 The market value of FedEx (2000–2002).
Source: Thomson Analytics

Partly as a result of the communications campaign, reporters wrote more positively about FedEx. Figure 11–4 shows the findings of an electronic content analysis of all media articles that referenced the FedEx and UPS in 2001. Media content was classified as positive or negative and aggregated into a net effect indicator that reflects the degree to which the content positively or negatively influenced the company's reputation. The results indicate that FedEx benefited from better relative reputational coverage than did UPS throughout 1991.

Finally, FedEx's positioning in reputational surveys also rose impressively since the communications campaign was implemented. In *Fortune*'s 2002 Global Most Admired survey, FedEx was ranked in seventh position, up from a lowly 74th in 2001. In *Fortune*'s survey of America's Most Admired companies, FedEx was ranked eighth, up from 16th in 2001, establishing FedEx in the survey's coveted top ten on both lists for the first time. In the *Financial Times* 2001 World's Most Respected Companies survey of CEOs, FedEx was newly ranked in 22nd position. Finally, in the 2001 Harris Interactive-Reputation Institute

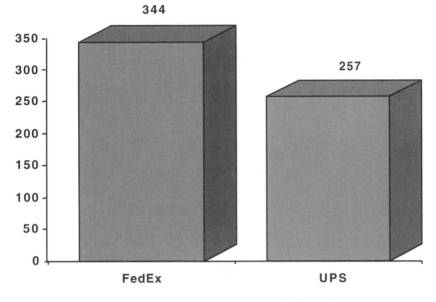

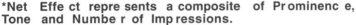

*Net Effe ct repre sents a composite of Pr ominenc e, Tone and Numbe r of Imp ressions.

Figure 11–4 Results of electronic content analysis of media coverage in 2001.

Source: Delahaye Medialink / Reputation Institute

survey of the Reputations of America's Most Visible Compa-nies, FedEx was ranked eighth in overall corporate reputation, up from 13th place in 2000. Figure 11–5 summarizes FedEx's rel-ative standing on the RQ survey conducted with the general public in 2001.

In more detail, Figure 11–6 shows how FedEx has improved on all underlying dimensions of the RQ rating provided by rep-resentative samples of U.S. consumers taken in 1999, 2000, and 2001. In the three years since FedEx's absorption of Caliber Sys-tems, the company has improved across the board on ratings of its emotional appeal—the degree to which consumers trust, like, and admire FedEx. ... As Fortune magazine recognized in March 2002, "...FedEx has successfully transcended its image as simply an air express carrier for business to become a one-stop-shop for any shipping need."[4]

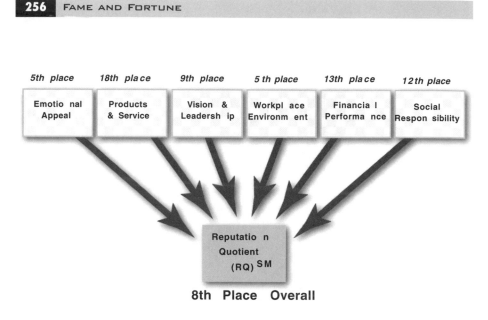

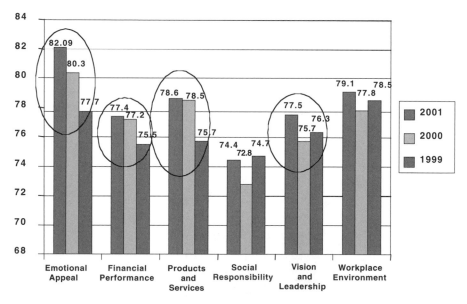

Figure 11–5 The relative ranking of FedEx on the different dimensions of the Annual RQ survey in 2001.
Source: Harris Interactive/Reputation Institute

Figure 11–6 RQ Dimensional ratings of FedEx by U.S. consumers (1999–2001).
Source: Harris Interactive/Reputation Institute

To celebrate the successes of its communications campaign in generating recognition for the company, FedEx released a series of global ads in 2002 that recognized the root source of those successes as the family of FedEx employees. Figure 11–7 shows a copy of the French version of the emotionally appealing ad. The campaign effectively signaled to employees the success of FedEx's planned expansion strategy, and the recognition of that successful implementation by external stakeholders. Without a doubt, FedEx had built a stronger business by acquiring lots of physical assets in a few short years. But FedEx had also addressed the

Figure 11–7 A FedEx ad series celebrating external recognition of its employees.
Source: FedEx Corporation

communications challenges posed by the integration of those assets into a coherent whole and, in so doing, had managed to build valuable reputation capital for all of its stakeholders.

HOW DOES A COMPANY BECOME BEST IN CLASS?

The FedEx experience exemplifies many of the key elements of the process through which companies can develop winning reputations. We suggest three key lessons.

Lesson #1: Reputation Management Must be Audited and Tracked

Despite the temptation to act quickly, there's seldom merit in launching reputation-focused initiatives without first benchmarking where you are. Effective reputation management begins with an audit of stakeholder perceptions, including employees, the public, and the relevant external groups concerned with the company's operations. Audits can be quantitative or qualitative. Quantitative data can help pinpoint more precisely problematic perceptual gaps with particular stakeholder groups. But qualitative audits carried out via management and stakeholder interviews can also help to portray the broad outlines of the reputational landscape.

The reputational audit should be matched by a communications audit—an assessment of the company's own reality—what the company is actually saying, and how well those statements are being conveyed through all of the channels of communication at its disposal. The purpose of the communications audit is to establish how and how well the company is speaking out to stakeholders. The audit also provides the basis for continual tracking of results.

Juxtaposing stakeholder perceptions against actual communications provides the raw material for a gap analysis—an examination of the degree to which perceptions of the company are in alignment with the reality of the company. Figure 11–8 describes the substance of the analysis that it suggests, as well as the change implications that derive from it. On one hand, if reality is ahead of stakeholder perceptions, then the company's challenge is to

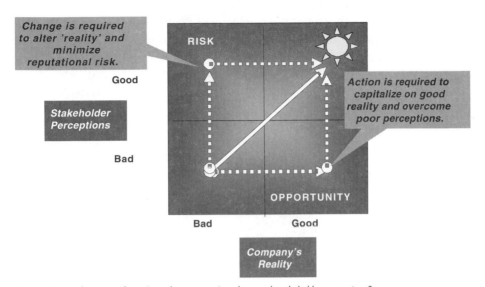

Figure 11–8 The gap analysis: Does the company's reality match stakeholder perceptions?

improve on its communications—to get the word out. On the other hand, if perceptions are better than reality, the company is in a high-risk position and its challenge is two-pronged: first, to launch fundamental initiatives designed to redress the company's reality and reduce the company's risky reputational position and, second, to communicate aggressively about the changes it has made.

Lesson #2: Reputation Comes from Within

Contrary to pat notions on the topic, corporate reputations are not manufactured wholesale by creative communications staff seeking to gain a strategic foothold in the executive suite. They are what scientists call *social facts*—a reflection of the company's actions and initiatives as they come to be mirrored in the eyes of stakeholders. As such, they come from within—they are partial reflections and partial distortions of what investors, publics, and partners perceive to be the company's history, culture, strategy, workplace, practices, and structure.

To build a company's reputation, or to rebuild it as FedEx did, to implement a new strategic direction requires far more than old-fashioned PR spin or advertising. It involves deep-seated change that is rooted in the company's cultural makeup.

That's why reputational initiatives have gained so much visibility in recent years: They cannot be compartmentalized into the traditional domain of specialized communications staff. They invariably require a collaborative effort across multiple functional areas in the company. As Figure 11–9 demonstrates, that means peeling back the layers of relationships the company has with stakeholders to identify the company's beating heart, rooted as it is in the company's history, identity, culture, and strategy. Conversely, reputation-building means identifying the historical elements, identity elements, cultural elements, and strategic elements that make a company distinctively different from rivals in the marketplace and finding ways to express those differences in communications and integrative initiatives that address the stakeholder concerns of employees, customers, investors, communities, and the media.

Lesson #3: Reputations Must Be Earned Over and Over

Tempting though it may be to think so, reputation management is not something you do once and then forget about. As companies regularly redeploy their hard assets in order to respond to new competitive conditions, as managers change the company's strategic direction, either organically or through merger, they have to work hard to keep alignment between the new visions and strategies they are pursuing and the existing corporate cultures that resist change. When the annual RQ results of 2002 were released in the *Wall Street Journal* on February 12, 2003,

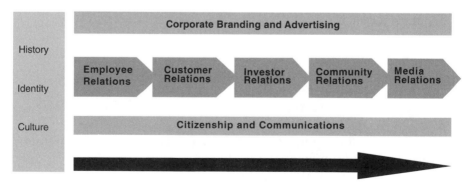

Figure 11–9 Exploring the internal roots of the company's reputation.

FedEx had slipped slightly in its RQ rating from 2001. It had also lost ground against rival UPS, whose aggressive advertising, communications, and workplace initiatives built significant visibility and credibility for the company throughout 2002. FedEx hadn't slipped much—but UPS had simply taken a bold leap forward. Clearly, reputation is a relative thing—it must be earned continuously and competitively. As the French saying goes, "vingt fois sur le métier remettez votre ouvrage."

****

What *Fame and Fortune* has emphasized is that companies must recognize the powerful constraining effects that stakeholder perceptions have on the ultimate success of their initiatives. Reputations are intangible assets that belong to the soft side of the balance sheet. As we have tried to show you throughout the book, however, reputations powerfully shape how well a company's strategy is received in the marketplace, and so the financial results it achieves. FedEx demonstrated insight and awareness of these effects, and its communications staff were buoyed by the top management support they received for integrative planning and execution of their initiatives.

Readers of *Fame and Fortune* should take these lessons to heart as they embark on their own reputational journeys. We hope to have inspired you.

ENDNOTES

1. This chapter benefited from extensive contributions by Bill Margaritis and his team of communications professionals at FedEx. We are extremely grateful for their collaboration here with the Reputation Institute's initiatives.

2. James S. Watson, Presentation to Goldman Sachs 18th Annual Transportation Conference, February 5, 2003.

3. Source: *http://www.fedex.com/us/investorrelations/financialinfo/financialreleases/Q4FY02.html?link=4.*

4. *Fortune*, March 4, 2002

INDEX

8 reasons why you should read the Financial Times for 4 weeks RISK-FREE!

To help you stay current with significant
developments in the world economy ...
and to assist you to make informed business
decisions — the Financial Times brings you:

 Fast, meaningful overviews of international affairs ... plus daily
briefings on major world news.

 Perceptive coverage of economic, business, financial and political
developments with special focus on emerging markets.

❸ More international business news than any other publication.

 Sophisticated financial analysis and commentary on world market
activity plus stock quotes from over 30 countries.

❺ Reports on international companies and a section on global investing.

❻ Specialized pages on management, marketing, advertising and
technological innovations from all parts of the world.

❼ Highly valued single-topic special reports (over 200 annually)
on countries, industries, investment opportunities, technology and more.

❽ The Saturday Weekend FT section — a globetrotter's guide to
leisure-time activities around the world: the arts, fine dining, travel,
sports and more.

FT FINANCIAL TIMES
World business newspaper

The *Financial Times* delivers a world of business news.

Use the Risk-Free Trial Voucher below!

To stay ahead in today's business world you need to be well-informed on a daily basis. And not just on the national level. You need a news source that closely monitors the entire world of business, and then delivers it in a concise, quick-read format.

With the *Financial Times* you get the major stories from every region of the world. Reports found nowhere else. You get business, management, politics, economics, technology and more.

Now you can try the *Financial Times* for 4 weeks, absolutely risk free. And better yet, if you wish to continue receiving the *Financial Times* you'll get great savings off the regular subscription rate. Just use the voucher below.

---

4 Week Risk-Free Trial Voucher

Yes! Please send me the *Financial Times* for 4 weeks (Monday through Saturday) Risk-Free, and details of special subscription rates in my country.

Name_____

Company_____

Address_____ ❏ Business or ❏ Home Address

Apt./Suite/Floor _____City _____State/Province_____

Zip/Postal Code_____Country _____

Phone (optional) _____E-mail (optional)_____

Limited time offer good for new subscribers in FT delivery areas only.

To order contact Financial Times Customer Service in your area (mention offer SAB01A).

The Americas: Tel 800-628-8088 Fax 845-566-8220 E-mail: uscirculation@ft.com

Europe: Tel 44 20 7873 4200 Fax 44 20 7873 3428 E-mail: fte.subs@ft.com

Japan: Tel 0120 341-468 Fax 0120 593-146 E-mail: circulation.fttokyo@ft.com

Korea: E-mail: sungho.yang@ft.com

S.E. Asia: Tel 852 2905 5555 Fax 852 2905 5590 E-mail: subseasia@ft.com

FT FINANCIAL TIMES
World business newspaper

www.ft.com

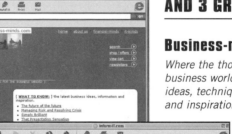